The Philosophy of Wilhelm Schapp

Also Available from Bloomsbury

The Phenomenology of Questioning, Joel Hubick
Structure Phenomenology, Herbert Witzenmann
Günther Anders' Philosophy of Technology, Babette Babich

The Philosophy of Wilhelm Schapp

From Phenomenology to Jurisprudence and the Hermeneutics of Stories

Edited by
Daniele De Santis and Daniele Nuccilli

BLOOMSBURY ACADEMIC
LONDON • NEW YORK • OXFORD • NEW DELHI • SYDNEY

BLOOMSBURY ACADEMIC
Bloomsbury Publishing Plc
50 Bedford Square, London, WC1B 3DP, UK
1385 Broadway, New York, NY 10018, USA
29 Earlsfort Terrace, Dublin 2, Ireland

BLOOMSBURY, BLOOMSBURY ACADEMIC and the Diana logo are trademarks of Bloomsbury Publishing Plc

First published in Great Britain 2025

Series design: Charlotte Daniels
Cover image: *The Waves* (1931), Edvard Munch
(Contributor: incamerastock / Alamy Stock Photo)

A catalogue record for this book is available from the British Library.

A catalog record for this book is available from the Library of Congress.

ISBN: HB: 978-1-3503-6783-8
ePDF: 978-1-3503-6784-5
eBook: 978-1-3503-6785-2

Typeset by Deanta Global Publishing Services, Chennai, India

Contents

Contributors

Daniele De Santis (PhD 2013, Rome) is Associate Professor of Philosophy at Charles University, Prague. His research focuses on the early phenomenological tradition and the history of philosophy, with a particular interest in ontology and theory of knowledge. He has recently co-edited (with A. Tropis) the volume *Rethinking Intentionality, Person and the Essence: Aquinas, Scotus, Stein* (2024) and published the monograph *Transcendental Idealism and Metaphysics. Husserl's Critique of Heidegger. 2 Volumes* (2023). He is the editor in chief of *The New Yearbook of Phenomenology and Phenomenological Philosophy*.

Francesca De Vecchi is Professor of Theoretical Philosophy at San Raffaele University, Milan, Italy. Her research topics focus on social ontology; phenomenology of the person, empathy, and social acts; and phenomenology of gendered personal identity. She outlined a phenomenologically embedded social ontology called *qualitative social ontology*. Her last book is *La società in persona. Ontologia sociale qualitativa* (2022). She is Co-editor in chief of the journal *Phenomenology and Mind* and Director of the *Research Centre in Phenomenology and Sciences of the Person* (PERSONA) at San Raffaele University.

Susan Gottlöber completed her studies at Technische Universität Dresden, Germany. She is Associate Professor in Philosophy at Maynooth University, Ireland, where she has until recently served as Dean of Teaching and Learning and currently serves as Associate Dean of Teaching and Learning for the Faculty of Arts and Humanities . Her current primary research interests revolve around philosophical anthropology, with a particular emphasis on Max Scheler, the influence of intellectual history on Scheler's philosophy, the importance of intersubjectivity, individuality, embodiment, and the question of human nature in relation to technology and other living beings. In addition to this, she is interested in philosophy of toleration and value theory.

Karen Joisten is Professor of Philosophy at the Rheinland-Pfälzische Technische Universität Kaiserslautern-Landau. Since 2020, she is the spokesperson of CEDIS (Center for Ethics and the Digital Society) and the head of the certificate study program: "Technoethik" at DISC (Distance and Independent Studies Center). She also is head of the international research group: "Narrative Ethics" and a member of the Ethics Committee of Saarland University Medical Center. Among other positions, Joisten has been a visiting professor at the University of Kassel, guest lecturer in Bogotá (Columbia) and a fellow at the Max-Weber-Kolleg (Erfurt). Her current research focuses on the ethical challenges that arise through digitalization. She has developed the integrative new approach of TEDS (Technoethics for Emerging Digital Systems), which deals in particular with the ethical questions caused by artificial intelligence systems from a basic theoretical as well as an application-oriented perspective.

Kristjan Laasik received his PhD in Philosophy from the University of Miami in 2011 and currently works as Associate Professor of Philosophy at Zhejiang University, China. His research concerns the intersection of Husserlian phenomenology and the philosophy of mind, with a special focus on the topics of perception and emotion—not to mention a recent foray into the philosophy of geography.

Sophie Loidolt is Professor of Philosophy and Chair of Practical Philosophy at the Technical University of Darmstadt, Germany. She is a recurrent visiting professor at Center for Subjectivity Research in Copenhagen and the president of the German Society for Phenomenological Research. Her work centers on issues in the fields of phenomenology, political and legal philosophy, and ethics, as well as transcendental philosophy and philosophy of mind. Her book *Phenomenology of Plurality. Hannah Arendt on Political Intersubjectivity* (2017) won the Edward Goodwin Ballard Book Prize in 2018. Currently, she is preparing a book with the working title *Public Experiences. A Phenomenological Theory of the Public Realm*.

Daniele Nuccilli is MSCA-CZ Post-Doctoral Fellow in the Department of Philosophy (Úfar) of Charles University, Prague. He works extensively on the early phenomenological tradition and the most recent developments of German philosophy. He has edited the Italian translation of Schapp's *In Geschichten verstrickt* and the collected volume *The Phenomenological Movemen*t (2020). Currently, he is completing the first English monograph on the philosophy of W. Schapp.

Wilhelm Schapp (1884–1965) studied with Dilthey (Berlin), Rickert (Freiburg), and Husserl (Göttingen). He is considered one of the main representatives of the early phenomenological tradition and one of the founders of the phenomenology of law. After the Second World War, he developed a unique narratological approach to classical phenomenological themes. Among his publications, see the volumes *Beiträge zur Phänomenologie der Wahrnehmung* (1910), *Die neue Wissenschaft vom Recht* (1930-32), *In Geschichten verstrickt. Zum Sein von Ding und Mensch* (1953), and *Philosophie der Geschichten* (1959).

Michela Summa is Professor of Theoretical Philosophy at the University of Würzburg. She received her PhD from the University of Pavia and KU-Leuven, with a dissertation on Husserl's phenomenology of temporal and spatial constitution. Before joining the University of Würzburg, she worked as a post-doc at the Clinic for General Psychiatry in Heidelberg from 2009 to 2015, and at the Institute for Philosophy in Würzburg from 2015 to 2018. In 2018, she also served as a guest professor for phenomenology and hermeneutics at the Institute for Philosophy in Kassel. She is the author of *Spatio-temporal Intertwining: Husserl's Transcendental Aesthetic*, published in 2014. Additionally, she has written several articles on topics in the philosophy of mind and phenomenology, with a focus on different classes of intentional experience, as well as in aesthetics, social philosophy, and phenomenological psychopathology. She has also edited various volumes and special issues on these subjects.

Nicole Thiemer is Research Assistant in the Department of Philosophy at the University of Kaiserslautern-Landau (RPTU) and in the Carl-Zeiss-Foundation-funded project *Sustainable Embedded AI* at RPTU. She is Managing Director of the Wilhelm-Schapp-Research-Center and Lecturer in the certificate study program *Technoethics* at DISC. Her research interests include ethics and digitalization, narrative philosophy, philosophy of science, and hermeneutics.

Alejandro G. Vigo (PhD 1994, Heidelberg) is Professor of Philosophy at the Universidad de los Andes. He has extensively published on ancient philosophy and the German phenomenological traditions. Among his publications, see *Zeit und Praxis bei Aristoteles. Die Nikomachische Ethik und die zeit-ontologischen Voraussetzungen des vernunftgesteuerten Handelns* (1996), and *Estudios aristotélicos* (2006).

1

On the Many Philosophies of Wilhelm Schapp

Editors' Introduction

Daniele De Santis, Daniele Nuccilli

Investigating the thought of an author such as Wilhelm Albert Johann Schapp (October 15, 1884, Großefehn–March 22, 1965, Sanderbusch) means journeying through some of the decisive milestones of the twentieth century, at least as far as the historical-philosophical sphere is concerned. Indeed, the philosopher from Aurich grew under the protective wings of crucial figures who inaugurated some of the dominant currents of thought in Germany and Europe at the beginning of the last century. These philosophers left an indelible mark on subsequent philosophical production even up to the present day: the historicism of Dilthey, the neo-Kantianism of Rickert, the phenomenology of Husserl, Pfänder, Reinach, and, alongside these, the lessons of Simmel, Lipps, and Scheler. The massive attempts to find new tools in the face of a universal crisis of knowledge and previously unseen social phenomena, of which the works of the authors just mentioned are emblematic examples, constitute the Cartesian axes within which Schapp's philosophical reflection is oriented. His doctoral dissertation, discussed under Husserl's supervision in 1909 and published in 1910 with the title *Beiträge zur Phänomenologie der Wahrnehmung* incorporates some insights of Husserlian phenomenology but also explores new thematic horizons, especially with regard to the perception and understanding of a thing on a cognitive level. The two books of *Die Neue Wissenschaft vom Recht* (1930/2) fit into the track of Reinach's phenomenology of law but inaugurate a new way of phenomenologically interpreting fundamental concepts such as that of contract and property. Additionally, his "philosophy of stories" takes up the examples present in the historicistic reflections of Rickert and Dilthey and explains them in phenomenological-hermeneutical terms, offering an alternative way of understanding human beings in contrast to the one offered by Heidegger since the 1920s. Amid the impressive theoretical architectures of his masters and fellow intellectual travelers, his thought thus moves in an original and independent manner, identifying new and unheard-of solutions to fundamental questions that were emerging in the cultural landscape of the time and that have not yet been extinguished. As we shall see in this book, to delve into his work, then, means not only to shed new light on glimpses and nodes of some of the fundamental paths of thought of the recent past, be it in the phenomenological-perceptual or theoretical-legal or narratological-hermeneutical spheres, but also to find alternative solutions and new interpretive options to that tangle of questions that still permeate the current theoretical debates.

Given the density of encounters and influences that characterize the author's lifetime, before moving on to the content exposition of the chapters in this volume, it is appropriate to offer here a brief intellectual biography of Wilhelm Schapp.[1]

Heir to a family of East Frisian boatmen, shipowners, and merchants, after receiving his diploma from the Gymnasium in Wilhelmshaven during Easter of 1902, at the age of seventeen, he went to Freiburg i. B. Beginning the Winter Semester of 1902/3, he studied philosophy and law[2] and attended lectures by Rickert and Cohn, among others. Thanks to Rickert, he became familiar with Hegel's philosophy of history and developed a fascination with Kant's work, which he would admit to having studied in such depth that he was able to memorize parts of the three critiques.[3] After three semesters, he moved to Berlin where he attended lectures by Dilthey, Simmel, Schmoller, Kohler, and Dernburg.[4] It was at Dilthey's house in 1904 that he had his first encounter with Husserl's phenomenology. Dilthey understood from the very beginning the "epochal" importance that the recently released (1900–1901) two-volume work (the *Logical Investigations*) would have in the philosophical landscape of Germany at the time.[5] The admiration that seeped from the Wiesbaden philosopher's lectures stimulated Schapp. About to pass his first bar exam at the Court of Appeals in Berlin and move to the neighborhood of Göttingen for his practicum, he got in touch with Husserl to plan the continuation of his philosophical studies.

It is important to note how the hermeneutical horizon in which Schapp's very first contact with phenomenology was populated by figures of stature. The solid training of the neo-Kantian school and the deep interest in the work of Kant[6] inherited from Rickert were part of a complex philosophical scenario in which reflection on the status of the spiritual sciences and their relation to the natural sciences had taken center stage. The two main philosophical movements that were animating this reflection at the turn of the century were psychologism and historicism, both, in different ways, called into question by Husserl's phenomenology. Especially the reflection on the historical dimension of human beings represented a point of convergence where the two different positions of Rickert and Dilthey intersected in what has been defined as the *südwestdeutschen Zuwendung zur Geschichte*, "the southwest German turn to history" (Marquard 1982: 112).

There are two aspects of the two authors' reflection in those years that left an enduring mark on the philosophical horizon of Schapp's work and paved the way for the recomposition, in his philosophy of stories, between the logical a priori motives of Husserl's early phenomenology and the historicist-hermeneutic instances of German historicism (Noack 1962: 213–26). The first aspect is related to Dilthey. In the 1900 writing *Die Entstehung der Hermeneutik*, he challenged some of the assumptions of his earlier works. His foundation of the sciences of spirit in the internal experience of the individual (*Erlebnis*), a recurring theme of his writings from the last two decades of the nineteenth century, was giving way to an intersubjective view of "understanding" (*Verstehen*) mediated by a symbolic component, fundamentally related to linguistic expressions, but also to mimic expressions (Dilthey 1996: 235ff.). This first attempt to shift from a psychological-descriptive and ego-centered view to a more purely hermeneutic one in Diltheyan historicist reflection directly merged with the recognition and theorization of an indissoluble link between history and individual life and placed the moment of understanding, especially historical understanding, at the center of his philosophical reformulation of the nexus between individuality and otherness, self, and the world (Cristin 1999: 23–4; Nuccilli 2018: 32ff.). The theoretical path briefly described and the wide span given to the analysis of the link between individual psychic experience and the history of other individual and collective subjects in the past cannot but be taken into consideration if one is to try to grasp the genesis and thematic background against which the concepts of entanglement (*Verstrickung*) and co-entanglement (*Mitverstrickung*) stand in Schapp's philosophy of stories (see Nuccilli 2018: 23).

The second element of the author's cultural background to be considered, which has not yet been emphasized in the secondary literature and yet finds strong parallels throughout his philosophy, is Rickert's critique of "concept formation" in the natural sciences as presented in the work *Die Grenzen der naturwissenschaftlichen Begriffsbildung* (1896). Within his argument on how universality should be understood in the historical sciences as opposed to the natural sciences, Rickert identifies a definition of the concept of species (*Gattung*) as a "concrete multiplicity of individuals" and then specifies that "something that is part of the concrete species is not to be considered simply as an exemplification of the concept of species" (Rickert 1896: 394). This Rickertian definition of the concept of species, which does not hinge on an ontological difference between the general and the particular but simply on a greater extension in numerical terms of a wholly historical and material reality, can be regarded, for all intents and purposes, as the forerunner of Schapp's critique of the phenomenological concept of species. This aspect represents a fundamental moment in the development of the latter because, since the *Beiträge*, the concept of history/story is regarded as an indispensable element for the understanding of things in their individuality.

It is with this background, therefore, that Schapp comes to Göttingen for the Winter Semester 1905–6. There, he is active as a lawyer and has, at the same time, the opportunity to attend the courses and exercises of Husserl, Müller, and Cohn. It is, however, the study of the *Logical Investigations* that catalyzes all his energies and, in particular, the phenomenological method proposed therein (Schapp 1959: 13, 2025: 228). Moreover, it was the phenomenological method that was slowly drawing various scholars from Germany and Europe to gather around the figure of Husserl. Schapp's years in Göttingen were also the rising years of the phenomenological movement (see Schuhmann 1977: 74; Spiegelberg 1994: 167). In 1905, the arrival of Reinach and Daubert inaugurated an actual pilgrimage to Göttingen by some of the Munich scholars philosophically formed by Theodor Lipps: this is the famous "invasion from Munich" (Schapp 1959: 20, 2025: 234). These Munich scholars came to Husserl's phenomenology, often criticizing the philosophical principles of their own training with one of the leading exponents of psychologism at the time (Lipps). The invasion culminated in 1907 with the arrival of Theodor Conrad and Dietrich von Hildebrand and the foundation, by Conrad and Alfred von Sybel, of the *Philosophische Gesellschaft Göttingen* (see Schuhmann 1977: 103). This was the very beginning of the Göttingen circle.

In the summer semester of that same year, Husserl delivered the famous lectures on *Ding und Raum*, part of the *Hauptstücke aus der Phänomenologie und Kritik der Vernunft*, identified later by himself and his students as *Dingvorlesung*. These lectures represent the center of an early dialectical phase between Husserl and exponents of the Munich and Göttingen circles (see Schuhmann 1987: 240–1). In particular, Conrad and Reinach began to express their doubts about the new direction Husserl was giving to his phenomenology, which was increasingly turning to a transcendental form of idealism, built on a new basic methodical element, that of reduction (*Reduktion*), extensively treated by Husserl (2008) already in the 1906/07 lectures *Einleitung in die Logik und Erkenntnistheorie*.

Vorlesungen, but whose genesis can be traced back to the famous meeting in 1905 in Seefeld between Husserl, Pfänder, and Daubert.[7] "A turn toward the Marburg school!" was Reinach's reproach.[8]

It was within the *Philosophische Gesellschaft Göttingen* that Schapp matured and developed the phenomenological assumptions that would flow into his doctoral dissertation *Beiträge zur Phänomenologie der Wahrnehmung*. In this dense period of encounters, the figures of reference for Schapp became Reinach and Conrad who, like Daubert and Pfänder, had already been students of Lipps in Munich. All of them, in different ways, were taking a critical distance from the new direction of Husserl's phenomenology.

The typical feature of the encounter between Husserl's early students in Göttingen, including Schapp, and Husserl's followers in Lipps's circle in Munich, is a different attitude toward phenomenology. Indeed, the Munich group was, on the one hand, less inclined to accept Husserl's theoretical proposal in toto and uncritically and, on the other hand, was strongly interested in the detection of proto-phenomenological roots in the history of philosophy and especially in Plato's philosophy. As Schapp attests, "their central focus was the Platonic theory of *methexis* (the theory of participation in concepts)"; "they no longer believed in sensation as a constituent of perception, and explained any statements claiming this as construction; however, they still believed in acts and psychology (the latter had not yet been placed in doubt)" (Schapp 1959: 21, 2025: 234). In this open debate on several fronts, Reinach must have played a fundamental role. In those years, he was not only establishing himself as an excellent teacher and a referential figure for the first phenomenologists (Ingarden 1992: 42–3), but was also developing his own idea of phenomenology often inspired by Plato. Both Schapp in the *Beiträge* (see Schapp 2013: 7–8) and Reinach later in his lecture *Über Phänomenologie* (see Reinach 1969: 198), identify the Athenian philosopher as the one who first shifted philosophical attention from the discursive-linguistic sphere of Socratic research to the visual-intuitive one of the doctrine of ideas (see De Santis 2014: 28–35). Within this persistent reference to the figure of Plato, a strong interest in issues related to perception began to emerge for Schapp, an interest that would be consolidated in the nine months Schapp spent in Munich between 1907 and 1908. During those months, he not only had fruitful exchanges with Pfänder and Daubert (see Schapp 1959: 21–2, 2025: 234–235), but also had the opportunity to attend the lectures by Moritz Geiger, Lipps, and Carl Stumpf. While Pfänder's thought would be influential in what concerns the acquisition of the phenomenological method, as far as the development of his own peculiar view of the occurrence of reality in the perceptual realm is concerned, Schapp's original and innovative position will benefit from the assimilation of some principles of Lipps's aesthetics. Indeed, from the Lippsian understanding of the perception of the external world, Schapp seems to inherit an interest in the materiality of things in the specific attitude they manifest in everyday life, especially concerning human practical activities.[9] Schapp's constant interest for the practical-poetic background of the comprehension of the thing is thus to be found in the intersection between Lippsian aesthetics and Husserlian phenomenology and not exclusively in the otherwise crucial influence of Heidegger's *Being and Time*.

The thematic lines briefly sketched above characterize Schapp's formative philosophical period, the "academic" one, and constitute the structural basis on which the author's various theoretical paths, from the "phenomenology of law" to the "philosophy of stories," would later be engrafted. This formative period ended with the discussion of his doctoral dissertation on June 16, 1909. Despite the immediate response to the publication of the *Beiträge*, Schapp decided to devote himself to the practice of law, for which he had qualified a few months after the dissertation was written, and thus moved to Aurich, his hometown, where he started his own private law practice with some success (see Joisten 2016: 365–6).

From that moment on, his attendance at the circles' activities became increasingly sporadic and occasional, even though he continued to keep a dense correspondence with other phenomenologists of the time. His philosophical production, indeed, had a long break until the publication in 1930 of the first volume of *Die neue Wissenschaft vom Recht*, which was followed by the second volume in 1932. These two volumes follow in the footsteps of Reinach's phenomenology of law but were originally intended to compose together with *Zur Metaphysik des Muttertums* (almost ready in 1937 but released posthumously in 1965), a trilogy devoted to "a new phenomenology of values."[10]

Although centered on entirely independent themes, these three texts set the stage for the turning point that was to take place with the philosophy of stories. Of relevance are at least two central junctures that should be mentioned. One concerns the discussion of the concept of work in the second volume of *Die neue Wissenschaft vom Recht*, and the other concerns the treatment of the mother-child relationship in *Zur Metaphysik des Muttertums*. The concept of work opens up the phenomenological front to the historical-hermeneutical problems of early Schapp's education between Freiburg and Berlin. Within the investigation of the constitution of "property" as a pre-givenness of positive law, which he sets up in the second volume of *Die neue Wissenschaft vom Recht*, the relationship between the creator and the work takes on a prominent place, investigated from a peculiarly historicist perspective. Indeed, in a central passage of his analysis, Schapp states, "The history of humankind is the history of its works. The relations we have identified between self, work, value, and production are fundamental relations for history; they represent the a priori of historical science" (Schapp 1932: 67). What may sound like a clear reference to the problems with which Rickert and Dilthey had confronted each other in the early 1900s, also opens a moment of crisis for Schapp's conception of the phenomenological method of intuition of essence to the point that in his phenomenology of law, Schapp prefers to adopt the comparative method and what he calls a "phenomenology of creation" (Schapp 1932: 38-39). It is from these elements that, following his conceptual acquisition in the 1950s of the entanglement of humans in stories, Schapp takes the starting point for his analysis of the concept of thing-for which we find later in the first section of *In Geschichten verstrickt*.[11] On the other hand, in *Zur Metaphysik des Muttertums*, we find a discussion of the "mother-child relationship" (*Mutter-Kind-Beziehung*) (Schapp 1965: 5 ff.) which will be later incorporated into the second section of *In Geschichten verstrickt* (Schapp 2012: 196 ff.), and its discussion of the problem of co-entanglement and entanglement of the I-stories (*Ichgeschichten*) in the we-stories (*Wirgeschichten*). According to Schapp, the mother-child relationship and the father-child relationship form the basis for any legal discourse to grasp civil law and the value context on which it is based, regardless of the different constitutions of the different states and peoples. Similarly, the story of the mother-child relationship and the story of the father-child relationship constitute the fundamental paradigmatic stories that entangle the whole of humanity regardless of their belief and nationality. This thematic plexus not only constitutes the theoretical apex of *In Geschichten verstrickt*, but also represents one of the central axes of *Philosophie der Geschichten*.

Overall, the 1930s passed peacefully for Schapp despite the political upset brought about by the rise of National Socialism in Germany and the gathering winds of war. Until 1939, he was active as a notary mainly in the field of tax law, having no close implications with the government. In 1940, after the outbreak of the Second World War, he was placed in the Civil Service Reserve of the Army High Command to serve as a judge in the Army Tribunal. He would not be called to serve until toward the end of the war in 1945 but was then immediately discharged because he fell ill with typhus (see Joisten 2016: 368).

Toward the end of 1945, Schapp resumed his study of Pfänder's *Die Seele des Menschen* (Pfänder 1933), and the following year devoted himself to the reading of the works of Ranke (Schapp 2017: 138 ff.). By the end of the decade, these readings led to new reflections, which formed the basis for a series of private meetings organized in his home office with the Aurich philosophical association, which he himself had founded: its members debated the major themes of early phenomenology from a new perspective (see Schapp, J. 2004: 18). Also, Hermann Lübbe attended these meetings with some regularity and, on a couple of occasions in 1954, Odo Marquard attended as well. At the time, both were part of Ritter's school at the University of Münster (see Marquard 2004: 45). In the first meetings, Schapp proposed to start afresh from the reading of his *Beiträge zur Phänomenologie der Wahrnehmung* in order to inaugurate a new philosophical beginning, made necessary by the devastating recent events of the Second World War (see Schapp, J. 2004: 16–17). The reworking of the meeting material provided the groundwork for his "philosophy of stories," a trilogy of works (*In Geschichten verstrickt. Zum Sein von Mensch und Ding* (1953); *Philosophie der Geschichten* (1959); *Metaphysik der Naturwissenschaft* (1965)) in which he interprets the question of the lifeworld and that of humans' "being-in-the-world" from the new philosophical perspective of the "entanglement in stories."

Having briefly discussed Schapp's intellectual trajectory, we can now present both the structure and the content of this volume. Although our ambition was not and cannot be that of covering all the different aspects and nuances of Schapp's philosophy, this volume has been thought and designed in such a way that its tripartite structure mirrors and follows the overall development of his thought.

However, before we get into a more detailed presentation of all the individual chapters, a crucial terminological-philosophical remark is here necessary concerning the German term *Geschichte*. As is known, the term can and should be literally translated with "history"; yet, Schapp's philosophical understanding of it is such that its meaning oscillates between *history* and *story*—also depending on how strong one's emphasis on the narratological implications of that concept is. Since then, the very understanding of the term is philosophically based (namely, based on how one interprets Schapp's own views on the matter), full freedom has been left to the authors on how it should be translated into English and then used. Accordingly, the reader will sometimes find the term left in German, sometimes translated as *history,* and sometimes as *story* (and sometimes even as both). The different linguistic options are nothing but the expression of the authors' different philosophical perspectives on the concept, thus on Schapp's philosophy itself.

The chapters have been organized and divided into three macro thematic sections, respectively dedicated to the three macro-phases of the development of Schapp's philosophy. The first section is in fact dedicated to Schapp's early phenomenological reflections, and it pursues three different, yet related aims. The first aim is that of elucidating some of the crucial concepts and acquisitions of his doctoral dissertations on the phenomenology of perception (Summa, Laasik); the second consists of putting Schapp's reflections back into the context of the early phenomenological movement so as to more properly understand his own views (De Santis); finally, a third aim can be identified, which is that of exploring some of the connections between Schapp's early philosophy and some of the later developments of his thought (Vigo). The second macro-section follows almost exclusively dedicated to Schapp's phenomenology-based philosophy of law and values. Three chapters have been included into this section, each of which has a quite specific goal and aim. Whereas Nuccilli's chapter tackles one of the most crucial notions of both Schapp's early and more mature philosophy, namely, that of *Ding* and *Wozuding*, Loidolt's contribution has the crucial function of providing the readers with a general introduction to Schapp's philosophy of law (the first ever of this kind published in English). Finally, De Vecchi has the chief merit of showing how relevant Schapp's qualitative ontology still is for contemporary debates. The third and last section is, on the contrary, dedicated to the *Philosophie der Geschichten*, with a special focus on the two volumes In Geschichten verstrickt and *Philosophie der Geschichten*. The opening chapter by Gottlöber makes the case for considering the importance of the concept of "story" for the crucial problem of "personal identity"; by contrast, the last two chapters provide the readers with a systematic discussion of the two volumes above, and are thus to be regarded as following upon one another. Whereas Thiemer focuses on the groundbreaking book of 1953 *In Geschichten verstrickt*, Joisten addresses the more systematic development that Schapp gives to his *Geschichten*-philosophy in the 1959 *Philosophie der Geschichten*.

The volume closes with the English translation (by Elizabeth A. Behnke) of Schapp's famous *Erinnerungen an Husserl*, a most precious autobiographical piece published in the 1959 collective book *Edmund Husserl 1859–1959. Recueil commémoratif publié à l'occasion du centenaire de la naissance du philosophe*, edited by Herman Leo Van Breda and Jacques Taminiaux. The decision to include the *Erinnerungen* in our volume should not be too difficult to fathom and understand. Not only is the *Erinnerungen* a crucial text in order to get a better insight into Schapp's interpretation of the development of his own thought vis-à-vis Husserl's phenomenology (among others), it is an important document on the beginning of the phenomenological tradition, therefore on Schapp's own position in it and in relation to the many figures who contributed to shaping it.

The overall structure of the book being outlined, a quick overview of the content of the chapters can now be offered to the readers.

Michela Summa's paper *Schapp on Perceptual Normativity* develops the most systematic analysis and discussion of Schapp's doctoral dissertation on the phenomenology of perception from the vantage point of one of the most debated issues of contemporary philosophy and phenomenology of perceptual experience: the problem of *normativity*. After she introduces the distinction between what she calls "bottom-up" (= pre-conceptual) and "top-down" (= conceptual) normativity, Summa makes the case for considering Schapp's approach to the normativity of perception to be a synthesis or conjunction of the two. In this respect, a crucial role is played by the last chapter of Schapp's dissertation on perception, the one in which the problem of the "idea in perception" is introduced and systematically dealt with. It is here, in fact, Summa argues, that pre-conceptual normativity (the one related to the structures of perceptual content) is combined with conceptual normativity (the one related to the recognition of the object *as* this or that object).

Summa's discussion of Schapp's early phenomenology is followed by Kristjan Laasik's chapter *Schapp on Color, Clarity, and Ideas*. In his analysis, Laasik pursues a quite strong aim, that of presenting and reconstructing Schapp's perspective on visual perceptual experience as a "deductive argument" (as he himself calls it) or, more precisely, as a "hypothetical syllogism supporting the view that visual perception can only give its objects in color." But the overall goal of his chapter is to clarify the relation of dependence between different aspects of Schapp's thought on perception, notably, his claim that visual perception can only give its objects in color (with a special emphasis on "adhesive" color), the concept of "clarity" and that of "idea" or, better: individual ideas (the ones that capture things in their individuality and utmost particularity). The chapter closes with a series of three objections which the author moves against Schapp. The first objection (during whose presentation Laasik resorts to Husserl's notion of phantom) targets Schapp's claim about adhesive color, namely, the argument to the effect that we always need adhesive colors to experience spatial objectivity; by contrast, the second and the third objections are about Schapp's use of Platonic Ideas, and the alleged role they would play in perception. Here Laasik resorts once again to Husserl, that is to say, to the distinction between Platonic Idea and Kantian regulatory idea to challenge Schapp's conception that perception is more or less like a "sudden epiphany."

If the first two chapters tackle Schapp's early phenomenology with the aim of presenting some of its immanent features and tensions, the third chapter by Daniele De Santis (*From* Sachverhalt *to Geschichte and Back: Remarks on Wilhelm Schapp and the Early Phenomenological Tradition*) sets out to achieve a different goal, that of assessing one of the possible origins of Schapp's *Geschichte*-philosophy from within the context of the early phenomenological discussions on the status and role of "states of affairs" (*Sachverhalte*). The ambition of the chapter is to make the case for regarding Schapp's concept of *Geschichte* as a further development and radicalization of some of the early phenomenological understandings (Husserl, Reinach, Ingarden, and Pfänder) of the problem of truth and, in particular, of the "state of affairs-object" relation. In this respect, De Santis maintains, the *Geschichte*-philosophy is not to be seen as an alternative to early phenomenology (as is epitomized, for example, by Husserl and Reinach), but rather as stemming out of some of its unresolved tensions.

Alejandro G. Vigo's chapter on *Perception and Stories. Schapp and Plato's* Theaetetus adds a new dimension to the discussion of Schapp's philosophy and, in particular, of what he calls the transition from "Schapp I" (to be identified with the early dissertation on perception) to "Schapp II" (resulting in the philosophy of stories and the departure from his early views). As Vigo explains in detail, the transition can be generally described as a departure from Husserl's phenomenology and, more specifically, from the basic and foundational role ascribed to "perception" in the constitution of experience. And if Plato comes to play a crucial function in Vigo's assessment, it is because Schapp seems to perceive "a secret link" between Plato (and Platonism, no matter what such label might mean) and the idea that perception should always represent the starting point of our analyses and discussions of experience. After a systematic discussion of the Platonic (and anti-Platonic)[12] elements that still characterize the doctoral dissertation, Vigo gratifies the reader with a thorough investigation of Schapp's reading of Plato's dialogue *Theaetetus* (along with *Cratylus* and the *Sophist*, though to a lesser degree). Schapp's goal is purely deconstructive: for what he tries to do is find in Plato the historical sources (of the notions of "meaning" and "concept") that would later lead to Husserl himself and some of his foundational claims about perception. As Vigo also poignantly explains, Schapp's intention is to go back to the very source of that conception of perception from which he himself had slowly moved away (= Schapp I).

With the chapter on *The Character of Things: Ding, Werk and Wozudinge. A Path in Wilhelm Schapp's Thought* by Daniele Nuccilli, we enter the second thematic macro-section of our book, the one dedicated to Schapp's phenomenology-based philosophy of law and values. Nuccilli has the ambition of outlining one of the internal evolutionary lines in the development of Schapp's thought. Unlike Vigo,

Nuccilli identifies three different periods in Schapp's philosophy and claims that to each of these periods corresponds a different interpretation of the concept of "thing." In the phenomenology of perception, the thing (*Ding*) is seen as the primary reference for perception and knowledge of the external world; in the philosophy of law, the thing is seen first and foremost as a "work" (*Werk*) and as a "value" (*Wert*), finally, in the philosophy of stories, the thing is seen as a "thing-for" (*Wozuding*), that is, as things that have a purpose of use and are embedded in the stories of the humans who have or have had to do with them. Nuccilli shows how the different ways in which the thing is interpreted in its character and properties has also methodological consequences and leads to a progressive questioning of the phenomenological method. It is through the notion of thing-for indeed that the cognitive model of classical phenomenology is questioned, and this is done by retrieving and developing further some of the arguments already present in the book on phenomenology of perception and especially in the treatment of the work in his philosophy of law. As Nuccilli further argues, it is not by chance that the concept of thing is from the very beginning to the end of Schappian reflection linked to the concept of history/story, one of the fundamental concepts around which revolves the turning point of his thought.

The chapter on *The New Science of Law* by Sophie Loidolt pursues a double goal. On the one hand, she provides the readers with a brief, yet systematic and clear assessment of some of the tenets of Schapp's phenomenology of law, on the other hand, she presents Schapp's position as consisting in a continuation and modification of Adolf Reinach's ("eidetic-realistic") phenomenological approach to jurisprudence.[13] As she explains, even if it is true that Schapp takes on Reinach's doctrine of social acts and promises, he pays far more attention to their being based upon values and valuing attitudes. The latter aspect is of particular importance since it is directly connected to Schapp's conviction that even positive law remains related to a substructure (the value) to which it "answers" as a pregiven in a specific way. Hence, jurisprudence is not and cannot be a science of mere legal constructs freely constructed; rather, it is a realm of abstraction which, however, refers to a "concrete reality." A reality which, in turn, can be grasped according to the a priori structures constituting the regional ontologies of "social reality and value reality."

Francesca De Vecchi closes the second section of our volume with her contribution on *Wilhelm Schapp's Qualitative Social Ontology: The Role of Values for the Law*. Here, De Vecchi claims that Schapp's phenomenology of law can be regarded as a fruitful example of "qualitative ontology," by which expression she means an ontology with an "existential" twist, so to say, able to account for our being, living, and acting as personal subjects in the world. In sum, it is an ontology that builds on a phenomenology-based account of the person. More specifically, the most important peculiarity of a phenomenology-based qualitative ontology is the emphasis on the role of values (construed as the actual correlates of our "personal" experience of the world). It is against such a backdrop that the author moves on to tackle Schapp's phenomenology-based philosophy of law, for the latter hinges on the correlation between law and values, or better: on the idea that the law is properly founded on evaluative experience and the person's capacity to "enjoy values." What was merely touched upon in the introductory chapter by Loidolt (the relation between the "world of values," as an ontological *Unterbau*, and the pre-givenness of contracts) is now looked at from the vantage point of qualitative ontology (as quickly characterized above). In this respect, De Vecchi's main claim can be summed up as the idea that there obtain "values" (both individual and collective) which are meaningful for us as persons in our everyday life, and they are the necessary condition in order for certain juridical formations (here, what Schapp himself calls "rational contract") to be at all possible.

With Susan Gottlöber's *The Power of Storytelling: Being Entangled in Stories as a Core Feature of Human Identity*, we enter the very last section of our book. Gottlöber's chief merit is to address Schapp's philosophy of *Geschichten* in a most systematic way, thereby also showing its significance and relevance for contemporary debates bearing upon issues of human-personal identity. Moreover, by comparing Schapp's approach to what she calls "classical hermeneutical tradition" (Dilthey and Gadamer in the first place, but also Ricoeur), she is able to highlight important analogies as well as differences. Gottlöber is rightly convinced that in times when the search for the structures of human existence becomes more and more challenging, Schapp's philosophy provides an interesting nuance in distinguishing the different human experiences both on individual and social levels: "the access (*Zugang*) is through the individual story or stories, encompassing not only the history of a culture, people, or group but also their interpretations and reinterpretations over time."

The chapter by Nicole Thiemer, *Philosophy of Histories I.* In Geschichten verstrickt. *Approaches and Reflections*, proposes to the reader a very systematic and in-depth introduction to the 1953 text with which Schapp inaugurates his *Geschichte*-philosophy trilogy: *In Geschichten verstrickt*. The chief merit of the author is that of touching upon all the most important topics and concepts first introduced by Schapp in his groundbreaking work: the notion of *Geschichte*, of course, but also that of *Wozudinge* and the idea of being entangled

(*Eigenverstrickung* and *Fremdverstrickung*) in stories or histories (Thiemer chooses not to choose between the two options). As she points out, it is crucial to keep in mind that the expression "*Verstrickung*" (the very key to understanding Schapp's own *Geschichte*-philosophy) does not have a negative connotation; rather, it refers to the irreducible fact that *Geschichten* are constituted as a network of relations and references in which human beings, as human beings in the world, are always and already embedded, in such a way that a detachment from being entangled in histories/stories is both "existentially" and "essentially" impossible.

The chapter by Karen Joisten (*Philosophy of Histories II: Philosophie der Geschichten. Approaches and Reflections*) brings the third macro-section of our book to conclusion, for here the discussion of Schapp's *Geschichte*-philosophy focuses on the later *Philosophie der Geschichten*, the second volume (published in 1959) of the *Geschichte* trilogy (the one in which the concepts and ideas first injected in the 1953 *In Geschichten verstrickt* are systematically cashed out). As she explains, the importance of the book lies in the fact that here Schapp's ambition is to show from a "historical perspective" the position of the "philosophy of histories." In a way that runs parallel to Heidegger's claim about the "oblivion of being" in Western metaphysics (or to Husserl's idea of the oblivion of the lifeworld due to the "mathematization of nature"), Schapp wants to show to what extent Western philosophy is dramatically marked by what he calls "the oblivion of histories." In this respect, the theoretical and systematic goal of hermeneutically elucidating our entanglement in histories cannot be divorced from the historical one which consists in tracing their "oblivion" back to the beginning and subsequent development of Western philosophy. The "hermeneutics" of our being entangled in histories goes necessarily hand in hand with the hermeneutics of that history (= the history of philosophy) which caused and resulted in the very *Geschichtenvergessenheit*.

* * *

When we editors (Daniele and Daniele) first set out the ambitious goal of putting together the first ever English collective volume on the philosophy of W. Schapp, we wanted to realize a book that could be both a presentation of the *many different aspects of his thought* and a discussion of *the manner such philosophy actually unfolded and developed*, moving from its early commitment to phenomenology to the later *Geschichte*-philosophy. The three thematic sections testify precisely to such double ambition, for the chapters here published do tackle some of the aspects and elements of Schapp's philosophy, while the book as a whole provides the reader with a picture and assessment of this philosophy's internal development, as it were. Of course, this does not mean *that all aspects or nuances* of Schapp's philosophy have been covered in this volume.[14] For example, the third volume of the *Geschichte* trilogy (*Metaphysik der Naturwissenschaft*) is mentioned and touched upon by more than one author, and yet never systematically delved into. The same can be said of *Zur Metaphysik des Muttertums*. On the contrary, there are topics that are addressed or even just mentioned by more than one chapter, such as the concepts of *Geschichte* and *Verstrickung*, that of *Wozuding*, the problem of the nature of perception, or the question as to the phenomenological foundation of contracts. This was of course unavoidable to the extent that these are some of the *Hauptbegriffe* and *Hauptprobleme* of Schapp's philosophy. Yet, the fact that the same concept or problem might appear more than once in the book does not result in a mere repetition of arguments and theses. For as long as the same concept/problem is tackled from within a different context, a different light is shed upon it and its significance within Schapp's thought. Last but not least, no satisfactory assessment of the development of Schapp's philosophy will ever be possible until open and full access is granted to the rich, yet still partially unexplored *Nachlass* preserved at the Bavarian State Library in Munich and in Schapp's former notary office in Aurich (in addition to the four *Nachlass*-volumes already published by Karl Alber), as well as to Schapp's personal library.

In this respect, the present volume wants to be primarily the expression of a hope, the hope to represent only the first of a series of volumes and studies to come on the many different aspects of Schapp's philosophy, on its (phenomenological) origins, and the great relevance it has (and can still have) for contemporary debates and discussions in philosophy.

Let us conclude this introduction by thanking all the authors for their contributions and efforts, and the publisher for its patience. A special thank goes to Jan Schapp, the son of Wilhelm Schapp, for the way he supported and encouraged our project from the very beginning.[15]

Notes

1 To find that this is not secondary to his philosophical production, we need only think of the famous metaphor of stories that "are not like drops in the middle of the sea" in *In Geschichten verstrickt* (see Schapp 2013: 94) or the phraseology that is linked to the German verb "auftauchen," literally "to emerge."

2 See Schapp (1964: 54).
3 See Schapp (1959: 12).
4 See Schapp (1964: 54).
5 In a meeting of the *Königlich Preußische Akademie der Wissenschaften* on March 2, 1905, Dilthey publicly expressed his esteem for Husserl and called the *Logical Investigations* literally *epochemachenden* (Dilthey 1905: 329).
6 See Schapp (1959: 9).
7 Testimony of this encounter is the Seefeld manuscript, in which the late Husserl claims to already find a "correct use of the concept of phenomenological reduction." See Husserl (1966: 237–68) and Spiegelberg (1974).
8 "Reinach reproached Husserl for turning toward the Marburg school, which was already attracting some attention in Munich at that time; he didn't think it was correct for Husserl to try to find support in the Marburg school for his metaphysical efforts. At that time, we had founded a phenomenological society in Göttingen that met almost every week" (Schapp 1959: 20, 2025: 234).
9 In his *Ästhetik*, Lipps defines the individual's projecting of the will into the working of a thing and the subsequent recognition of aspects of the subject in the thing as the "character of the thing" itself (see Lipps 1903: 201). See Schapp (2013: 121 ff.), where the very idea of a character of the thing plays a crucial role.
10 During a private conversation which took place in Aurich on September 4, 2021, Jan Schapp, the son of Wilhelm Schapp, explained to Daniele Nuccilli that this trilogy was conceived by his father as *eine Phänomenologie der Werte, der Schöpfung und der Liebe*, "a phenomenology of values, creation, and love." (D. N.)
11 Let us emphasize that a later confirmation of the importance of the connection between the concept of "work" and that of "thing-for" can be found in Schapp (2005: 64ff). Here, the author addresses the relation between the *Wozuding* and the problem of the juridical foundation of "property" (*Eigentum*).
12 For an in-depth discussion of Wilhelm Schapp's Platonism and anti-Platonism in relation to the phenomenological tradition, see also Nuccilli (2020).
13 See also Salice (2023), for a recent assessment of Schapp's "theory of exchanges" (and more generally the entire vol. XIX of *The New Yearbook for Phenomenology and Phenomenological Philosophy* dedicated to Reinach). For a more comprehensive assessment of the early phenomenology of law (Husserl, Reinach, Scheler, Stein, and Schapp), see the seminal work by Bobbio 2018 (originally published in 1934). More specifically, see the editor's introduction to the new edition of Bobbio's work (Bobbio 2018: xi–xxxiv), where the reader is gratified with a fine-grained discussion of the different positions adopted by the early phenomenologists. Let us remark that the nature of the relation between Schapp's philosophy of law and Reinach's can be interpreted in different ways; whereas Loidolt stresses the elements of continuity between the two, others would lay emphasis on their differences instead. For a different perspective, Di Lucia (1997: 150–63).

14 In this regard, it might be helpful to consult the three collected volumes that have been published in Germany in the past twenty years: Lembeck (2004); Joisten (2010); and Joisten, Schapp, and Thiemer (2020).

15 This work was supported by the Czech Sciences Foundation, financing the project "Rediscovering a German-Czech Member of Early Phenomenology: Intentionality, Consciousness and the Mind in the Philosophy of Maximilian Beck" (GAČR 24-10611S) and by the *Cooperatio* program provided by Charles University (field: philosophy), and implemented by the Faculty of Arts. This work was supported by the European Regional Development Fund project "MSCA Fellowships CZ—UK2" (reg. no.: CZ.02.01.01/00/22_010/0008115). This work was supported by the European Regional Development Fund project "MSCA Fellowships CZ - UK2" (reg. no.: CZ.02.01.01/00/22_010/0008115).

References

Bobbio, N. (2018), *L'indirizzo fenomenologico nella filosofia sociale e giuridica*, a cura di P. Di Lucia, Turin: Giappichelli.

Cristin R. (1999), *Fenomeno e storia*, Napoli: Guida editori.

De Santis, D. (2014), "L'idea della fenomenologia come fenomenologia delle Idee," in D. De Santis (ed.), *Di idee ed essenze. Un dibattito su fenomenologia e ontologia (1921-1930)*, 7–130, Milano: Mimesis.

Di Lucia, P. (1997), *L'universalità della promessa*, Milan: Giuffrè.

Dilthey, W. (1905), "Studien zur Grundlegung der Geisteswissenschaften," *Sitzungsberichte der Königlich Preußischen Akademie der Wissenschaften*, 14: 322–45.

Dilthey, W. (1996), "The Rise of Hermeneutics,"trans. R. Jameson and R. A. Makkreel, in *Selected Works Vol. IV*, trans. R. A. Makkreel and F. Rodi, 235–60, Princeton: Princeton University Press.

Husserl, E. (1966), Hua X, *Zur Phänomenologie des inneren Zeitbewusstseins (1893-1917)*, ed. R. Bohem, Den Haag: Nijhoff.

Husserl, E. (2008), *Introduction to Logic and Theory of Knowledge: Lectures 1906/07. Collected Works, Vol. 13,* trans. C. O. Hill, Dordrecht: Springer.

Ingarden, R. (1992), *Gesammelte Werke, Bd. 4: Einführung in die Phänomenologie Edmund Husserls: Osloer Vorlesungen (1967)*, Tübingen: Niemeyer.

Joisten, K., ed. (2010), *Das Denken Wilhelm Schapps*, Freiburg i. Br.: Karl Alber Verlag.

Joisten, K. (2016), "Wilhelm Schapp. Eine biographische Skizze," in W. Schapp, *Philosophischer Nachlass, Bd. I: Auf dem Weg einer Philosophie der Geschichten*, 360–72, Freiburg/München: Karl Alber Verlag.

Joisten, K., Schapp J., and Thiemer, N., eds (2020), *Die Rezeption Der Geschichtenphilosophie Wilhelm Schapps: Kommentare und Fortsetzungen*, Freiburg/München: Karl Alber Verlag.

Lembeck K.-H., ed. (2004), *Geschichte und Geschichten. Studien zur Geschichtenphänomenologie Wilhelm Schapps*, Würzburg: Königshausen und Neumann

Lipps, Th. (1903), *Ästhetik: Psychologie des Schönen und der Kunst,* Hamburg: Leopold Voss

Marquard, O. (1982), *Schwierigkeiten mit der Geschichtsphilosophie,* Frankfurt am Main: Suhrkamp.

Marquard, O. (2004), "Die Philosophie der Geschichten und die Zukunft des Erzählens," in K.-H. Lembeck (ed.), *Geschichte und Geschichten. Studien zur Geschichtenphänomenologie Wilhelm Schapps*, 45–56, Würzburg: Königshausen und Neumann.

Noack, H. (1962), *Die Philosophie Westeuropas,* Darmstadt: Wissenschaft Buchgesellschaft.

Nuccilli D. (2018), "History and Stories: Schapp's Ontological Conception of the Entanglement," *Kritika & Kontext*,22: 27–43.

Nuccilli, D. (2020), "Species, Ideas, and Stories. Schapp between Phenomenological 'Platonism' and 'Anti-Platonism'," *Azimuth*, 15 (VII): 61–75.

Pfänder, A. (1933), *Die Seele des Menschen: Versuch einer verstehenden Psychologie,* Tübingen: Niemeyer.

Reinach, A. (1969), "Concerning Phenomenology," trans. D. Willard, *The Personalist*, 50 (2): 194–221.

Rickert, H. (1896), *Die Grenzen der naturwissenschaftlichen Begriffsbildung*, Freiburg im Breisgau und Leipzig: J. C. B. Mohr.

Salice, A. (2023), "Wilhelm Schapp and the Standard Theory of Exchange," *The New Yearbook for Phenomenology and Phenomenological Philosophy*, Special Issue: "Reinach and Contemporary Philosophy," XIX: 132–50

Schapp, J. (2004), "Erinnerungen an Wilhelm Schapp," in K.-H. Lembeck (ed.), *Geschichte und Geschichten. Studien zur Geschichtenphänomenologie Wilhelm Schapps*, 13–25, Würzburg: Königshausen und Neumann.

Schapp, W. (1930), *Die neue Wissenschaft vom Recht. Eine phänomenologische Untersuchung. 1. Bd. Der Vertrag als Vorgegebenheit*, Berlin-Grunewald: Rotschild.

Schapp. W. (1932), *Die neue Wissenschaft vom Recht. Eine phänomenologische Untersuchung. 2. Bd. Wert, Werk und Eigentum*, Berlin-Grunewald: Rotschild.

Schapp, W. (1959), "Erinnerungen an Husserl," in AA.VV., *Edmund Husserl 1859-1959*, 12–25, Den Haag: M. Nijhoff.

Schapp. W. (1964), "Kleine Autobiographie des Verfassers," *Eckart-Jahrbuch 1964/65*: 54–6.

Schapp, W. (2009 [1965]), *Metaphysik der Naturwissenschaft*, Frankfurt a. Main: Vittorio Klostermann.

Schapp, W. (2012[1953]), *In Geschichten verstrickt Zum Sein von Mensch und Ding*, Frankfurt a. M.: Vittorio Klostermann.

Schapp, W. (2013), *Beiträge zur Phänomenologie der Wahrnehmung* [1910], Frankfurt am Main: Klostermann.

Schapp, W. (2015 [1959]), *Philosophie der Geschichten*, eds. K. Joisten and J. Schapp, Frankfurt am Main: Klostermann.

Schapp, W. (2017), *Philosophischer Nachlass. Teilband II: Auf dem Weg einer Philosophie der Geschichten*, hrsg. von K. Joisten, J. Schapp, and N. Thiemer, Freiburg, München: Karl Alber Verlag

Schapp, W. (2025), "Recollections of Husserl," trans. E. A. Behnke, in D. De Santis and D. Nuccilli (eds), *The Philosophy of Wilhelm Schapp: From Phenomenology to Jurisprudence and the Hermeneutics of Stories*, 227–238, London: Bloomsbury.

Schuhmann, K. (1977), *Husserl-Chronik. Denk- und Lebensweg Edmund Husserls*, Den Haag: Martinus Nijhoff.

Schuhmann, K. (1987), *Husserl und Reinach*, in K. Mulligan (ed.), *Speech, Act and Sachverhalt*, 239–56, Dordrecht: Springer.

Spiegelberg, H. (1974), "Neues Licht auf die Beziehung zwischen Husserl und Pfänder", *Tijdschrift voor Philosophie*, 36: 565–73.

Spiegelberg, H. (1994), *The Phenomenological Movement*, Kluwer Academic Publishers: Dordrecht.

Part I

Phenomenology

2

Schapp on Color, Clarity, and Ideas

Kristjan Laasik

Wilhelm Schapp wrote his dissertation, titled *Beiträge zur Phänomenologie der Wahrnehmung*, under Edmund Husserl's guidance at the University of Göttingen, defending it in 1909 (Schapp 1976a). Attesting to Schapp's intellectual potential and his burgeoning reputation, Herbert Spiegelberg speaks of Schapp as Husserl's most notable Göttingen *Urschüler*, that is, a student before 1905 (Spiegelberg 1965: 169).[1] He also writes that Schapp's "highly original" dissertation, "exploring in detail the way in which physical things and phenomena which are not substantial things appear, is one of the best examples of early phenomenologizing; it also attracted considerable attention among psychologists" (Spiegelberg 1965: 219).

As far as I know, Schapp's dissertation is his only published text dealing with his early views of perceptual experiences. It is comprised of three sections. In the first, he argues that our senses of sight, hearing, and touch, all present us with a world of "things." The sense of sight, in particular, presents things by means of color. In the second section, he proceeds to discuss just the sense of sight, focusing on how color presents things, or the relationship between the presenting and the presented. He argues that color presents things by contributing a certain order, or form, that manifests itself in the orderly, predictable variation of perspectives in the course of experience. In the third section, he asks what invests the perceptual order with a higher worth than that belonging to mere chaos, and what renders it real. He argues that this is because, in its orderliness, the presented participates in something akin to Platonic Ideas.

In the dissertation, Schapp approaches philosophical issues in a manner that involves hardly any discussion or citation, of other philosophers' works, with only an occasional mention of Goethe, Husserl, or Plato. Instead, he appears to accord importance to giving close consideration to his own actual experiences—even concluding his *Preface* with a kind of expression of methodological commitment, "I only hope that I wrote nothing I did not myself see" (Schapp 1976a: IX). Also, instead of engaging in philosophical theorizing or formulating his theses and defining his terms at the outset, he permits his discussion to progress from insight to insight, raising further issues and addressing them as it goes along, aiming toward the deeper understanding that can only be articulated and brought to the reader in the fullness of time.

I have already considered Schapp's views in another paper, in which I approach his discussion very much on these, its own terms (Laasik 2015). Here, by contrast, I will undertake to reconstruct his views as a deductive argument, while also covering somewhat broader thematic ground than in my other paper, and invoking Husserl's views as part of my criticisms of Schapp's position. Specifically, I will be arguing for the following three theses:

(A) Schapp's overall argument can be reconstructed as a hypothetical syllogism supporting the view that visual perception can only give its objects in color.
(B) Considerations of clarity perform important roles in that argument.
(C) There are, however, problems with various aspects of the argument, centering on the color and spatiality of things, and their relations with what Schapp refers to as "Ideas."

I will be working with the following reconstruction of Schapp's argument:

(1) Whenever there is a visual perceptual experience, it involves intending an Idea.
(2) If an experience involves intending an Idea, the Idea confers upon the experience a form.
(3) If a conferral of form thus takes place, the experience is directed to a thing.
(4) If an experience is directed to a thing, it gives it with spatial properties.
(5) If an experience gives a thing with spatial properties, it also gives it in color.
(6) Whenever there is a visual perceptual experience, it gives things in color.

Some clarificatory remarks are in order. Schapp, as I have indicated, hones and refines his terms as he goes along, and it is therefore important to note that the main conclusion, (6), actually concerns not just any kind of color, but what he comes to refer to as "adhesive" color (*anhaftende Farbe*)—meaning, roughly, constant color—to be discussed in more detail in part II of my paper (Schapp 1976a: 86). Also, he at one juncture narrows the scope of his views to a specific kind of "observational" perception (*beobachtende Wahrnehmung*), but I have not incorporated this qualification into my statement of his argument, since he almost does not consider other kinds of perception, and generally concerns himself with perceptual experiences as such (Schapp 1976a: 66). It should also be clarified that when he speaks of Ideas (*Ideen*), he means, specifically, "individual Ideas" (*Einzelideen*), that is, capturing things in their utmost particularity, not in terms of their species or salient properties (Schapp 1976a: 133–5). Clarity (*Klarheit, Deutlichkeit*) is yet another notion which evolves through the different stages of Schapp's discussion, being at first left intuitive, then connected with the notion of form, and finally traced to its putative source in Ideas (Schapp 1976a: 61–3). I have not incorporated it into my above reconstruction of Schapp's main argument, but have nevertheless given it prominence as part of my thesis B, because it seems to me an important part of Schapp's various subsidiary arguments. I take it to be a kind of noetic notion, that is, pertaining to the experience, considered as one side of the experience-object correlation. As such, it has a noematic correlate, namely, in this case, in perceptual form, which mirrors it to the point that it is possible to recast certain claims or arguments in either noetic or noematic terms, conducing to insight into the problems at hand.

I am reconstructing Schapp's argument in deductive terms, since I believe that doing so may help us to better assess Schapp's views, namely, by drawing into focus relations of dependence between different aspects of experiences, something a phenomenologist could perhaps also articulate in terms of eidetic variation. But doing so will also require me to considerably reorganize Schapp's ideas. Notably, Schapp's actual discussion does not progress from the above premise 1 toward the conclusion, but instead, on the whole, the other way around, namely, from the conclusion and premise 5, toward premise 1. It is also not obvious to me that he even regards 6 as his main conclusion, instead of, say, a point that is established at the outset and then made the starting point of the entire ensuing discussion. However, I believe that my construal is, in this regard, vindicated by giving closer heed to the details. Thus, while Schapp may, indeed, establish at the outset that visual perception involves color of some kind or other, his ideas should be seen as requiring additional support as soon as he specifies that he has in mind adhesive color specifically, and that such adhesive color is indispensable for us to be able to experience things and their spatiality.

The main body of my chapter consists of three parts, with Part 2 mainly dedicated to connecting premises 3–5 of the reconstructed argument with Schapp's actual discussion of the color and spatiality of perceived objects, and Part 3, to establishing a connection between premises 1 and 2, on the one hand,

and Schapp's discussion of Ideas, on the other. In Part 4, I will make three criticisms of Schapp's views.

1

I will now present aspects of Schapp's view to provide support for my theses A and B, namely, that Schapp's argument can be reconstructed as a deduction, supporting the view that visual perception can only give its objects in color, and that considerations of clarity perform important roles in that argument. As the reader will see, the below discussion importantly leads up to Schapp's consideration of what I will call the distant things scenario, which I take to be at the core of his subsidiary arguments for premises 3–5 of his main argument. I will not be offering criticisms of his uses of the distant things scenario, since I have already done so elsewhere, but keeping it in view should help the reader assess whether we have, indeed, correctly reconstructed his main argument (Laasik 2015).

Although I will be drawing attention to Schapp's ideas roughly in the order in which he presents them in his Sections 1 and 2, I will not be aiming to give a complete overview of these parts of his dissertation—only highlighting the ideas and passages that bear on my take on his argument, especially his discussion of color, the physicality of things, and his appeals to perceptual clarity.

To begin, in Section 1 of his dissertation, he argues that the sense of sight presents things through color, while not yet being very clear as to the nature of that color or why he takes it to be so indispensable and important: "Now, what is sensuously given to us in the colored world, which we 'see,' what is perceived? The first answer will be, 'Color.' And color surely occupies a distinguished place in this world" (Schapp 1976a: 17). He next notes that we do, indeed, perceive space as well as things in space (Schapp 1976a: 18). He makes a kind of phenomenological argument to the effect that things are indeed experienced in their physicality and can in no way be reduced to complexes of color. We see, for example, "how elastic the iron of a tuning fork is; we see the lightness of a feather, of smoke, which the wind carries away. We see the consistency and heaviness of an iron weight, which bores itself into the sand. In seeing, all this stands before us in person" (Schapp 1976a: 20).

So, it should be intuitively compelling that visual perception gives us things and their physical properties—we are in a position to appreciate this if we stay away from undue theorizing and philosophize, as it were, with our hands in pockets. Schapp affirms with emphasis that many properties of things reveal themselves under favorable circumstances in the world of color.

More generally, Schapp discusses visual and other perceptual experiences in terms of the distinction between what he refers to as "the presenting" (*das Darstellende*) and "the presented" (*das Dargestellte*). Colors present; things are what is presented. Indeed, color also presents space, and space, in turn, presents things or makes a necessary contribution to presenting things. The general view is that while something can, in different regards, be both presenting and presented, nothing can ever present itself. Schapp is thus led to speak of a kind of "tear in the world," or a "cleft" between the presenting and the presented (Schapp 1976a: 41, 52). In Chapter 7, Section 1, Schapp adds to this discussion by introducing a new distinction between the presenting and the presented, which turns on the idea of causality, as he asserts that "the presenting—colors, tones, data of the senses of touch and pressure—is dropped when one views the thing-world from the viewpoint of causality; it finds no place in the world of causality, as the presented does" (Schapp 1976a: 46–7).

To clarify, this new, causality-based distinction is introduced to enable us to conceive of a unified world of things, as what is presented by our different senses, because there are considerable differences between what can be intuitively given, for example, by sight, hearing, and touch. To attain a conception of a unified thing-world, we need to conceive of it in terms of the causal relations among things. Schapp argues that many causal relations are perceivable, making a direct and simple appeal to the effect that this idea is intuitively compelling (Schapp 1976a: 48–9).

At the start of Section 2, Schapp gives a somewhat widely-ranging introductory discussion, setting the stage for the distant things scenario, namely, by sketching aspects of the worldview of "the Ancients," such as their beliefs that there existed Olympian gods, fixed stars in the firmament, and, somewhere in the nether regions, an Underworld, Tartarus. Schapp contends that, by and large, these superstitious and false beliefs were not due to perceptual failures. We might nowadays easily believe that they were because of certain preconceived ideas about the world we experience. Modern science has taken a certain idea of clarity (*Deutlichkeit, Klarheit*) from ordinary experience and applied it beyond ordinary experience, while using microscopes and telescopes to open up micro- and macroscopic realms. For example, when we adjust the focus in a microscope, we take ourselves to have attained the correct view when our sample begins to look clear in the same way that ordinary things do under normal viewing conditions. The result is a homogenization of the world, and a misconception regarding perceptual experience, namely, that it can similarly take as its objects both near and far things, objects microscopic, middle-sized, and macroscopic, and perceive all of them either correctly or incorrectly. This is why we would naturally regard the stars in the sky as material things, and charge the Ancients with letting their senses deceive them as they looked into the night skies. Schapp, however, believes that it is a mistake for a philosopher to take for granted the legitimacy of the broad application of this idea of clarity. Instead, he embarks on an inquiry into the nature of such perceptual clarity—leading him, in Chapter 1, Section 2, to argue that we fail to perceive a house far down in the valley qua thing because it is experienced unclearly.

> The house that we see on top of the mountain, and next to which we stand, is really as it appears. The house that we see deep down in the valley, is really not as it looks from afar. What we see where the house really stands, a bluish spot, does not even appear as if it were really the way it looks. It is something unclear, indistinct. It is not as if, instead of the house, we are distinctly seeing another thing, a small cloud. What we instead see, does not at all appear as if it were a thing, which could be relegated to the same level as the house beside which we stand. What we see down there does not appear as a small cloud, in the same way as what is standing next to us appears as a house. And, for the main thing, this is not because we know that the eye does not carry so far, but has instead to do with the perceived. To be drastic, one representation looks distinct and the other indistinct. It is not that the second representation does not earn our trust. Instead, by its own content, it makes no claim on our trust. This requires no further reflection, it only requires watching the phenomenon itself. (Schapp 1976a: 63)

As Schapp explains in the quoted passage, the distinguishing mark between the ways of givenness of the two houses is clarity, or the lack thereof. Color sometimes fails to present things: the putative distant things are thus, in fact, categorically different from nearby things. This is because the nearby things are clear, while the putative distant things are unclear.

Next, in Chapter 2, Schapp argues that "observational perception" and "thing" are correlative terms. He conceives of observation as an intrinsic aspect of a kind of perception, namely, seeking to overcome perceptual obstacles and difficulties, and to attain things as they really are (Schapp 1976a: 66). He contrasts observational perception with aesthetic perception, which revels in unclarity and has no interest in overcoming it.

Observation, or penetration into the thing, is possible only under favorable circumstances, namely, in good lighting and at a suitable distance. "We do not see in this way that which is far away, however much we exert ourselves. There, the glance slips off that which is seen. The seen permits no entry, as a thing does" (Schapp 1976a: 70). He further adds that in the case of "darkness, twilight, phenomena of distance" (Schapp 1976a: 71) there can be no observation, because "here the observer finds no object that would offer an aim for the observation" (Schapp 1976a: 71).

Schapp is here still operating with a notion of clarity that is merely intuitively understood. He raises the question of the nature of clarity but addresses it only by offering further examples: how a tree, or a house, looks to us as we view them at an increasing distance until it becomes a mere black dot in the distance (Schapp 1976a: 72). These are transitions from clear to unclear givenness. However, we are not told when the experience becomes so unclear that we can no longer speak of the givenness of things.

Yet Schapp also argues that the relevant kind of clarity can be better understood when we take a closer look at the kind of color that he has in mind, namely, adhesive color, which invests perceived objects with a form, enabling us to achieve a conception of clarity as possession of form. Thus, Schapp contends that a thing's constant color, or adhesive color, as he calls it, needs to be distinguished from the perspectival color, or the lighting effects—but the presentation of adhesive color nevertheless requires perspectival color, and it can never be given "purely" (Schapp 1976a: 87). We learn that the adhesive color is univocal (*eindeutig*), whereas the lighting effects are equivocal (*mehrdeutig*). The adhesive color resists my will, whereas I can whimsically make what I like of the perspectival lighting formations. Schapp argues that the ability to provide resistance is due to having a form: "The difference between lighting effects and the actual color is a *difference of form*. The lighting effects lack a solid form, the actual color is univocally formed" (Schapp 1976a: 89). A form governs the ways in which color changes through time, while being itself timeless, "A form is something absolute. Nothing in it permits of a construal, nothing of it can be taken away from it. It is the absolutely simple, qualityless, transparent" (Schapp 1976a: 96). The wrong color may be forced into the form of a particular thing's color and can deceive us for a while, until the course of its modulation reveals that we have been subject to an illusion (Schapp 1976a: 95). In twilight, or at a distance of a thousand feet, however, we merely experience switching from one presentation to the next, without any of them attaining to a position of privilege among the others, that is, providing the basis for relegating the others into the realm of the illusory (Schapp 1976a: 95).

Having put before the reader these various aspects of Schapp's view, let us connect them with our premises 3–5. From the material in Schapp's Section 1, we learned, first of all, that visual perception gives us color, space, and things. We were also assured that while the perception of color does, in a sense, come first, this should not be taken to mean that physical things are reducible to color. Instead, the relations between color and things should be viewed in terms of the presenting-versus-presented dichotomy. This dichotomy is ultimately underpinned by the concept of causality, further underscoring the irreducibility of the presented to the presenting, namely, of things, to mere constellations of color. We now have in place all the main elements of premises 4 and 5, but it may still not be entirely clear whether it is correct to attribute to Schapp the ideas captured therein. This does, however, become evident when we reach Schapp's discussion of the distant things scenario—inviting us to consider the case of the house far down in the valley, where the right kind of color fails to obtain, and to agree that, for this reason, we cannot make good sense of its shape and its spatial relations with the surrounding scenery—and are therefore not really perceiving it as a thing at all. So, the distant things scenario is used by Schapp to make subsidiary arguments for what we have rendered as premises 5 and 4—ordered, now, to align with the actual overall trajectory of Schapp's discussion.

(5) If an experience gives a thing with spatial properties, it also gives it in color.

(4) If an experience is directed to a thing, it gives it with spatial properties.

From Schapp's Section 2, we also learned more about the kind of visual perception, and color, that Schapp has in his sights, namely, observational perception and adhesive color. The notion of observational perception is helpful in that it further elucidates the process, and possible progress, of visual perception. But observational perception is for Schapp the main kind of perception, basically a stand-in for perceptual experience in general, since any alternatives to it are barely mentioned. I have therefore opted not to explicitly incorporate it into my reconstruction, but to speak of (visual) perceptual experiences in general. Adhesive color is contrasted, on the one hand, with perspectival color, but also, on the other hand, with color that is not sufficiently alive with the play of lights and shadows. Schapp connects adhesive color with the notion of form, which turns out to be of crucial importance for the presentation of things. It seems fair to say that things are given *if and only if* they are invested with a form, but, to give our hypothetical syllogism a cleaner look, we have emphasized just one side of the biconditional:

(3) If a conferral of form thus takes place, the experience is directed to a thing.

However, our discussion has not quite attained premise 3 yet, insofar as we have not yet said anything about the sources of form to enable us to speak about its "conferral" upon the sensuous multiplicity. We are, at this point, only able to say that if there is form, the experience is directed to a thing.

What about the role of clarity in all this? As I have already indicated, I believe that clarity is a kind of noetic notion, capturing an aspect of the experience, and yet closely mirroring an aspect of the experienced object, in the context of the experience-object correlation. We may say, roughly, that an experience is clear, insofar as its object has a form. If this is correct, we should, in principle, be able to state the main argument without explicitly invoking clarity, and yet rely on considerations of clarity to gain a different perspective on some of its core ideas, putting us in a better position to appraise the argument. Indeed, we can see that Schapp moves the consideration of clarity center stage when he first advances the distant things scenario to support his views concerning the dependence relations among experienced color, space, and things.

2

Let us continue our presentation of aspects of Schapp's view, aiming to support our theses A and B. We will now be mainly considering premises 1 and 2, in light of Schapp's discussion, in Section 3 of his dissertation, of Platonic Ideas, the manner in which Ideas are understood by perceivers, and their role in furnishing the boundaries of things.

In Chapter 1, Section 3, Schapp turns his attention from color, and what is presented in color, to the non-sensuous aspect of perception. He draws our attention to "a peculiar moment, which seems of great importance to [him], indeed, which first confers upon every perception the peculiar light, without which, to speak with Kant, every perception would be blind and have nothing to do with sensuous givenness" (Schapp 1976a: 130). He further clarifies that he has in mind "the Idea in perception," and that he uses the designation "Idea" to make a connection with Plato (Schapp 1976a: 130). Otherwise, instead of "Idea," one could also say, "concept," or "essence." We must, accordingly, distinguish in every perception between an intention (*das Meinen*) and an intuition (*das Anschauen*), the former concerned with an Idea, and the latter, with a thing's sensuous givenness. However, the Idea and the sensuous givenness are inseparably bound together, and can be rent apart only by abstraction.

He further emphasizes that an Idea is to be distinguished from a species:

> We have, indeed, said that the thing stands before us as "potsherd"—by this it is not meant that it stands before us under the species *potsherd*. Because that, as which it stands before us, [or] what we mean of a thing, is connected with the utmost individuality of the thing; we have an intention of everything we objectify of a thing, down to its last peculiarities. (Schapp 1976a: 133)

So, an Idea should not be designated by a general term but by a proper name, if not for the fact that we seem to lack suitable proper names for most things, leaving us little choice but to designate each individual thing with an "X." It can be seen that by "Idea" Schapp means an "individual Idea" (*Einzelidee*), or we might also call it the individual essence of a thing.[2] In relation to the contrast between Ideas and species, he also invokes a case where we may seemingly willfully impose different notions on something like a cloud formation—for example, as it seems now like a mountain, now like some kind of animal—as having to do with subsuming the nebulous sensuous given under different species, but contends that this subsumption under species presupposes that something has, in the first place, been perceived in terms of an individual Idea (Schapp 1976a: 133). Thus, one may speculate as to the nature of the lighter patch in the hotel room ceiling, subsuming it now under this, now under that species, but it is only when one opens the curtains in the morning that it really strikes one, say, as a lighter stroke of whitewash. Schapp explicitly distinguishes two closely related aspects of this occurrence. On the one hand, when the curtain came open, the color "took on forms, the form of the adhesive color etc. This then presented me with the stroke of whitewash" (Schapp 1976a: 138–9). On the other hand, an Idea is revealed to me, insofar as all "indeterminacy" about this patch of ceiling is suddenly gone (Schapp 1976a: 139). So, the form and the Idea, though closely related, are distinct from each other. Schapp also repeatedly and emphatically connects the notion of an Idea with clarity of perception, "Now, there is such an Idea of each thing that we perceive clearly (*deutlich*), and we cannot perceive any thing without this Idea" (Schapp 1976a: 134). Also, the things that are seen clearly are "univocally determined" (*eindeutig bestimmt*)—as if they were telling us, "Thus are we, this is the essence we have" (Schapp 1976a: 139). By contrast, "[t]hat, which we see unclearly, hides from us its essence" (Schapp 1976a: 139). It leaves open many possibilities of seeing itself, with the consequence that we see mere chaos, and no thing at all. So, in sum, one perceives a thing "in its Idea." Only insofar as things "participate" in Ideas, or "embody" them, are they knowable, and do they amount to anything at all: "The Idea is what first provides the world with a sense, what makes it a cosmos" (Schapp 1976a: 142).

In Chapter 2, Section 3, Schapp begins to discuss our understanding (*Verstehen*) of Ideas. It is precisely the Idea, and not the perceived thing, that is understood when one has a perceptual experience of a thing. Schapp makes a connection between clarity and understanding: "As a confused story is described as incomprehensible, so too is the perception of what is distant, of the world enveloped in twilight. But a clear perception is understood, just as a well-delivered story is understood" (Schapp 1976a: 145). So, I take it that when he speaks, as he sometimes also does, of clear perception's being "understandable," he does not mean that, at a minimum, the mere possibility of understanding is there. Instead, what he means is that the understanding is actual, already attained. Indeed, it appears to be his view that, once there is understanding, it leaves no room for further clarification, or any kind of progress, within the perception: "The perception in which something is understood, has thereby reached its goal. It would be senseless to demand more of the perception or to excogitate a perception which accomplished more" (Schapp 1976a: 146).

It may seem somewhat counterintuitive that there can be no perceptual progress, whether stepwise or by degrees. To address such a concern, Schapp proceeds to hammer home the point by proposing to consider perceptual experience as a special case of the more general phenomenon of learning, "All learning—and we learn in this sense daily—is an epiphany (*Erleuchtung*). It is a leap into the truth, an understanding. To speak of stages there, makes no sense" (Schapp 1976a: 147). We do not make gradual educational progress by patient drudgery, for example, by endless repetition of the material. Instead, grasping is always sudden, "One does not know where the understanding comes from; it is there in one blow" (Schapp 1976a: 147).

He elaborates on this point further, for example, by underscoring the difference between the sudden attainment of knowledge and the gradual development of organic life. However, we also find a gesture at a way of explaining any seeming cases of gradual progress of understanding: "It may well be that in everything we understand, there remains a residue of what is not understood. We can understand incompletely" (Schapp 1976a: 148–9). Thus, the entire body of mathematics is certainly not completely understood. But the parts of it that are understood, *are* understood.

In Chapter 3, Section 3, Schapp introduces the notion of a boundary (*Grenze*), with the stated aim of establishing the correctness of the foregoing discussion, insofar as a boundary stands in a close relation with an Idea—while also objecting to physical and psychological accounts of boundaries (Schapp 1976a: 149).

Schapp, accordingly, presents his readers with descriptions of various surfaces (*Flächen*), to make the point that these surfaces may not yet amount to the outer surface (*Oberfläche*) of a thing. A surface is something that can be understood without any relation to a body (*Körper*). It is also without reference to a body that we may already speak of "directions" (*Richtungen*). However, amid the various directions, we can also come to experience a boundary, for example, between something brown and something gray, insofar as we see something as "still" (*noch*) brown, and then brown "no more" (*nicht mehr*). Schapp contends, "This 'still' and 'no more' has sense only in regard to a boundary. It is, namely, not the simple perception of different qualities that gives us the boundary; they must be looked at from the aspect of 'no more' and 'still'" (Schapp 1976a: 152). Schapp further draws a connection between the notions of the boundary and the figure (*Gestalt*). It is figures that are bounded, and figure and boundary are likewise overlooked if one just sees a mere surface (Schapp 1976a: 155).

But now, how to account for there being boundaries? On the penultimate page of his dissertation, Schapp proposes an account in terms of Ideas:

> Insofar as we see a thing in its Idea (*in seiner Idee*), it stands before us as bounded. It is not that the "sensuous" somehow ceases; instead, the Idea cuts through the sensuous.
>
> So far as (*sofern*) a thing embodies the Idea *inkwell*, *pencil*, or *cigar*, an Idea which incorporates itself in the same way in all things that are exactly the same, (*sofern*) the thing has a boundary. (Schapp 1976a: 156)

Indeed, Schapp eventually suggests that the boundary is only an example of an array of categorial concepts, such as *identity*, *unity*, and *totality*, of which we must conceive by recourse to Ideas and their functioning toward the sensuous.

Let us now consider how Schapp's actual discussion, as we have just presented it, connects with our reconstruction of his argument. First of all, remember that in part II of our paper, we conceded that we had not yet completely justified our inclusion of premise 3.

(3) If a conferral of form thus takes place, the experience is directed to a thing.

The problem was that our talk of "conferral" of form was not born out by the substance of Schapp's Section 2, although certainly emphatic about the importance of form in perception. However, Schapp's invocation of Ideas in Chapter 1, Section 3, puts premise 3 on a firm footing, namely, as part of our reconstruction of Schapp's argument. Indeed, based on Chapter 1, premises 2 and 1 should appear in the same light.

(2) If an experience involves intending an Idea, the Idea confers upon the experience a form.
(1) Whenever there is a visual perceptual experience, it involves intending an Idea.

I say so because it is in Chapter 1 that Schapp puts forward his views concerning the need for Ideas in perceptual experience, conceiving of Ideas as individual Ideas, instead of species or genera. We are also advised that Ideas cannot simply be identified with a sensuous form, while endorsing a close relation of one-sided dependence of forms on Ideas. Indeed, Chapter 1 probably sets forth stronger claims than are captured by our conditionals, insofar as Schapp probably commits himself to bi-conditionals where we have opted to articulate one-sided conditional claims as premises 2 and 3, to set up our hypothetical syllogism.

So, I believe that Chapter 1, Section 3, enables us to complete the justification of our reconstruction of Schapp's argument, but what have we learned about the justification for Schapp's views, as represented by us? As far as I can tell, Schapp makes two subsidiary arguments for premises 1 and 2 combined, namely, in Chapters 2–4, Section 3. The first is the argument from learning in Chapter 2. In this argument, the notion of clarity again plays an important role, insofar as Schapp appeals to the intuitive legitimacy of a sharp demarcation between the clear and the unclear, as he effectively urges us to accept a separation between the sensible realm and the Platonic supersensible realm, while impressing it upon us that the sudden, epiphanous attainment of complete, unsurpassable clarity is a remarkable phenomenon which calls for an explanation in terms of the thing's participation in, and our grasping of, an Idea. Second, in Chapters 3 and 4 we can find an argument from boundaries. Schapp introduces the notion of a boundary while arguing that it is in need of an explanation by recourse to Ideas—and could not possibly be accounted for in physical or psychological terms. I take the argument from boundaries to be his second subsidiary argument for premises 1 and 2 of the main argument.

3

If one accepts premises 1–5 in the argument we have attributed to Schapp, the conclusion deductively follows. I do, however, believe that there are problems with various premises and lines of thought which make up this argument—a contention I have set forth as my thesis C. To show that this is the case, I will now make three Husserl-inspired objections to Schapp's argument—while sketching the relevant Husserlian views quite briefly, and not concerning myself with the overall justification of the Husserlian phenomenological approach.

My first objection targets Schapp's ideas concerning the visual perception of color, space, and things—premise 5 specifically,

(5) If an experience gives a thing with spatial properties, it also gives it in (adhesive) color.

I have already noted that Schapp argues for this idea by invoking the distant things scenario, which I have critiqued elsewhere (Laasik 2015). Here, I will, instead, target premise 5 directly. My objection is that in light of the conceivability of what Husserl calls the perceptual "phantoms," Schapp's requirement of adhesive color, for perceptually experiencing things and their spatial properties, should appear as extremely implausible. As is well-known to phenomenologists, Husserl believes that we can conceive of experiences of phantoms, that is, objects with spatial properties (or "determinations"), but lacking all physical properties, that is, involving causality and actual or possible causal relations. According to Husserl, we experience spatial properties in terms of visuo-kinesthetic anticipations, concerning the ways in which the object would appear if we moved relative to it, and physical properties in terms of environmental anticipations, that is, concerning the ways in which the object would appear upon its interacting with its environment, for example, by colliding with another object. In the case of constant or adhesive color, however, its physicality is attested to by the fact that our experience concerns anticipations with regard to the ways in which the color interacts with a changeable lighting environment.[3]

Whether or not we actually experience phantoms, I find it compelling that experiences of phantoms are conceivable. It seems that we do not always need adhesive color in order to experience spatial objectivity. Instead, we need a kind of color that will, at a minimum, enable us to draw lines of demarcation, and this may be enough, for example, for it to appear to us that one object is occluding another, giving us at least a rudimentary sense of their three-dimensional spatiality. It might be that there is a dazzling color-confusion on the one side of the demarcation line, and a somewhat different dazzling color-confusion on the other side—or perhaps, on both sides, just different shades of gray, as in the dark of the night. Such an experience would be devoid of constant color, and we could, by keeping the lighting conditions fixed, namely, as a methodological device, consider the experience apart from all, or most, anticipations concerning the ways in which the color-confusion or the shade of gray would present itself in different lighting conditions. Notice that we may concede that, in these circumstances, it could be very difficult to make out an object's shape or to experience any objects at all. We only need to argue that it is not impossible.

If we can do that, then phantoms are conceivable, and it is possible to experience spatial properties without adhesive color. At this point, it might be suggested that this consideration does not damage Schapp's view, since we have been talking about objects in a broader sense than Schapp does, insofar as he concerns himself specifically with things, whatever the case may be with other kinds of sensuous objects, for example, phantoms. In connection with this, it is also worth remembering that he cashes out the presenting-versus-presented distinction in causal terms, tailoring it specifically to physical things. But I believe that my point would carry over from phantoms to physical things. So long as we are granted the barest color resources needed to draw some lines of demarcation, is it not possible to imagine one relatively obscure mass hurtling toward another in the dark and to have at least a vague anticipatory sense of the consequences of an impending collision?

Now, someone might grant this, yet object that while we seem to be considering fairly remote possibilities, Schapp's project might perhaps be concerned more specifically with something like our actual experiences. His phenomenology might simply be less "pure" than ours by incorporating some (not illegitimate) assumptions, which we, on our part, have chosen to eschew. However, I believe that we, on our part, do not need to reach for any particularly remote possibilities of experience. We can see this by considering a pertinent argument of Schapp's, which can be turned against his own view. Namely, Schapp sometimes brings up the case of distant things together with other cases like looking into a dark night or a thick fog, or seeing things in twilight (Schapp 1976a: 71, 95, 102). Just as with distant things, it is emphatically the case that we do not experience rich color modulation in twilight, or in the dark of the evening. According to Schapp, this means that we do not perceptually experience the things around us, even though we see their outlines, shades of gray and shades of dark, and perhaps some clues to their color. Yet Schapp's view that we, inevitably, never see things in the dark of the evening renders perceptual experience unacceptably failure-prone, as it breaks down all around us on a daily basis, effecting a chimerical transformation of the environment that we experience around us. I would therefore suggest that we can, at least sometimes, to some extent, experience things in the dark of the evening, albeit with difficulty, yielding a real-life counterexample to Schapp's premise 5.

Our second and third objections are concerned with the role Schapp accords to Platonic Ideas in perceptual experience, taking aim at the arguments from learning and from boundaries, respectively. To introduce the objection to the argument from learning, let us begin by briefly comparing Schapp's view with Husserl's. We have seen that, according to Schapp, a visual perceptual experience of a thing must involve "intending"—to be read as a success term!—an individual Idea, or essence, which will confer clarity and form upon the experience. On Husserl's mature view, however, there lies, at the core of the thing, as perceptually experienced, not its essence, but the "idea" of its essence, where "idea," now, signifies not a Platonic Idea but a Kantian regulatory idea, something toward which we strive, and which, accordingly, guides and motivates our epistemic pursuits, but always, inevitably remaining out of our reach (Husserl 1950: §143). More concretely, it will always be possible for us to achieve more fulfillments and closer determinations with regard to a thing, as our perceptual anticipations are fulfilled, and new, unexpected details revealed—for example, as I find out that the back of the fruit does indeed have brown spots as anticipated, but also that there are neither more nor less than three such spots, having had no anticipations as to their number (Husserl 1973: 58–9, 100–2). So, Husserl's view is motivated by the consideration that it is always possible to experience a thing better and more completely, and there is no privileged perspective which could yield the definitive, unsurpassable experience. But notice that we do not need to embrace this view in its full strength, in regard to its *always* being possible to improve on an experience. We just need to appreciate the fact that the Husserlian leitmotifs of fulfillment and closer determination, both of which can be thought of as occurring in processes, or series of stages, militate against Schapp's commitment to a sudden, epiphanous, unsurpassable perceptual revelation. For Schapp to be wrong, it is enough if some fulfillments and closer determinations are possible.

Now, Schapp supports this view by appealing to the argument from learning, which involves regarding perceptual progress as a special case of the more general phenomenon of learning. But this will scarcely help, because if the possibilities of gradual fulfillment and closer determination are intuitively compelling, this will also call into question Schapp's general view of learning, with its emphasis on Gestalt switch-like revelations. True, an object can be thought of as having a form, which has its source in its essence, its *Einzelidee*, and the revelation of which will conduce to the clarity of the experience—but we must allow for the possibility that the revelation takes place gradually, instead of in a sudden epiphany, as well as for a gradual increase in clarity along the dimensions of fullness and determinacy.

Based on the above presentation of Schapp's Chapter 2, Section 3, Schapp might try to address such criticisms by conceiving of perceptual clarity and progress, in mereological terms, with complete clarity being attainable in regard to one item at a time, while the whole can be somewhat unclear, insofar as it has some clear parts and some unclear parts. Someone could try to think in this way about the perceived object and its various parts, whatever they may be. But this idea does not work, because the perceptual object cannot be partitioned in terms of possibly completely clear parts. One could, in principle, keep achieving clearer, that is, fuller and more determinate, views of any parts of the object, as one keeps taking ever closer looks and experiencing these parts in an inexhaustible set of different circumstances.

Notice, further, that Schapp himself speaks some of the time as though in agreement with us, namely, when he invokes the idea of observational perception. In speaking of observation, he seems precisely to espouse the idea that we can perceptually experience things either clearly or unclearly, or even more or less clearly, by degrees. According to Schapp, as we have learned, it is precisely a hallmark of observational perception that it engages with what is unclear and aims to overcome unclarity where it finds it. For example, in this context, Schapp takes the crucial difference between near and far things to be that the former are amenable to observation but the latter are not, that is, with the nearby things, clarification is possible, but the distant things could not possibly be rendered any clearer (Schapp 1976a: 75–6). This suggests that Schapp, too, is at times bound to admit that perception is not like a sudden epiphany. However, such admissions are inconsistent with his "official" view, which he tries to defend by means of the argument from learning.

The argument from boundaries is, likewise, designed to support the view that visual experiences of things must involve intending Platonic Ideas, where "intending" is meant as a success term. I would construe this argument in terms of distinct, though related, ontological and epistemological lines of thought. First, an individual Idea determines a thing's boundaries. Second, we regularly have perceptual experiences that are quite clear as to things' boundaries, and this is possible because "a thing embodies [for us] the Idea *inkwell*, *pencil*, or *cigar*." We therefore "see a thing in its Idea" (Schapp 1976a: 156). (I am borrowing from the block quotation in our discussion of Schapp's Chapter 3, Section 3.) But the ontological consideration alone is insufficient to establish the conclusion, because a thing's boundaries do not determine its individual Idea, or individual essence. An individual essence encapsulates an object's identity criteria, but objects' identity criteria generally involve a great deal more than their boundaries. In the above Husserlian terms, if two members of a repetition series have the same boundaries, it does not follow that they are the same object (Husserl 2012: 134). However, it may also be that Schapp conceives of Ideas as indispensable sources of evidence, or epistemic guidance, concerning where a thing's boundaries are: we are able to experience the thing's boundaries because we are guided by Ideas like *inkwell*, *pencil*, or *cigar*. But if this is his argument, it should also be possible to attribute this guiding function to general (sortal) concepts which the perceiver brings to bear on the perceptual situation, enabling him to make sense of individual objects, including ones that are new to him. There is a hint of this view in Schapp's choice of the examples that we have just listed. In sum, the argument from boundaries does not succeed in showing that visual perceptual experiences must involve seeing a thing "in its Idea," in Schapp's sense.

4

I have been arguing that Schapp's overall argument can be reconstructed as a hypothetical syllogism supporting the view that visual perception can only give its objects in color and that considerations of clarity perform important roles in that argument. I have also pointed out three problems with various aspects of the argument, centering on the color and spatiality of things, and their putative relations with Platonic Ideas, construed by Schapp as individual Ideas, or essences. I hope that this attempt at reconstruction and critique will make it easier for readers to engage firsthand with Schapp's rich contributions to the phenomenology of perception.

Notes

1 Spiegelberg's account appears to be slightly chronologically inconsistent with Schapp's own. In his philosophical memoir, Schapp says that he came to Göttingen, and, by implication, became Husserl's student, in 1905 (Schapp 1976b: 18, 2025: 227).

2 According to Husserl, the individual essence (*das individuelle Wesen*) is "an identical that can be 'extracted' from a repetition series (*Wiederholungsreihe*), but is given only in 'identification'" (Husserl 2012: 134).

3 For a contrastive discussion of the levels of spatial objectivity (i.e., the phantom) and material thinghood, see Husserl (1952: Sect. One). Regarding color, see especially Husserl (1952: § 15 c).

References

Husserl, E. (1950), *Ideen zu einer reinen Phänomenologie und phänomenologischen Philosophie. Erstes Buch: Allgemeine Einführung in die reine Phänomenologie* (Hua. III), ed. W. Biemel, The Hague, The Netherlands: Martinus Nijhoff.

Husserl, E. (1952), *Ideen zu einer Reinen Phänomenologie und Phänomenologischen Philosophie. Zweites Buch: Phänomenologische Untersuchungen zur Konstitution* (Hua. IV), ed. M. Biemel, The Hague, The Netherlands: Martinus Nijhoff.

Husserl, E. (1973), *Ding und Raum. Vorlesungen 1907* (Hua XVI), ed. U. Claesges, The Hague, The Netherlands: Martinus Nijhoff.

Husserl, E. (2012), *Zur Lehre vom Wesen und zur Methode der eidetischen Variation. Texte aus dem Nachlass (1891-1935)* (Hua. XLI), ed. D. Fonfara, Dordrecht, Holland: Springer.

Laasik, K. (2015), "Wilhelm Schapp on Seeing Distant Things." *Studia Phaenomenologica*, XV: 394–412.

Schapp, W. (1976a), *Beiträge zur Phänomenologie der Wahrnehmung.* Wiesbaden, Germany: Heymann.

Schapp, W. (1976b), *Erinnerungen an Edmund Husserl. Ein Beitrag zur Geschichte der Phänomenologie.* Wiesbaden, Germany: Heymann.

Schapp, W. (2025), "Recollections of Husserl," trans. E. A. Behnke, in D. De Santis, D. Nuccilli (eds), *The Philosophy of Wilhelm Schapp: From Phenomenology to Jurisprudence and the Hermeneutics of Stories*, 227–238, London: Bloomsbury.

Spiegelberg, H. (1965), *The Phenomenological Movement. A Historical Introduction*, 2nd edn, Vol. I, The Hague, Netherlands: Martinus Nijhoff.

3

Schapp on Perceptual Normativity[1]

Michela Summa

A distinctive feature of phenomenological philosophy is its reliance on description. However, phenomenological descriptions should not be understood as simply aiming to present individual objects according to their qualities and characteristics. Rather, phenomenologists have often maintained that one of their main tasks is precisely to develop a *method* of description that is philosophically appropriate. But appropriate for what? To put it briefly: for recognizing the structures of experience and distinguishing between types of experience on the basis of their respective constitutive structures.[2] Accordingly, the starting point of phenomenological inquiry is taken to be the description of what makes up everyday experiential occurrences: for example, how things are given in perception or imagination, how we emotionally react to certain situations, how we shape our actions within a social context, etc. Building on such descriptions of everyday experience to obtain structural descriptions requires a sophisticated method involving analytical considerations, reflection, and imaginative variation on what is given in experience.

This descriptive method, aimed at finding the structures of experience itself and of what is manifested in experience, is endorsed by Wilhelm Schapp in the dissertation he wrote under the supervision of Edmund Husserl in Göttingen, published in 1910 as *Beiträge zur Phänomenologie der Wahrnehmung* (*Contributions to the Phenomenology of Perception*) (Schapp 2013). Schapp's book focuses on perception as the type of act that is taken by several phenomenologists—including Husserl himself and Maurice Merleau-Ponty—to exemplarily embody the features of the pre-predictive and intuitive constitution of objects as experientially given "in the flesh" (*leibhaftig*). Within the phenomenological cartography of consciousness, which draws the "essential lines of demarcation" (Husserl 2004: 6) among different kinds of acts, perception is first distinguished, as an intuitive act, from acts that intend their objects emptily, that is, without presenting them (signitive acts). At a further level of specification within the class of intuitive acts, perception is distinguished from a variety of other kinds of acts, such as memory and imagining, which, though also intuitive, do not present their objects in the flesh, but only re-present them.

Given its reliance on such a description-based methodological approach, can phenomenology also provide insights into normative questions concerning experience and its relation to cognition? This question is relevant for Schapp's work on perception, as for many others in the phenomenological tradition. To be sure, Schapp's *Beiträge* stands out as a work that draws almost exclusively on very concrete descriptions of perceptual experience in its multisensorial character. I will argue, however, that the *Beiträge* also raises normative issues, although this may not be an aspect of the book that strikes readers on first reading. Specifically, I believe that the main contribution of this book regarding the just mentioned set of problems consists in paving the way for a consideration of perceptual normativity that, while mostly proceeding bottom-up, does not exclude that there are questions to be addressed top-down.

In order to shed light on what I consider to be Schapp's contribution to questions concerning perceptual normativity, I will begin with a clarification of what I mean by "bottom-up" and "top-down" normativity by addressing two main strands in the current debate (Section 1). Approaches that defend a bottom-up view of normativity try to elaborate on the normative implications of normal perception. In this context, "normal perception" does not imply a generalization on the most frequent empirical occurrences; rather, it recognizes as "normal" those perceptual occurrences that meet the standards of appropriateness or adequacy that are entailed by what perception as such is. Approaches that defend a top-down view of normativity are also concerned with standards of adequacy, but they assume that such standards are to be found in conceptual formations, which therefore must play a role in perception, if perception is to be considered epistemically relevant.

Following this, I will then explain why I believe that Schapp's account of perceptual normativity paves the way for a melding of these two approaches. I will argue that the perceptual normativity related to the structures of perceptual content can be considered pre-conceptual, inasmuch as it relies on the sensible structures that are constitutive for perception as such (Section 2). I will thereby show how normative claims are developed from a consideration of normal experience and its immanent teleology. In this context, the structures of normal experience assume a normative significance not because they prescribe how we should perceive, but rather because they reveal the features that an act must have in order to be best realized (i.e., realized according to its intrinsic form) in a given situation.

Finally, I will consider how Schapp introduces in the last section of the *Beiträge*, focusing on the "idea of perception," a further assessment of perceptual normativity by bringing in concepts (Section 3). Here, the normativity envisaged is the normativity related to the adequate perceptual recognition of the object *as* this or that object. Accordingly, Schapp here addresses perceptual normativity within a cognitive framework. To be sure, within this framework, Schapp is concerned only with empirical concepts, or maybe even only with types. Nevertheless, the reference to what Schapp calls "ideas," which I take to correspond to empirical concepts, is a prerequisite for perception to be taken up in a higher-order cognitive act, that is, in a judgment of perception, and thus also to be normatively assessed in terms of epistemic justification.

1. Perceptual Normativity: Two Strands of Discussion

What does it mean to ask whether phenomenological analysis of perception has a normative dimension? To answer this question, it is not sufficient to recall, as I did in the introduction, that phenomenological description is more than ordinary description. For the question also arises in recent debates about perceptual normativity, crossing different philosophical traditions. In the philosophy of perception, the discussion of perceptual normativity has often been developed within the framework of a theory of knowledge inspired by Kant.[3] In this framework, considering perception from a normative point of view means investigating what are the conditions for perception to be epistemically relevant and thus legitimately taken as a moment of cognition. The normative approach to perception is therefore tied to questions about the justification of knowledge; it is assumed that answering these questions requires an inquiry into the conditions of possibility of knowledge itself. The source of cognitive normativity, according to Kant, is conceptual, and the unity of conceptual synthesis relies on subjectivity, or transcendental apperception, as the "standpoint of liability" for human knowledge, or as the "authority to claim something" (Pollok 2017: 220), which also entails that one is accountable for one's cognitive claims (Kant 1998; CPR A84/B116–A130/B169). Against this background, it is also understandable why questions about the normativity of perception conducted in a Kantian framework are connected with debates about conceptualism in perception.

Within phenomenology too, recent studies have focused on perceptual normativity.[4] Several of these emphasize the differences between the phenomenological account of perceptual normativity and the Kantian views sketched out above (see Crowell 2013; Doyon 2015; Hopp 2011). Thereby, it is assumed that, while approaches to perceptual normativity inspired by Kant are concerned with problems related to epistemic justification, the phenomenological approach assesses normative structures from the bottom, as experienced norms that make up, for instance, more or less adequate configurations of experience. Within this framework, the meaning of normativity is considered to be tied to the meaning of normality (see Wehrle 2015: 265–73; Summa 2014; Wehrle 2022). As Merleau-Ponty observes, from this perspective it is the object itself—or the thing in its mode of givenness—that prescribes, as it were, how proper perception should proceed, becoming "the goal of a bodily teleology" or "the norm of our psycho-physiological setting" (Merleau-Ponty 2005: 376). Phenomenologically oriented researchers tend to emphasize the non-conceptual nature of perceptual normativity: at least to a certain extent, perceptual processes can be considered to be appropriate or adequate to what they perceive, independently of any conceptual functions. This does not necessarily mean that concepts have no role to play in perceptually based cognition; rather, the claim is that such cognition should be considered a stratified process, and that even the lower levels, though not conceptually structured, yield a specific and *sui generis* kind of normativity.[5] In bringing to the fore the essential structures of perception in relation to the appearing of things, the description of perception bears normative implications that are independent of and presupposed by the typically conceptual formations that pertain to the predicative sphere of judgment.

Against this background, the approach to perceptual normativity oriented toward questions of justification tends to be thought of as proceeding top-down, whereas the phenomenological approach to perceptual normativity is typically spoken of as a bottom-up approach.

2. Schapp's Characterology of Perception and Bottom-Up Normativity

The first context in which Schapp seems to lean toward a normative consideration of perception is his discussion of the order of perceptual content and of how this order makes the presentation of the perceived possible. This discussion is notable for its frequent allusions to aesthetics, in several ways close to those later developed by Merleau-Ponty, who was also a reader of Schapp (see Merleau-Ponty 1964, 1993, 2005: 266–7, 303–5, 348–402). On the one hand, Schapp considers the activity of the phenomenologist—notably, that of the phenomenological philosopher who reflects on perception—to be comparable to the activity of a painter, inasmuch as both are "immersed" in the sensible world (Schapp 2013: 12); on the other hand, he contends that the immersion of the phenomenologist reflecting upon experience discloses the most basic and pre-reflective aesthetic immersion of perception itself. It should be emphasized that Schapp compares the perceiver not with a receiver of a work of art but rather with a painter (Schapp 2013: 77). This might seem quite puzzling: after all, isn't perception the receptive kind of experience par excellence? To what extent can it be compared with the productive activity of a painter?

The answer to these questions, I wish to argue, lies in Schapp's characterological view of perception and the perceptual thing, and on the conception of perception as an activity. With the idea of characterology, Schapp subscribes to a view of perception that rules out what is now referred to as the "sense data plus belief" account of perception and contends rather that the senses present things according to their proper Gestalt, or configuration. Characterology is thus at odds with the view that there is a dichotomy between objective properties and subjective sense data. Against this latter view, Schapp conceives of perceptual configurations as the particular mode of givenness of the thing according to its proper *character*, that is, that which typically and morphologically connotes it. The character of the thing is not something that can be determined conceptually, defined by a strict delimitation, or fixed by a set of rules; rather, it is something that can be grasped only aesthetically, by considering the qualities of the thing, its vague contours, etc. Such a non-conceptual grasp is similar to how we perceive and recognize the style of a painter or a writer (see Merleau-Ponty 2005: 382). According to Schapp, the thing is nothing beyond its mode of appearance; it is rather a unity of configuration within a "texture" of sensible appearances. This unity, as Thomas Rolf emphasizes, "derives its characterological density directly from the natural order that characterizes the sensible world of experience as a whole" (Rolf 2004: 91).

Against this background, we should also understand one further aspect of the analogy between the ordinary perceiver and the painter. The painter is here primarily considered as a particularly refined perceiver who is capable of attentively and explicitly recognizing distinctions that an ordinary perceiver sees but may not recognize. This becomes clear if one considers how the painter and the ordinary perceiver grasp light formations and light variations. What characterizes the painter's gaze is the ability not only to see the shape of things and the way in which, for example, color is distributed in a certain form but also to identify the variations of light in this particular appearance of the perceptual thing. Thus, the painter does not merely see a red book but can also identify the adumbrations that characterize this experience of this red thing in these circumstances. Such identification clearly has a more specific active and even pragmatic component because the painter not only grasps the color adumbrations but also reproduces them while painting. However, what Schapp seems to be most interested in emphasizing is that capturing, for instance, the play of light and adumbrations in the perception of colored things the way a painter does amounts to making explicit the configuration that perception has for ordinary perceivers. Accordingly, these observations are significant because they bring to the fore an underlying structure of morphological co-belonging and relationality that pertains to perception as such. From an ontological point of view, this structure relies on mereological distinctions between nonindependent parts (or moments) of a whole and independent parts or pieces (see Husserl 2001c: 4–46).[6] After all, we never perceive red in general, but this red in this situation of brightness or lack of light. Our experience of red is never without a certain adumbration, which in turn is correlative to a situative context and environmental and bodily conditions that precisely modulate the appearance of things (Schapp 2013: 76–98; see also Husserl 1989: 60–95, 1997: 37–88).

The characterology of perception thus establishes the primacy of the unity and structured interconnection of the senses and of concordant sensory appearances. This is even more evident if we consider Schapp's observations regarding intramodal synesthesia. According to Schapp, we *see* the smoothness or the elasticity of certain things; in the same way, we *bodily feel* the roughness of a street on which a heavily laden wagon is passing by, and we make this rough street intuitively present to our minds together with the wagon, even if we are not on it and may not even see either it or the street.[7] On this view, then, the distinctions made within perception according to the human senses are derivative; what is primary is a synoptic or holistic perception that takes up and grasps together, even intersensorially, the variety of sensible appearances of things. Such intersensorial and holistic unity is precisely what underlies our experience of the character of the perceptual thing.

But to what extent does this holistic and intersensorial view of perception, which is obtained by means of a descriptive analysis of the character of perception, have normative implications? Answering this question will make clear another aspect of the analogy between perceiver and painter: perception too is an activity. Schapp's view on perceptual normativity seems to be at least partly inspired by the ideas of optimality and concordance, which Husserl began to develop in the years of his activity in Göttingen.[8]

According to Husserl, who considers perception as the first moment of cognition, perceptual normativity is to be understood in relation to the presentation of the thing as it is in itself, which ideally refers to its most complete presentation. However, such a complete presentation is in principle impossible, and as a result, perception seems to contain within itself a contradiction between its constitutive perspectival and limited nature—for we perceive things always from a particular point of view—and the aspiration to completeness (e.g., Husserl 2001a: 3). Accordingly, Husserl suggests evaluating the adequateness of perception in relation to two criteria: the approximation of perception to the optimum of the presentation of the thing as it is in itself (ideally, the most complete appearance of the thing), and the intersensorial and intersubjective concordance among different perspectives on the thing itself. What matters here is that the perceptual optimum, as something that finite perception cannot in principle achieve, is nevertheless what guides perception. The optimum thus might well be a conceptual or idealized structure (Pradelle 2000: 153–92), but it is a structure that is prefigured within perception itself. If it were not, perceivers would remain satisfied with their partial perception of the thing and would not be moved toward a closer and more complete exploration of the thing.

One may certainly be suspicious concerning the phenomenological assessment of the concept of an absolute optimum—asking, for instance, whether this assumption retrospectively introduces within perception an idealized structure that actually does not belong to it. However, Husserl is not saying that we *always* undertake such a closer exploration aimed at completeness; we do not do so, for instance, when our perception is animated by pragmatic interests. We *can* nevertheless undertake such exploration and closer determination, and we do so when perception is oriented at purely theoretical interests (see Husserl 1997: 104–7).

Husserl connects the pragmatic and theoretical orientations of perception (or perceptual cognition) each with a different conception of the optimum. These can be thought of as (1) the infinite or absolute optimum, or the optimum as complete appearance; and (2) the finite optimum, or the optimum as the best appearance of the thing given the interests of this particular perceptual situation (Pradelle 2000: 153–92; Summa 2014: 213–33). Admittedly, Husserl ultimately underestimates the importance of the finite optimum as compared with the infinite optimum, just as he subordinates pragmatically-oriented cognition to theoretical cognition. But I would argue that the assumption of situated optimality introduces a pragmatic twist to Husserl's theory of perceptual normativity: the best perception may sometimes not be the most complete one, but rather the one that best suits the present situation and my interests in this situation.

Husserl also discusses perceptual normativity as based on concordance. This is a weaker view of normativity, according to which the standard is not an idealized optimum, but rather a concordant presentation that is arrived at progressively through a perceptual process. In this presentation, singular parts fit the whole, and subjective empty intentions, in the form of implicit protensions or even of more explicit anticipations, find intuitive confirmation. Normatively relevant concordance obtains when what is anticipated or protended is confirmed by actual experience, when we experience order in what appears, when appearances conform with what is implicitly anticipated on the basis of kinesthetic experience, or when there is intersubjective agreement about how different subjects perceive things, maintaining that everyone has their own unique perspective on the thing (Crowell 2013: 124–46; Summa 2014: 265–73; Wehrle 2015). Such a concordance is progressively established within perception considered in its process-like unfolding. Accordingly, the standard of concordance allows for a diversity of perspectives and sensible appearances, thereby maintaining the standard of synthetic unity or unification.

In the reading I wish to propose, Schapp takes up several aspects of Husserl's account of perceptual normativity and translates them into his own account of the perceived world as a network of things that appear with their own vague morphological characters. Schapp agrees with Husserl in considering perception as the first moment of cognition or as a proto-form of cognition (Schapp 2013: 65–6). Against the background of such an understanding, he also thematizes the normativity of optimal perception and perceptual concordance. However, compared to Husserl's analyses, the idea of a perceptual optimum seems to undergo some significant modifications in Schapp's account.

As an "advocate of common sense" (Rolf 2004: 90),[9] Schapp develops his normative remarks on the adequacy and appropriateness of perceptual acts starting from the consideration of how the experienced thing and world *normally* appear. Such normality, which is based on the concordance of appearances and on what we have seen to be the synesthetic counterpart of this concordance, is the basis for the sense of familiarity (or lack of familiarity, when such concordance is broken), which everyone forms on the basis of perception and which the painter is able to capture and reproduce on canvas. The normative implications of such an account of normal perception are partly related to the phenomenology of concordance and partly related to the orientation to optimality, which is nevertheless understood, as we will see, as a finite optimum.

I have already sketched out what Schapp understands as (mostly intersensorial) concordance in perception. We may say that what Schapp has in mind is the associability—or to use a Kantian term, the "affinity"—of sensible content. Sensible connections, in this sense, are not subjective add-ons; rather, they are rooted in the very mode of appearance of the object. Admittedly, as both Hume and Kant observe, this alone does not rule out that the concordance or affinity of content is merely coincidental; for this reason, the account of normativity developed on the basis of the description of normality does not suffice to establish epistemic justification. But, in this context, what interests Schapp is not justification. I am here limiting my considerations to the first two sections of the *Beiträge*, entitled, respectively, "The means by which the world of things is presented" and "The presentation of the world of things by color in detail. The order that color must keep in order to present things." Both titles, in particular the subtitle of the second section, provide some clues as to how normative considerations fit into the discussions of these two sections of the *Beiträge*. Schapp's observations concerning bottom-up normativity are related to the necessary or constitutive conditions to be investigated on the basis of descriptive analysis of the order of sensible contents. Accordingly, these descriptions are aimed at showing that a certain order needs to be assumed if perception in general is to be possible. Thus, to the extent that without such an order no perception at all would be possible or even conceivable, this sensible order itself, which is uncovered through description, takes on a normative significance. Despite these normative implications, however, the assumption of such an order of sensibility does not rule out illusions and perceptual mistakes, nor by itself does it allow us to uncover them (Schapp 2013: 98–108, 129–42). This already suggests that such normative implications alone do not provide grounds for epistemic justification.

The normative implications of the sensible order have rather to do with the assumption that the affinity or associativity of content is a prerequisite for us to have a perceptual relation to the thing as it is. Thus, this is a prerequisite to be considered bottom-up. The aim of perception—its inner orientation, or its proper form—is precisely to present the thing just as it is. However, this does not mean "presenting the thing in its completeness," as the ideal of the infinite optimum suggests; rather, it means presenting the thing in the way that, in the present situation, best renders that thing's character.

For this reason, the optimality of perceptual givenness that Schapp has in mind here comes close to a conception of the finite optimum as the standard of adequate perception, but gives it an aesthetic or characterological connotation. Consider, for instance, the following passage:

> It is as if perception, by its most proper nature, always aims at things and, where it does not find them, struggles to penetrate the veils that seem to lie over things. It immediately comes to rest where things are favorably given; where they are not, a moment of restlessness remains. Perception seems to reach out for things even in the distance. It seeks to possibly find something that may withstand its gaze. But what it attempts at a distance is elusive. (Schapp 2013: 74–5)

This passage suggests that perception should be understood as an *activity* that needs to be considered in normative terms according to its own teleology. In fact, Schapp is here referring to the normativity of perception according to what we can call the "constitutive standard" of perception, which also turns out to be a standard of efficacy, perfection, and self-realization. I borrow this terminology from Christine Korsgaard (2009), who introduces the concepts of constitutive standard and standard of efficacy in her metaphysics of normativity and then adapts them in order to explain the normativity of autonomous agency as self-constitution. Considered apart from Korsgaard's more demanding approach to self-constitution, and limiting ourselves to a general and somewhat formal consideration, constitutive standards are the "normative standards to which a thing's teleological organization gives rise." They are standards that "apply to a thing simply in virtue of its being the kind of thing that it is" (Korsgaard 2009: 29). Applied to perception, the constitutive standard, understood formally in this way, coincides with the realization of perception according to its own essence or nature. However, since Schapp assumes that the essence or proper nature of perception consists in tending to present things according to their own proper character, such optimal presentation also functions as the normative standard for evaluating the efficacy of perception itself. Accordingly, the optimal appearance of the thing, that is, the appearance that presents the thing according to its own character, coincides with the self-realization of perception—which, in accordance with Aristotelian teleology, brings the tensions in perception, its striving for fulfillment, to rest. Such an optimal appearance is not to be understood as a complete manifestation of the thing or an idealized optimum of maximal fullness; instead, optimal appearance is the most "fitting" (*günstig*) appearance in *this* perceptual context. Optimal appearance and the standard of efficacy of perception thus correspond to the appearance that is most suitable to presenting the thing according to its proper nature, given the present perceptual conditions of the given situation.

This view of the situative normativity of perception is presented by Schapp according to what we might call the parameters of proximity or distance adequate to seeing the thing with clarity and distinction. Regarding these parameters, we should not think of an absolutization of the normative standard, but rather of what best presents the thing according to its proper nature in this situation and in relation to the contingent bodily conditions of the percipient. In this sense, orienting oneself to the perceptual standard may mean, for instance, searching for the most appropriate position, trying out what is the most suitable distance, focusing, varying the brightness, etc.

The orientation to a perceptual standard described here precedes conceptualization, including empirical conceptualization. In the first and second sections of the *Beiträge*, as I mentioned, what interests Schapp is not the perception of something *as* something, nor the determination of the properties of the thing; rather, the aim in these two sections is to analyze the constitution of the world of perceptual things just as they appear, possibly even considered apart from positing them as really or materially existing. This is a world that, for the perceiver, is not made up of "conceptually sharply delineated objects, but rather represents a closely meshed network of characterological references" (Rolf 2004: 91). However, the claims Schapp makes in these two sections are not meant to be the last word on perceptual normativity. Notably, they do not exclude the possibility that on the basis of characterological perception we may arrive at a determination of the thing according to what Schapp calls its "idea," and thus replace the vague contours of the characteriologically experienced thing, which Schapp addresses in the first two sections of the book, with sharper boundaries (*Grenzen*) between them (Schapp 2013: 149–53).

3. Ideas in Perception

Schapp develops his account of perceptual normativity when discussing the question of the adequateness of perception in relation to the meaningfulness of the perceptual act and the "idea" of the object in the third section of his *Beiträge*, entitled, precisely, "The Idea in Perception." What is such an idea? And what does it mean to claim that there is an "idea" *in* perception? Schapp introduces the concept of idea partly as a continuation of what he has already discussed in the previous sections regarding optimal presentation. Optimal presentation, as we have seen, is determined with reference to the proper nature or character of the thing: the optimal presentation is the one in which the nature of the thing is best displayed to the perceiver. The concept of "idea" expands on what it means to perceive a thing according to its proper nature or essence.

Schapp also explains that making such idea or essence explicit and discussing its function in perception have further epistemically relevant normative implications. According to Schapp, we may perceive things without focusing on or being explicitly aware of what their proper nature is. However, we can also turn to the "idea" of the thing, perceiving it "as such": we can grasp in the perceptual instance its *quid*, that is, what makes this thing precisely what it is. Schapp takes his concept of *idea* to be equivalent to the concept of *essence*, even making explicit reference to Plato (Schapp 2013: 130). But he seems also to have in mind the complex discussions of the different kinds of idealities, from eidetic singularities to higher general ideas, which were the subject of lively discussion in early phenomenology. Additionally, Schapp's discussion of the idea of perception is reminiscent of Husserl's discussion of ideation and ideating abstraction, notably in the Second Logical Investigation (Husserl 2001b: 235–313). In order to understand how the reference to the idea in perception can be taken to have an epistemically relevant normative function, we should consider how Schapp addresses the idea in perception by reassessing perceptual illusion—roughly, a form of deviation from what he takes to be the norm, or standard of efficacy, of perception.

The topic of perceptual illusion is, in fact, already a topic of discussion in the second section of the *Beiträge*, devoted to the inner order of the world of perception. There, Schapp considers illusion in the context of the discussion of proximity and distance in perception and argues that it is incorrect to assume that the remoteness of a thing is a source of perceptual illusion (e.g., by presenting things to us as smaller than they really are); it is more correct, he argues, to say that perception eventually "abandons" us when things get more and more distant from us, and it "does not pretend to give us things" (Schapp 2013: 64). Schapp turns again to perceptual illusion in the second section when considering the dependence of what is perceptually presented on the order of the presenting content. He describes a situation in which we first perceive something as a shard of pottery and then realize that the object is actually a bacon rind. The apprehensional change in perceiving an object as a shard of pottery or a piece of bacon rind is also understood holistically, inasmuch as it goes hand in hand with a change in the apprehension of the nexus of meaningful connections in which the object is perceived, and thus also of the meaningfulness of the surrounding world. However, Schapp admits that the considerations developed at this stage are not intended to provide an exhaustive discussion of perceptual illusion (Schapp 2013: 105). In particular, as I will make clear in what follows, in this context, Schapp is not yet considering what it means to perceive something *as* something and how correction in this perceiving of something as something can take place.

What interests him here is to show what remains identical in the two perceptions—namely, precisely the order of perceptual contents. The structural commonality of content between two acts is thus presupposed by the very possibility of the phenomenon of perceptual illusion. This also means that perceptual illusion is possible only insofar as there is a structural ordering of sensible contents, which may bear in itself a certain ambiguity and thus allows the object to be apprehended as one thing or another. Both the illusion and its uncovering presuppose a certain embedding of the experience of a singular object within a context, and thus require a holistic understanding of perception. Such an oscillation between two possible apprehensions on the basis of the same configuration and order of perceptual givenness, and the experience of a conflict between the two apprehensions, is what underlies the formation of a consciousness of problematic possibility as a logical form and lays the ground for a genetic understanding of the emergence of even categorially structured doubt from the structures of experience (see Husserl 2001c: 135–139, 1973: 87–102). Neither in Husserl (at least not in his later texts) nor in Schapp should this be read in the sensualist terms. The claim is not that we have some sensible content which is in itself chaotic and acquires meaningfulness only insofar as it is apprehended or interpreted in one way or another; rather, sensible givenness is ordered, and what underlies possible illusions are unitary sense configurations that lend themselves, by virtue of their appearance in a meaningful context, to being grasped "as" something or something else. Seeing-as, then, is a relational phenomenon, to the extent that it is always embedded in a meaningful perceptual situation.

Schapp expands on these considerations of perceptual illusion in the third section of the *Beiträge* with a more decided epistemological interest and in connection with his discussion of the idea in perception. His claim is that the apprehension of an object *as such*, for instance, as a shard of pottery or as a piece of bacon rind, is based on an intention directed at the "idea" of the object. Accordingly, Schapp emphasizes, it is in the perception of the thing *as such*, or as being a thing of a certain kind, that illusion can arise, be recognized, and then be corrected:

> When I perceive a thing, I perceive it as something or, which is the same, under an idea. I have a certain intention (*Meinung*), an idea of it. I can be mistaken in such an idea. The thing may be under a different idea than the one under which I perceive it, such as when I take is for a shard of pottery while it is a piece of bacon rind. (Schapp 2013: 142)[10]

On the reading I am proposing, this passage makes clear how reference to at least an empirical form of conceptualization must be presupposed in order for us to be able to recognize a perceptual mistake not just as a rupture in perceptual concordance, but also as a failed identification or recognition—that is, to recognize that our meaning-intention in perceiving something *as* something is mistaken. Sensible perception, considered apart from the conceptual formation that Schapp calls an idea, could not produce illusions. To be sure, Schapp speaks of ideas as operative in perception; but if one agrees that ideas are analoga of empirical concepts, and thus understands perceiving *something as something* as a process of interpretation or subsumption under a concept, then Schapp seems at least partly to agree with Kant that "the senses do not deceive [. . .] not because they always judge correctly, but rather because they do not judge at all" (Kant 2007: 258). In this sense, what is mistaken in perceptual illusion is not the order of perception itself, but rather the way we interpret and judge that order, the stance we take, or the cognitive claims we make on the basis of that order.

Schapp may well wish to include such interpretative and conceptual moments in perception itself, but in his own analysis of perceptual illusion, he himself appeals to judgment, or more precisely, to intention in judgment:

> When I saw the shard of pottery in the courtyard, the object stood before me in its determinateness with many properties. I perceived its character. In this perception, the pottery shard stood before me in the flesh and sensibly given. However, with such facing sensibly and in the flesh, the content of the perception I had is not exhausted. There is another element in perception, which must not be confused with this facing sensibly and in the flesh. We called intuition the mental attitude in which I experience this facing sensibly and in the flesh. However, I did *know*, I did *mean*, that what was facing me was precisely a "shard of pottery." Such "being a shard of pottery" cannot be intuited: it can be intended (*gemeint*). Intending is something different from intuiting. In turn, it is also a particular kind of intending, closely connected with intuiting. If someone had said to me right at the beginning: "What I see there is a bacon rind," I would have known and also meant in a certain sense that it was a bacon rind and not a shard of pottery. Nevertheless, I would have continued to see the thing—albeit in a different way—as a shard of pottery, as long as I myself had come to "see" that it

> was a "bacon rind." Here we are dealing with two different kinds of meanings, which in this case we have surprisingly clearly next to each other so that we can compare them. Let us designate the one as "intending in seeing" (*sehend meinend*) and the other as "intending in judging" (*urteilend meinend*). (Schapp 2013: 131)

I quote this passage at length because, on my reading, it contains the core of Schapp's phenomenological account of perceptual normativity, as implying both the order of sensibility and the order of conceptual apprehension, thus connecting his otherwise usual bottom-up approach with a top-down approach to perceptual normativity. On the one hand, the order of sensibility is not only necessarily presupposed by any conceptual formation, as Schapp highlighted in the first two parts of the book; it is also necessary because only through sensory experience is it possible to give substance, fullness, and concreteness to concepts that, however empirical, would otherwise be empty to the experiencing subject. On the other hand, the conceptual order, or the order dictated by what Schapp calls the idea in perception, is necessary for things to be perceived as things of a certain kind, and thus according to a rule.

The double bind between the sensible order and the—empirical—concept is linked to the formation, motivation, and even legitimation of perceptual belief. As Schapp suggests, I may well understand what another person tells me in pointing to my perceptual error, and I may even start to doubt or modify my own perception; however, until I come to identify and recognize the error by myself, and thus to connect the conceptual structure with the content of experience in a way that allows me to revise my previous belief, I will maintain my old perceptual belief and thus continue to see the thing according to my illusory apprehension. It is therefore necessary to seek out a form of autonomy of judgment based on the fit between sensibility and concept.

This implies a conception of perception that goes beyond sheer receptivity, or a conception in which receptivity bears in itself active functions that can be assessed as judgmental or proto-judgmental. Under such a conception, perception will include the capacity to subsume the individual appearance under the generality of the concept, and then to apprehend and posit something *as* something. This conceptual order then defines the measure against which we regard a perception as either veridical or illusory. It is against the background of this conceptual formation that we can form beliefs—not only in the sense of an implicit familiarity but also of a stance that is expressed in a judgment which can be true or false.

4. Conclusion

Schapp's discussions of perceptual normativity proceed mainly bottom-up, that is, from the order of sensible content. However, I believe that it would be a mistake to read his analysis of perception and perceptual normativity as developing an exclusively bottom-up account relying on the normality of concordant perception. For not only does Schapp explain the normality of perception within the framework of a teleological orientation toward efficacy, perfection, or self-realization of the perceptual activity, he also develops some—admittedly scattered—insights about the normativity of perception within a logic of justification; that is to say, he also proceeds top-down. However, it would be equally mistaken to read into Schapp a form of justification inspired by Kantian theory of knowledge. There are several reasons for this: in particular, because sensible content for Schapp has its own material lawfulness that does not require it to be grounded in a formal unity of synthesis, and because the concepts which Schapp refers to as normative are only empirical concepts. In other words, I do not think that Schapp's account of normativity suggests that he subscribes to a form of transcendental idealism.

Whether this is sufficient to develop a robust theory of perceptual normativity is a matter that would certainly require further investigation. But what can be found in Schapp is at least an attempt to conceive of a form of justification that, although it proceeds descriptively from the order of sensibility, is ultimately based on the successful interrelation between intuition and concept.

Notes

1 Funded by the Deutsche Forschungsgemeinschaft (DFG, German Research Foundation)—Project ID 446126658.

2 In this, I endorse Giovanni Piana's (2016, 2020) conception of phenomenological description, and more generally the phenomenological method, as oriented to the search for structures of experience. See, in the English translation, Piana (2016, 2020).

3 See, for example, Doyon and Breyer (2015); Ginsborg (2008, 2015); McDowell (1996); Pollok (2017); Sellars (1992, 2007a, 2007b).

4 See, for example, Carta (2021); Crowell (2013); Doyon and Breyer (2015); Heinämaa, Hartimo, and Hirvonen (2022); Hopp (2011); Smith (2002); Summa (2014: 265–73; 2023); Wehrle (2010, 2017).

5 Against this background, we can also understand Walter Hopp's (2011: 190–225) distinction between intuitive fulfillment and epistemic fulfillment as a distinction between the pre-conceptual fulfillment of an intention that occurs at the level of perception and the conceptual fulfillment that occurs when perception is taken up in a cognitive act.

6 I am referring here to the formal ontological relation between (independent and nonindependent) parts and wholes, not to the analysis of the perceptual phenomena of contrast and fusion. See §§ 8–9 of the Third Logical Investigation (Husserl 2001c: 13–17).

7 "If you hear a wagon loaded with iron bars driving over a rough road without seeing it, you immediately have in mind the roughness of the road, the weight of the loaded wagon, the quantity of the loaded bars and other characteristics of the object" (Schapp 2013: 28). Here again, we can find a similar claim concerning the primacy and indispensability of unitary and intermodally synesthetic perceptual experience in Merleau-Ponty when he writes about visual perception: "A color is never merely a color, but the color of a certain object, and the blue of a carpet would never be the same blue were it not a woolly blue" (Merleau-Ponty 2005: 365).

8 For a more extensive discussion, see Claesges (1964); Doyon (2015); Pradelle (2000: 153–92); Summa (2014: 181–246); Wehrle (2010, 2015).

9 Interpreting Schapp as an "advocate of common sense" might seem to be at odds with his use of a comparison with the activity of a painter in order to describe perception, which, it might be objected, is not a particularly commonsensical understanding of perception. However, I think that such an objection is misguided, and that with that comparison, Schapp makes explicit an aspect of common sense that tends to remain implicit or is generally not recognized. We speak, for instance, of finesse, delicacy, or sensitivity in perception, which correspond to the capacity for perceiving wholes and their parts, how parts fit in a whole, etc. Thus, we use terms that are not unrelated to the aesthetic dimension (finesse, sensitivity, delicacy). This suggests that Schapp's comparison with the painter is an explication of a form of common sense regarding perception and not an intellectualist analogy.

10 The German concept *Meinung* is somewhat ambiguous, and the quoted passage mirrors its ambiguity. In the most general sense, and in phenomenological texts in particular, *Meinung* designates an intention, that is, the directedness at something considered as meaningful. However, *Meinung* often means opinion, thus taking a stance on something as something. I decided here to translate *Meinung* as "intention," as it is the more usual term in phenomenological texts. However, some remarks on the ambiguity of the term are in order here. In saying, "I have a certain intention, an idea" of the thing, Schapp is saying more than just "I am intending a thing": he is saying that he is taking a position on what the thing is. *Meinung* is related, on the one hand, to the ideal meaning and, on the other hand, to the stance I take with

respect to the state of affairs of "this thing being this or that," embodying this or that idea. Accordingly, the intention under consideration here is directed both at the ideal meaning and at the individual thing, and the position-taking suggested by *Meinung* allows for a margin of uncertainty. This margin of uncertainty is precisely what is at stake in the discussion of our noticing perceptual illusion. On the variety of meanings of intention and fulfillment in early phenomenology, see Salice (2012).

References

Carta, Emanuela. (2021), "Husserl on eidetic norms." *Husserl Studies*, 37: 127–46. https://doi.org/10.1007/s10743-020-09284-5.

Claesges, Ulrich. (1964), *Edmund Husserls Theorie der Raumkonstitution*, Vol. 19, *Phaenomenologica*, The Hague: Martinus Nijhoff.

Crowell, Steven. (2013), *Normativity and Phenomenology in Husserl and Heidegger*, Cambridge: Cambridge University Press.

Doyon, Maxime. (2015), "Perception and Normative Self-consciousness," in Maxime Doyon and Thiemo Breyer (eds), *Normativity in Perception*, 38–55, London: Palgrave Macmillan.

Doyon, Maxime and Thiemo Breyer, eds. (2015), *Normativity in Perception*, London: Palgrave Macmillan.

Ginsborg, Hannah. (2008), "Was Kant a Nonconceptualist?" *Philosophical Studies*, 137 (1): 65–77.

Ginsborg, Hannah. (2015), *The Normativity of Nature: Essays on Kant's Critique of Judgement*, Oxford: Oxford University Press.

Heinämaa, Sara, Mirja Hartimo, and Ilpo Hirvonen, eds. (2022), *Contemporary Phenomenologies of Normativity. Norms, Goals, and Values*, London and New York: Routledge.

Hopp, Walter. (2011), *Percetion and Knowledge: A Phenomenological Account*, Cambridge: Cambridge University Press.

Husserl, Edmund. (1973), *Experience and Judgment: Investigations in a Geneaology of Logic*, trans James S. Churchill and Karl Ameriks. Evanston: Northwestern University Press.

Husserl, Edmund. (1989), *Ideas Pertaining to a Pure Phenomenology and to a Phenomenological Philosophy. Second Book. Studies in the Phenomenology of Constitution*, trans. Richard Rojcewicz and André Schuwer, Vol. 3, *Edmund Husserl Collected Works*, Dordrecht/Boston/London: Kluwer.

Husserl, Edmund. (1997), *Thing and Space: Lectures of 1907*, trans. Richard Rojcewicz. Vol. 7, *Edmund Husserl Collected Works*, Dordrecht: Springer.

Husserl, Edmund. (2001a), *Analyses Concerning Active and Passive Synthesis: Lectures on Transcendental Logic*, trans. Anthony J. Steinbock, Vol. 9, *Edmund Husserl Collected Works*. Dordrecht/Boston/London: Kluwer.

Husserl, Edmund. (2001b), *Logical Investigations. First Volume. Prolegomena to Pure Logic. Investigations I and II*, trans. John Niemeyer Findlay, London and New York: Routledge.

Husserl, Edmund. (2001c), *Logical Investigations. Second Volume. Investigations III, IV, V, VI*, trans. John Niemeyer Findlay, London and New York: Routledge.

Husserl, Edmund. (2004), *Wahrnehmung und Aufmerksamkeit: Texte aus dem Nachlass (1893–1912)*, eds. Thomas Vongehr and Regula Giuliani, *Phaenomenologica*. Dordrecht: Springer.

Kant, Immanuel. (1998), *Critique of Pure Reason*, trans. Paul Guyer and Allen W. Wood, *The Cambridge Edition of the Works of Immanuel Kant*, Cambridge: Cambridge University Press.

Kant, Immanuel. (2007), "Anthropology from a Pragmatic Point of View," in Robert B. Louden (ed.), *Anthropology, History, and Education*, 227–429. Cambridge: Cambridge University Press.

Korsgaard, Christine M. (2009), *Self-Constitution: Agency, Identity, and Integrity*, Oxford: Oxford University Press.

McDowell, John. (1996), *Mind and World*, Cambridge MA: Harvard University Press.

Merleau-Ponty, Maurice. (1964), "Eye and Mind," in James M. Edie (ed.), *The Primacy of Perception*, 159–91, Evanston: Northwestern University Press.

Merleau-Ponty, Maurice. (1993), "Cézanne's Doubt," in *The Merleau-Ponty Aesthetics Reader: Philosophy and Painting*, 59–75, Evanston: Northwestern University Press.

Merleau-Ponty, Maurice. (2005), *Phenomenology of Perception*, trans. Colin Smith, London and New York: Routledge.

Piana, Giovanni. (2016), "Phenomenology as Philosophical Method," *Metodo: International Studies in Phenomenology and Philosophy*, 4 (1): 183–204.

Piana, Giovanni. (2020), "The Idea of a Phenomenological Structuralism," *Phenomenological Reviews*, 1. https://doi.org/10.19079/PR.s1.2.

Pollok, Konstantin. (2017), *Kant's Theory of Normativity: Exploring the Space of Reason*, Cambridge: Cambridge University Press.

Pradelle, Dominique. (2000), *L'archéologie du monde: Constitution de l'espace, idéalisme et intuitionnisme chez Husserl*, Vol. 157, *Phaenomenologica*, Dordrecht/Boston/London: Kluwer.

Rolf, Thomas. (2004), "Der dichtende Gegenstand. Wilhelm Schapps Beiträge zur Phänomenologie der Wahrnehmung," in Karl-Heinz Lembeck (ed.), *Geschichte und Geschichten: Studien zur Geschichtenphänomenologie Wilhelm Schapps*, 87–113, Würzburg: Königshausen & Neumann.

Salice, Alessandro. (2012), "Phänomenologische Variationen: Intention and Fulfillment in Early Phenomenology," in Alessandro Salice (ed.), *Intentionality*, 203–42, Munich: Philosophia.

Schapp, Wilhelm. (2013), *Beiträge zur Phänomenologie der Wahrnehmung*, Frankfurt a.M.: Klostermann.

Sellars, Wilfrid. (1992), *Science and Metaphysics: Variations on Kantian Themes*, Atascadero: Ridgeview.

Sellars, Wilfrid. (2007a), "The Role of Imagination in Kant's Theory of Experience," in Kevin Scharp and Robert Brandom (eds), *In the Space of Reasons: Selected Essays of Wilfrid Sellars*, 454–66, Cambridge MA/London: Harvard University Press.

Sellars, Wilfrid. (2007b), "Some Remarks on Kant's Theory of Experience," In Kevin Scharp and Robert Brandom (eds), *In the Space of Reasons: Selected Essays of Wilfrid Sellars*, 437–53, Cambridge MA/London: Harvard University Press.

Smith, A. David. (2002), *The Problem of Perception*, Cambridge, MA and London: Harvard University Press.

Summa, Michela. (2014), *Spatio-Temporal Intertwining: Husserl's Transcendental Aesthetic*, Dordrecht: Springer.

Summa, Michela. (2023), "Is Imagination a "Necessary Ingredient of Perception"? Sellars's and Husserl's Variations on a Kantian Theme," In Daniele De Santis and Danilo Manca (eds), *Wilfrid Sellars and Phenomenology: Intersections, Encounters, Oppositions*, 177–210, Athens: Ohio University Press.

Wehrle, Maren. (2010), "Die Normativität der Erfahrung. Überlegungen zur Beziehung von Normalität und Aufmerksamkeit bei E. Husserl," *Husserl Studies*, 26: 167–87.

Wehrle, Maren. (2015), "Normality and Normativity in Experience," In Maxime Doyon and Thiemo Breyer (eds), *Normativity in Perception*, 128–39, London: Palgrave Macmillan.

Wehrle, Maren. (2017), "The Normative Body and the Embodiment of Norms," *Yearbook for Eastern and Western Philosophy*, 2017/2: 323–27.

Wehrle, Maren. (2022), "(Re)turning to Normality? A Bottom Up Approach to Normativity," In Sara Heinämaa, Mirja Hartimo and Ilpo Hirvonen (eds), *Contemporary Phenomenologies of Normativity: Norms, Goals, and Values*, 199–218, London: Routledge.

4

From *Sachverhalt* to *Geschichte* and Back

Remarks on Wilhelm Schapp and the Early Phenomenological Tradition

Daniele De Santis

0. Introduction

In a famous discussion of Wilhelm Schapp's 1953 book *In Geschichten verstrickt*, the philosopher Hermann Lübbe strives to explain the emergence of the narratological perspective from within the phenomenological tradition in two manners. On the one hand, Schapp is said to walk a path that is "diametrically opposed" to "classical phenomenology"—by which Lübbe means that strand of early phenomenology that reaches its peak (*Höhepunkt*) in, and is paradigmatically epitomized by (among others), Adolf Reinach's *Platonism*. Such Platonic phenomenology rests on the conviction that the "world's proper being is a cosmologically unified multiplicity of essentialities," and "the task of all philosophy" amounts to "presenting such a cosmos theoretically" (Lübbe 1954: 654). Here Lübbe refers to Reinach, but one could mention Hedwig Conrad-Martius as well. She affirms, "World and being are in themselves full sense. They are pervaded by it. The totality of all *res*, of all *entia*, of all givennesses forms a cosmos, a cosmos of sense, a *kosmos noetos*. Within it, everything has its own determined, unmovable sense-place—even what is meaningless" (Conrad-Martius 1965: 377).[1] In her introduction to Reinach's collected works, she had already gone so far as to write that what is at stake here is not the existence of "isolated essentialities, essentiality-monads, as it were, which would have nothing to do with one another"; rather, "there obtains here a *lawful cosmos* which—*in virtue* of these essentialities [. . .]—forms the prodigious sphere in which they all possess their unique and unmovable position" (Conrad-Martius 1921: xix).

On the other hand, Lübbe points out that Schapp was pushed toward such a "radically new starting point" for phenomenology by the aporias in which classical phenomenology ends up: "In effect," he adds, "it can be shown how the essence-phenomenology bumps again and again into difficulties, which can be solved within Schapp's phenomenology of stories"; such "difficulties" emerge where "the set of a priori essentialities is not only presupposed, but their peculiar mode of being is also explicitly called into question" (Lübbe 1954: 655). As one could expect when discussing essentialities, Lübbe is here referring to a quite famous text of the early phenomenological tradition: Jean Hering's 1921 "Remarks on Essence, Essentiality and the Idea."[2] Lübbe quotes from the very end of the first chapter of Hering's essay, where he addresses the problem of the alterability of an individual essence such as the essence of a house. Here is the passage to which Lübbe refers: "If a house that was previously brown were painted white, we would surely say: the being-white does *not* belong to its essence; and we substantiate this by pointing out that the house could also have been painted some other color without anything having changed in the specific character of the essence constituting it" (Hering 1921: 504; Hering 2021: 63). This passage—Lübbe hastens to underline—is perfectly in line with the classical doctrine's distinction between the object's "unalterable essence" and the external, mutable, "'contingent' accidents." However, a footnote is added by Hering to the above passage, to which Lübbe immediately draws the reader's attention:

> Needless to say, an attitude is also possible in which, in contrast to the house in its previous state, we grasp the house in its current state as something isolated and new, without bothering about the factual identity of the two—as, for instance, when gathering examples of brown and white houses, we present the house as it was before and the house as it is now under two separate rubrics. We then certainly have before us objects to whose essence also the being-white or being-brown belongs. (Hering 1921: 504; Hering 2021: 63–64, trans. modified)

Lübbe takes this to be an actual confession upon the part of Hering: despite his Platonism, Hering willy-nilly has to admit that a "thing" (here, a "house") could essentially be "grasped" in various modes depending on the "properties" (*Eigenschaften*) that we decide to single out and regard as its own essence. In so doing, Hering ends up being caught in an insurmountable aporia. On the one hand, he clings to the Platonic idea to the effect that a thing's identity consists in an "inalterable essence" (which plays the role of the underlying unjustified presupposition); on the other hand, he seems to concede that "nominalism" is right in claiming that a thing's essence ultimately derives from the modality in which we "conceptualize" (*Begreifen*) it (Lübbe 1954: 655–6).[3]

In contrast, Schapp's approach is immune to such aporias because from the very beginning, he renounces the idea of the thing having a stable identity (and "inalterable essence"). Instead, Schapp understands things as always being "entangled" in stories (*von vornherein aus dem Zusammenhang der Geschichte*), with their "identities" consisting of the very course of the "story" to which they belong. As he writes,

> The being of the house does not consist in such a What, but in the fact that it has been whitewashed and so on and so forth [. . .]; its being a house is determined exclusively by the sense-connection of the story-like event (*geschlichtlichen Geschehens*) to which it owes its origin, place, and existence, the fact that it is new, old, or that it has been renovated. (Lübbe 1954: 656)

According to this second line of interpretation, Schapp's "narratological" perspective would not walk a path that is *diametrically opposed* to classical phenomenology; rather, it would emerge from the tradition of classical phenomenology in order to overcome the difficulties and aporias in which it necessarily ends up being caught (= they are aporias revolving around the "identity-alterability" dichotomy). On such a view, Schapp's phenomenology of stories would not be an alternative to the one epitomized by Reinach and Hering (as the previous reading presented by Lübbe to suggest); rather, it would represent the one and only way in which classical phenomenology could actually overcome (Lübbe speaks of "*überwinden*") its own aporias—thereby also overcoming itself.[4]

Now, although only in passing and without expanding on it, Lübbe does recognize that Schapp himself makes exactly the same claim regarding the way "classical phenomenology" thought of the relation between "act" and "state of affairs": "Schapp points out that he was led toward this radically new starting point for phenomenological research about the problem of story through the aporias that necessarily derived from the classical approach to 'act' and 'state of affairs'" (Lübbe 1954: 655). In the present chapter, I will try to elaborate upon this brief remark by Lübbe. Indeed, as we shall see by drawing on Schapp's published books and posthumously published *Nachlass*, the same duplicity of interpretation characterizes his view on the relation between his phenomenology of stories and the notion of "state of affairs" that was central to classical phenomenology.

To this end, the chapter will be divided into three parts. While the first part will be dedicated to an analysis of the way in which Schapp generally frames the *Sachverhalt-Geschichte* relation, in the second, I will propose an overview of the function that the concept of "state of affairs" (hereafter *SV*) plays in early phenomenology, but with no ambition whatsoever of covering all of the possible positions. The aim of this section is merely to highlight commonalities and differences among the many views. Finally, the third part will tackle Schapp's concept of *Geschichte* in order to show in what sense it is meant to offer a solution for the aporias into which classical phenomenology falls.

1. From *Sachverhalt* to *Geschichte* . . .

In his groundbreaking 1953 book *In Geschichten verstrickt* (see §17), Wilhelm Schapp presents the differences between "classical phenomenology" and his view as a series of four main bullet points:

1. The object of phenomenological analysis and investigation (states of affairs) "turns (*wandelt sich um*) into stories, stories that always include and entail someone/something entangled in them (*einen Verstrickten*)" (Schapp 2012: 178).
2. "While for the phenomenologist every state of affairs participates—via the proposition—in the proposition's and the concepts' eternal being, this sort of being is nowhere to be found in the case of stories. Stories consist always and solely in the entanglement [. . .]. Outside such entanglement, it does not make any sense to speak of being" (Schapp 2012: 178).
3. "For the phenomenologist, proposition and state of affairs stand in close connection with the object. The proposition refers to the object through the concept. The state of affairs is built up around the object (*Der Sachverhalt baut sich auf über dem Gegenstand*). The object is all one can talk about. The object ultimately dissolves into the something in general, and by a further change of focus, into the all-encompassing world" (Schapp 2012: 178).
4. "For us the object is reframed (*deutet sich um*) as stories, yet not as stories of objects; rather, as stories with someone/something entangled in them" (Schapp 2012: 178–9).

Although they do not exhaust what Schapp has to say on the matter, these four bullet points already provide us with some of the basic coordinates we need in order to begin orienting ourselves.

If we look at *2*, we are confronted with a radical opposition and *aut aut*: *SV* is recognized a form of "eternal being" that is nowhere to be found in the case of "stories." In the case of both *1* and *4*, the relation between the two seems instead to be more nuanced and complex. The verb *wandelt sich um* suggests an actual transformation (not a mere replacement or succession), and the grammar used in *4* does in fact outline a very interesting perspective. As I might understand Schapp's point here, the (phenomenological) concept of *Gegenstand* is reframed, or better, it *reframes itself* and *clarifies itself* (*deutet sich um*) as *Geschichte*, story. If I am on the right track, the sense of both *1* and *4* could be understood as follows. The concept of *Sachverhalt*—regarded as the subject-matter of classical phenomenology—*turns into* the concept of *Geschichte*—as what the new phenomenology is about (= *1*)—because what used to be understood as *Gegenstand* has *clarified itself* as *Geschichte* (= *4*).

The difference is not a minor one. As *3* recognizes, for classical phenomenology, *Sachverhalt* and *Gegenstand* are not to be identified: *SV* is what does the mediation between the proposition and the object itself (the former refers to the latter through *SV*[5]); "*Gegenstände*" designate what one can talk about and *Sachverhalte* stand for the formal-ontological correlates of what is stated about them. The claim that the object dissolves into what I have here translated with the expression "something in general" (*Etwas*) is in line with a well-known Husserlian refrain, the one according to which—taken as the highest formal-ontological category—the *Etwas überhaupt* = *Gegenstand* in the broad sense of a "*subject of possible true predications*" (Husserl 1976: 15; Husserl 2014: 12). As Schapp seems to contend (= *4*), given the state of affairs-object relation, "classical phenomenology" assumes the "world" to be nothing else than the totality of *somethings*, that is, *world* = the totality of subjects of possible true predications and of states of affairs as their formal-ontological correlates.[6]

Now the fact that both *SV* and the object make way for *Geschichte* means that we replace, say, a *two-term ontology* (states of affairs/objects[7]) with a *one-term ontology* (if I am allowed to say it in this way, using a jargon alien to Schapp's own language[8]). In other words, a world populated by both "objects" and (eternal) "states of affairs" (Schapp 2015: 57), and in which states of affairs are "founded upon" objects (Schapp 2016: 69), is replaced by (or turns out to be) a world full of stories and exclusively of stories.[9] Two more points could also be made regarding this. First of all, it needs to be noted that—in line with an early phenomenological mode of speaking—both propositions and states of affairs are regarded by Schapp as correlates of "thought," *Denken*:[10]

> When one thinks of propositions, one has the proposition conceptually (*in der Art des Denkens*). Thinking, one relates to the states of affairs that correspond to the proposition. Probably one could roughly express this by saying that insofar as the proposition is thought, the state of affairs is represented. The state of affairs emerges. In turn, the state of affairs is in relation to the objects that emerge along with the state of affairs. (Schapp 2012: 169)

Second of all—and as a variation on what has just been said—Schapp quickly raises the question about the relation between stories and the phenomenological concept of "act." As Schapp remarks in passing, "One could try to construe the entanglement as an all-encompassing act of experience, probably as the most all-encompassing act of experience (*Erlebnisakt*)"; thus one could strive "to break this act down into several acts," and—finally—one could try, "from the standpoint of the being-entangled," "to build stories out of all such acts, perhaps thereby clarifying more precisely the peculiar unity of the story as a sort of superstructure [which embraces all the acts] or as an interaction between acts" (Schapp 2016: 271). But he is clear about the outcome and the possibility of such attempt:

> This and similar enterprises never took us to the stories' nucleus. [. . .] We can neither dissolve stories into acts nor regard the psychic moments, at which one aims with the act-doctrine, as components of the stories. In other words, the act-doctrine cannot serve in any way whatsoever to clarify the stories, and more specifically, to shed light on the very being-entangled-in-stories moment (*das Moment des Verstricktseins in Geschichten*). (Schapp 2016: 272)

All the passages discussed so far date from 1953; a few years later, in his famous "Recollections of Husserl" of 1959 (see the translation published in this volume), Schapp will explicitly present the distinction between the following five "strata" and "layers" as one of the major outcomes of the "phenomenological method" as it was originally employed by Husserl in the *Logical Investigations*:

> 1. The objective, the objects, the matters (*Sachen*), or the world of objects and their relation to each other;
> 2. The states of affairs and
> 3. The propositions corresponding to the states of affairs, and
> 4. The judgments and acts of judging once again corresponding to the propositions, and then further in general
> 5. The sphere of cognitive acts in which a world is presented: representing, perceiving, intuiting, empty representation, questioning, doubting
>
> (Schapp 1959: 14; Schapp 2025: 228).

And yet, as should be clear from what I have been stating thus far, the system of these five layers and strata (namely, their relations) is exactly what Schapp's *Geschichte*-philosophy does somewhat abandon—in the sense that none of them is recognized per se as having any validity within it. For if the two-term ontology (= *1* + *2*) is replaced by the one-term ontology of stories,[11] the latter cannot in turn be said to be composed of propositions (= *3*), nor can they be regarded as made up of acts (= *4* + *5*) in the sense in which Husserl's "act-phenomenology" of the *Logical Investigations* regards the acts as the very phenomenological-psychological origin of a given sense-formation.

Now since we will have to come back to this over the course of §2, yet another fundamental point is to be made before we move on. In a 1954 posthumously published note entitled "The Way into Stories" (*Der Weg zur Geschichte*)—to which we will have to pay attention later on—Schapp admits that "Halfway to the story stands the state of affairs–formation. This had to be discovered first, and then dismissed once again if one wanted to get to the story-formation" (Schapp 2016: 203). Schapp is clear. To use Lübbe's own language, the philosophy of *Geschichte* is not simply to be regarded as walking a path diametrically opposed to that of the "object/state of affairs"; rather, the very idea of *Geschichte* follows from both the discovery and the subsequent dismissal of *SV*. The latter is in fact regarded as a preliminary and yet necessary step on the way to the former—as though without the preliminary discovery of *SV*, one could not arrive at the concept of *Geschichte*

2. . . . and Back

SV plays a crucial role in the history of early phenomenology, which could be written or rewritten from the perspective of the problem of both the function and the nature of *SV*.[12] The idea of mapping out all the possible views on *SV* goes far beyond the limited scope of this chapter; my goal is far more modest, yet no less crucial and important for the sake of my problem here, namely, that of better determining Schapp's view so as to more properly understand the *SV*-*Geschichte* relation.

One point needs to be recognized immediately. Despite Schapp's general way of talking about *SV*, it is quite difficult to deny that the position(s) he has mainly in mind stem from Reinach. Or better, what he seems to have in mind whenever he talks of *SV* (in general or without any specification) is the view propounded by Reinach and understood as a radicalization of what Husserl argues in, for example, §§17 and 28 of the *Fifth Logical Investigation*. In §17, Husserl distinguishes between "*the object as it is intended*, and the *object sic et simpliciter that* is intended" (Husserl 1984: 414; Husserl 2001b: 113, trans. modified). And *SV* is here described as "the full and entire object corresponding to the whole judgment" (Husserl 1984: 416; Husserl 2001b: 114). Let us also add that as far as the judgment-*SV* relation is concerned, Husserl speaks only of *erscheinen*: "In the judgment a state of affairs appears before us" (Husserl 1984: 461; Husserl 2001a: 139). In this respect, then, for Husserl *Gegenstand* ("object") and *Sachverhalt* ("state of affairs") do not fall under two different formal and ontological categories (as in contrast seems to be the case with Schapp); rather, *SV* is understood as the "object"[13] that properly corresponds to a judgment. In the descriptive-psychological language of the *Logical Investigations*, one could simply affirm that *SV* is the object corresponding to (or appearing in) that kind of complex (and in this sense *founded*) act that is called a *propositional act*. In Husserl's words, "Each act has its own appropriate, intentional objective reference: this is as true of complex as of simple acts. *Whatever the composition of an act out of partial acts may be, if it is an act at all, it must have a single objective correlate*, to which we say it is 'directed,' in the *full*, *primary* sense of the word" (Husserl 1984: 415; Husserl 2001b: 114). Hence it could simply be called a founded-complex object. Translated into the act terminology that Husserl is using here, *SV* is the objectual correlate corresponding to what, within the immanent and real structure of an act, is the "intentional matter" (*Logical Investigation V*, §20[14])—understood as the individualization of an "ideal meaning"—or to go the other way around and use the language of a former student of Husserl, Erich Heinrich, the "ideal meaning" stems from "the ideation of the spiritual *phansis*" (Heinrich 1910: 20).

Now Husserl's position leaves us with at least three major problems to address (and the history of early phenomenology could also be written from the angle of how they were respectively tackled):

(A) The problem of how to account more precisely for the (propositional) act–*SV* relation;
(B) The nature itself of *SV*, also with respect to the (propositional) act to which it corresponds;
(C) The function that *SV* is supposed to play.

(A) The only two expressions used by Husserl to describe the judgment-*SV* relation are *correlate* and *appearing*—by which he *exclusively means* to point in a minimal way at *SV*'s correspondence with a relevant act of consciousness (or system thereof).[15] As far as I can tell, the case is similar with Reinach, who speaks of "correlate" (Reinach 1989: 114; Reinach 1982: 338). In his reconstruction of Daubert's position, Schuhmann speaks, probably too strongly, of "constitution" (*Konstitution von Sachverhalten*) (Schuhmann 2004: 213), whereas Daubert seems to limit himself to describing it as "posited by the copula" (*durch die Kopula gesetzt*) (quoted in Schuhmann 2004: 214). Pfänder is the one who commits to a more robust terminology, as it were. In his *Logic* of 1921 (Part One: The Theory of Judgment; First Chapter: Preliminary Considerations, §4), the verb used is "projecting" or *entwerfen*: "To each particular judgment there corresponds a state of affairs. [. . . .] *The judgment projects (*entwirft*) this state of affairs out of itself.* It posits it over against itself in such a way that the projected state of affairs (*entworfene Sachverhalt*) is always kept exterior to the judgment that projects it, always beyond or 'transcendent' to it." Or by resorting to the language of intentionality, "the state of affairs is the counterpart, the 'intentional correlate,' of the judgment that projects it" (Pfänder 1963: 35; Pfänder 2009: 35). *SV*, Pfänder points out at the end of §4, is like "a movie image": "By projecting the state of affairs, the judgment distinguishes itself from it—in this respect, the judgment is *primary* and the *state of affairs, secondary.* Understood exclusively as projected by the judgment, the state of affairs is totally dependent upon it. It is projected the way a movie image is projected by the projection lamp" (Pfänder 1963: 36: Pfänder 2009: 36–37). Taking up this terminology, Ingarden will speak of a "*merely intentional state of affairs*" to designate the "intentional correlate of both the content and the form of a judgment" (Ingarden 1925: 127; see also what he writes to Jean Hering in Ingarden 1958b: 1).

(B) The answer to the question about *SV*'s nature derives from how one has already preliminarily understood *A*. In this respect, Husserl's and Reinach's positions seem to diverge quite widely. Reinach's view on *SV* is usually presented as a form of Platonism: "The totality of *Sachverhalte* Reinach conceives as an eternal realm comprehending the correlates of all possible judgments [. . .]. Objects, it is true, may come and go, but *Sachverhalte* are immutable"; "Platonism, here, means that *Sachverhalte* are transcendent not only to the mind but also to the world of spatio-temporal objects. It means that they are entirely independent of all mental activities" (Smith 1989: 60).[16] With Husserl the situation is quite different. For him, to affirm that a truth obtains means that there is an ideally (not a really) possible consciousness in whose act(s) that truth is instantiated as an "intentional matter" (Taieb 2018; De Santis 2021: 50). Yet in my opinion, Reinach's position is less easy to characterize than is usually said. It is true that in "On the Theory of Negative Judgments," he says that "negative states of affairs subsist precisely as do positive states, quite independently of whether or not they are presented to anybody or come to be apprehended, believed, meant, or asserted" (Reinach 1989: 130; Reinach 1982: 361). But it is also true that what Reinach is trying to dispel here is the false belief that *SV*s (primarily the "negative" ones) can be regarded as a mere production (*erzeugen*) by thought. It is also worth pointing out that when Reinach maintains that *SV*s subsist "wholly independently of any conscious subject which may grasp [them]," the example is that of an "a priori" proposition ("2 x 2 is equal to 4," along with the negative one, "2 x 2 is not equal to 5"). Moreover, in the famous Marburg lecture "On Phenomenology," Reinach will remark that "states of affairs obtain indifferently of which consciousness apprehends them, and of whether they are apprehended by any consciousness at all" (Reinach 1989: 544–545). Nevertheless, in this case, the example under scrutiny is also that of the a priori (and the relevant state of affairs[17]). Far from me, of course, is the ambition to dismiss the interpretation of Reinach on *SV* in terms of "Platonism" (regardless of whether such a label is really apt to express his position); what I am trying to do is to indicate the complexity of his view. And let me add one more element to this puzzle. In the posthumously published manuscript entitled by the editors "Notwendigkeit und Allgemeinheit im Sachverhalt," the following tripartition is proposed (Reinach 1989: 351):

Proposition:	Form: Extra-temporal	Content: Extra-temporal
Judgment-Act:	Form: Temporal	Content: Temporal
State of Affairs:	Form: Temporal and Extra-temporal	The Content Decides

As far as I understand his remarks here, whereas "judgments" (understood as "propositional acts" of the individual subject) are always temporal with regard both to their content and to their form (because both of them come and go together with the act), the opposite is the case with the "proposition" (= the ideal content instantiated in the former). In contrast, in the case of *SV*, they can be either temporal (like acts) or extra-temporal (like propositions), depending upon the content of the *SV* itself (= the objects out of which *SV* is composed or which it includes within itself). This is what Reinach means to say when he writes, "*Inhalt entscheidet*" in the right column. (If one wants to stick with the expression "Platonism" to refer to Reinach, it would be a Platonism of propositions, which are extra-temporal in both their form and their content, and not of states of affairs.) That, this is the case is corroborated by a still unpublished text composed in the mid-1950s by another member of the Göttingen circle, Theodor Conrad.

The text offers a retrospective survey of the "phenomenological method" as originally practiced by the "Munich-Göttingen circle" and in opposition to Husserl's. Most of the manuscript's analyses revolve around the question of knowledge, with particular focus upon the relation between *SV* and what Conrad calls here *Tatbestand*, "the intuitive substrate itself" (that is, what is "propositionally" grasped, and thus articulated in the form of a state of affairs) (Conrad 1954: 4).[18] The α-appendix to the text is dedicated precisely to the issue of *SV*'s temporal determination. Let us quote a few short passages: "Temporality or timelessness belong to that which is intuitively facing the researcher in a way that is still amorphous, and they do so as immediately graspable characteristics of it, *prior to* any statement being attempted about it. That which is still amorphous is either temporal or non-temporal"; "it is obvious that calling the [state of affairs] temporal is merely something *derived*, *transferred*; it transfers what is to be found in something real or ideal (*real oder ideell*) that is non-articulated to the state of affairs articulating and explicating this material, presenting it as precisely this material" (Conrad 1954: 12). In the β-appendix, Conrad goes on to explain that "Therefore the temporality or timelessness cannot be regarded as a quality of the state of affairs as such; instead, it belongs to the state of affairs' amorphous basis" (Conrad 1954: 13). Unlike Reinach, Conrad does not seem to make (at least here) any distinction between the *SV*'s "form" and its "content"; yet in a way that seems to be line with the former's view, Conrad *apertis verbis* denies that "temporality" could be regarded as a "quality" of *SV*. Quite the opposite is true. Only what is "presented" in and by *SV* (the amorphous basis) is either temporal or timeless depending on its real or ideal nature. Of course, the two positions do not perfectly match. For if both agree upon the fact that the "content" decides, Reinach concedes that temporality (and the lack thereof) can be directly attributed to the state of affairs. In contrast, for Conrad, *SV* is per se neither temporal nor timeless. It can be attributed a temporal determination only "*derivatively*." Now the point is important for us in order better to characterize, even if only *per viam negationis*, Schapp's way of understanding the (phenomenological) notion of *SV*. Whereas Schapp regards (the phenomenological notion of) *SV* as eternal—regardless of whether this means timelessness or omnipresence, according to the two senses of the Greek *aei*—this does not seem to be prima facie the case with Reinach or Conrad. In sum, Schapp's understanding of *SV*, hence of the *SV-Geschichte* relation, is based on a (Platonizing) *radicalization* of Husserl's and Reinach's position on the matter. He seems to extend what Reinach contends about "a priori" states of affairs to *SV* in general. By the same token, he seems to strip Husserl's position from the reference to the idea of a "possible consciousness." If among the figures mentioned above, there is anyone with whose position Schapp's view seems to match, it could be Pfänder's. Schapp writes that "for the phenomenologist every state of affairs participates—via the proposition—in the proposition's and the concepts' eternal being" (Schapp 2012: 178). In turn, Pfänder points out that, "To each particular judgment there corresponds a state of affairs. [. . .] *The judgment projects this state of affairs out of itself*" (Pfänder 1963: 35; Pfänder 2009: 35). But he had also already clarified that judgments consist of ideal formations called "thoughts," and thoughts are not real "occurrences, but ideal, *timeless structures*" (Pfänder 1963: 3; Pfänder 2009: 3). Yet, it is one thing to speak of "eternity" (Schapp), while "timelessness" is quite another thing (Pfänder).

(C) If one were to express in just a few words what *SV*'s "function" is, one could say: it fulfills the crucial function of the "truth-maker" (Mulligan 2009), or—as Johannes Daubert would say—*das Erfüllende und Wahrmachende* (Schuhmann 2004: 211). As Schuhmann remarks, "The world is the sum-total of objects; states of affairs arise (*entstehen*) only as long as a conceptually thinking being directs its gnoseological interests (*Erkenntnisinteressen*) to them" (Schuhmann 2004: 215). If this is the case—and if *SV* = truth-maker[19]—a question imposes itself that bears on the relation between *SV*'s function and its being the correlate of our judgments/propositions. For if, as Pfänder contends, *SV* is "projected" by the judgment "out of itself" and is "posited" by it over against itself, how can there be a case in which to a given judgment there "corresponds" no *SV*? Differently framed, how can a judgment not correspond to what it itself "posits" or "projects" out of itself? In the case of Husserl, we can conceive of *SV* "as the creature of a naturalistic ontology: the *Sachverhalt* is a truth-making segment of reality that is 'thrown into relief' through an act of judgment"; therefore "the Husserlian *Sachverhalt* is dependent upon consciousness for its demarcation, but is independent in the sense that what gets demarcated [. . .] exists independently of the act which brings this demarcation about" (Smith 1989: 63). The problem becomes apparent here. Let me add, however, that in the present context, I am less interested in the truth-making problem than in the question regarding the (ontological) status that one is bound to ascribe to *SV* in order for it to be able to play that role. Are *SV*s a part of the world's furniture along with objects (as Schapp seems to say)? Or, are they the result of a mere subjective and consciousness-dependent "demarcation" of it? If we accept the first alternative, then we seem to be bound to drop the talk of *SV* as posited or constituted by thought. If, in contrast, we opt for the latter option, we seem to be bound instead to abandon the idea of *SV* as truth-making principles, for in this case thought itself would posit its own truth-maker—or even better, thought and the proposition would be at the same time the "verified" (by the state of affairs) and the "verifier" (indirectly and via the state of affairs that they themselves posit).

Pfänder seems to have clearly perceived the difficulty I am pointing out. In his *Logic*, in fact, the tension just evoked appears in full light. In his attempt at rethinking the idea of truth as *adaequatio intellectus et rei* (Pfänder 1963: 80; Pfänder 2009: 83), Pfänder writes that "no other relationship remains that can be identified with the claim to be true except the *relationship of the judgment to the objects and the states of affairs posited by it*" (Pfänder 1963: 79; Pfänder 2009: 83). A few lines later, the objects–states of affairs duality is resolved by speaking of the "*comportment* (Verhalten) *of the objects referred to by the judgments*" and of "the *self-comportment* (Selbstverhalten) *of the object*" (Pfänder 1963: 81; Pfänder 2009: 84). *SV* is no longer the result of the judgment's position, rather, the judgment refers to an object that "comports itself" (*Selbst-Verhalten*) in a certain manner. Other phenomenologists have resolved the tension by somehow doubling *SV* itself. Daubert, for example, speaks of both *Sachverhalt* and *Kenntnisverhalt*: the former designates "the actual comportment of the matters" (*das eigentiche Verhalten der Sachen*); the latter is the "subjective state of affairs," the one that corresponds to our subjective grasp (*Auffassung*) of the world (Schuhmann 2004: 207). But the most paradigmatic case is certainly Ingarden. He explicitly distinguishes between the judgment's *objectum formale* and the *objectum materiale*. The former is the "purely intentional" state of affairs, the purely intentional correlate of the judgment; the latter is "the objective state of affairs that exists independently of the knowing subject and the judgment's proposition" (Ingarden 1925: 128).[20] In this case, there obtains not only the object–state of affairs duality; there is also a duality within the very idea of *SV* between a subjective state of affairs and an objective-independent state of affairs (a more systematic assessment of these problems is offered in Ingarden 1965: 292–315).[21] For Ingarden, the notion of truth does not equal a correspondence of the judgment with the *SV* it posits; it does consist in the correspondence between two *SV*s, the "formal" state of affairs (posited by the judgment) and the "material" one (subsisting independently of it).

At the end of this short history of the phenomenological concept of *SV*, a sort of dualism (if I can characterize it in this way) turns out to be affecting it. Or better, what seems to emerge is a dual conception (one that runs parallel to Lübbe's argument about the essence-*Geschichte* relation).

On the one hand, *SV* seems to be nothing other than the ideal-objectual correlate of propositions, whose (main) function is that of carving out or throwing into relief "segments of reality." On the other hand, a strongly objective conception of it can be identified, one according to which states of affairs subsist independently of any subjective act (= propositional projection). In the former case, a dualism obtains between objects (independent of any act) and *SV*s understood as the ideal-objective correlates of subjective acts. Here, phenomenologists hesitate between a mere talk of "appearance" or "correlate" and the stronger idea of "projection." In the latter case, the dualism is between a two-term objective ontology (both objects and *SV*s exist independently of our propositional acts)—this seems to be the case for Ingarden and Conrad; and an ontology according to which there are (only) objects, which nevertheless comport themselves in such and such a manner (Pfänder). Here, states of affairs are not ontological entities over and above objects but rather they do designate the object "comporting" itself in a certain way.[22] One could speak either of an object-ontology without *SV*s (they are the objects' own comportment) as a separate kind of entity, or of a *SV*-ontology into which objects dissolve (objects do not exist prior to their own self-comportment).

3. Stories and States of Affairs **(A Preliminary Conclusion)**

As seen in §1, in his note on "The Way into Stories," Schapp admits that the discovery of *SV*, and its subsequent dismissal, was necessary in order to arrive at the *Geschichte*-formation. In other words, no *Geschichte* without *SV*. However, what Schapp means in general when he talks of discovery is not easy to say. An answer could nevertheless be sketched based on what I said in §2. Schapp is right in holding *SV* as what is said about objects (bullet point *3* from §1); in fact, all the phenomenologists mentioned above seem to regard states of affairs (primarily) as the correlates of our judgments and propositions. And if—as seems to be the case with Pfänder and Ingarden—the notion of *SV* is doubled in such a way that *either* objects are identified with their "comportment" (*Selbst-Verhalten*) (Pfänder) *or* they are understood as the sum total of the (material) *SV*s that can then be said about them based upon how they are carved out by our propositions and their "formal states of affairs" (Ingarden, Daubert), then a (radical) conclusion could be drawn: the conclusion according to which the discovery of *SV* results in the world (= the sum total of objects) turning into (or being implicitly assumed as) the sum total of what *can be said about it*. Now, if I am right in making such a claim, then Schapp's conception of *Geschichte* is (also) to be understood as a radicalization of *SV* as it was presented in the previous section. This is confirmed—I believe—by what Schapp himself affirms in bullet points *1* and *4* from §2. Let us quickly recall them.

1. The object of phenomenological analysis and investigation (states of affairs) turns into stories, stories that always include and entail someone/something entangled in them (Schapp 2012: 178).
2. The object is reframed (*deutet sich um*) as stories, yet not as stories of objects; rather, as stories with someone/something entangled in them (Schapp 2012: 178–179).

The subject-matter of phenomenology (= states of affairs) *turns into* stories because the very notion of "object" *has clarified itself as Geschichte*: (a) a two-term ontology (a world that includes both objects *and* states of affairs) (b) turns into a one-term ontology (a world with only states of affairs into which all objects dissolve), (c) which is eventually replaced by the *Geschichte*-philosophy (a world made up only of stories). The transition can be presented in the form of a simple sequence.

(a) Objects/States of Affairs → (b) States of Affairs (Objects) → (c) Stories

A diagram could also be proposed to illustrate this point (Figure 4.1).

Of course, the transition or actual transformation of classical phenomenology into the philosophy of stories (the downward arrow) presupposes that the subject's own role changes accordingly as well. Schapp is right in affirming that "the act-doctrine cannot serve in any way whatsoever to clarify the stories, and more specifically, to shed light on the being-entangled-in-stories moment." But he is right because the act-doctrine he has in mind (Husserl's) conceives of

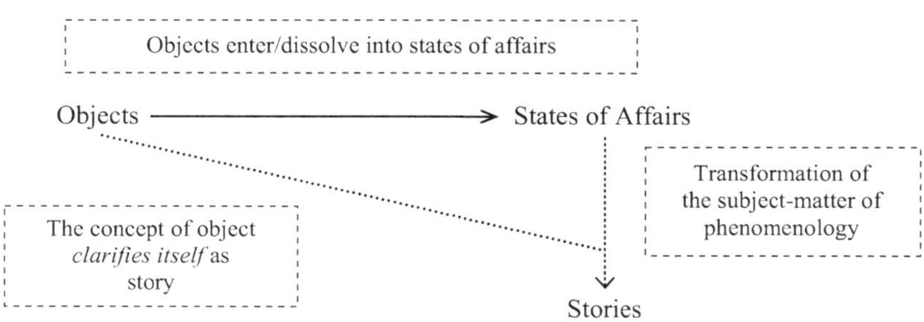

Figure 4.1 From *SV* to Stories

the act's matter as the very instantiation and realization of a (Platonic) eternal meaning. And yet it is difficult not to see in the "carving out"–function proper to our propositional acts something that anticipates what Schapp calls "the being-entangled-in-stories moment" (Schapp 2016: 272). For does not the *carving out*–idea presuppose that we are always and already immersed in and surrounded not by objects, but precisely by states of affairs? And is this not presupposed in a way that precisely anticipates—and points toward—our being-entangled-in-stories (= the world as the sum total of what *can be said about it*)?

Now, even if my tentative reconstruction so far is on the right track, an objection arises that needs to be addressed immediately. In fact, while my reconstruction hinges on the possibility of regarding *SV* as a transition-formation, so to speak—one that will eventually lead to the *Geschichte*-philosophy—Schapp is always adamant about sharply contrasting or opposing them. *Either SV or Geschichte*—this always seems to be his position on the matter. But we have also seen him admitting that without the discovery of *SV*, the very *Geschichte*-philosophy he is proposing would never have been possible. Thus, my reading here presupposes that *at least at some point*, Schapp has indeed identified *SV* and *Geschichte*, or at least that he has tried to construe the latter in terms of the former. Now, such a text does indeed exist, although it is still unpublished. I am actually referring to two typescripts (preserved at the Bavarian State Library) composed on June 7, and 13, 1951, and respectively entitled: "Once Again, State of Affairs" (*Wieder Sachverhalt*), and "Stories" (*Geschichten*) (Schapp 1951a; 1951b).[23] *The texts cannot be quoted here due to copyright issues*. They are nevertheless crucial. In them, Schapp still admits that the world only becomes a world with the emergence of states of affairs. Moreover, in a manner that he will later reject, Schapp maintains that in every story, every proposition is connected with every other proposition within an indissoluble nexus. What Schapp is already rejecting here is the thesis that propositions actually represent the ultimate elements out of which stories are made, for the question is whether in this case, one really does justice to the matters and does not commit a mistake similar to the one made when one says that propositions are made out of concepts. In this way, one destroys the story's unity, that of the *total state of affairs*. It is apparent that Schapp is not rejecting the (more general) thesis that stories consist of *SVs*; rather, here he is dismissing the (more specific) claim to the effect they are made out of *SVs* understood as "ultimate," atomic elements.[24] It should come as no surprise that the unity of the story is called total state of affairs. And he directly refers to such a total state of affairs as a nexus of sense: for Schapp, every "state of affairs" that corresponds to a proposition is embedded within a "total state of affairs" or a greater nexus of sense—which in turn always has the totality of the world as its own necessary background. However, doubts already seem to emerge. For example, since every story (in our sense) is unique and concrete, then one has to recognize that in its structure, the story does not seem to refer to general states of affairs.

The above two 1951 typescripts contribute, I believe, to shedding additional light upon Schapp's claim about the importance of the preliminary discovery (and subsequent dismissal) of the notion of state of affairs for the *Geschichte*-philosophy. *SV* is crucial because—as the notion of *Gesamtsachverhalt* expresses—it introduces the very idea that objects do not exist per se, but are always part of a more embracing "nexus of sense." They are nothing per se; they exist only insofar as they belong to a given state of affairs, which in turn is part of the all-encompassing total state of affairs (the world itself). But in order for the *Geschichte*-philosophy to be possible at all, *SV* had to be rejected. And these are the two reasons that seem to motivate the rejection of *SV*. In the first place, there is the risk that one ends up (mis-)understanding stories as composed of *SV*s as ultimate elements (which is parallel to the mistake of construing propositions out of single concepts). In the second place, there is Schapp's mistrust about *SV*'s "Platonic" implications. If stories are always *einmalig und konkret*, then the idea of *SV* as correlate of propositions (= the individualization of an ideal meaning in the act's intentional matter) must necessarily be abandoned once and for all.

* * *

The goal of the present paper was to shed light on the relations between Schapp's concept of story and the phenomenological concept of state of affairs from the standpoint of his own perspective on the matter. My ambition has not at all been to justify his thesis that *Geschichten* and *Sachverhalte* are necessarily incompatible and that the former has to replace the latter. The assessment of such an issue would also require me to discuss Schapp's own interpretation of "classical phenomenology," and in particular, of its alleged underlying "Platonism." But this is a problem that goes far beyond the scope of this text, whose sole aim has been to make the case for regarding Schapp's *Geschichte*-philosophy if not as a part of the early phenomenological tradition, at least as stemming out of it and some of its tensions.[25]

Notes

1 On this topic, see Nuccilli (2020); on Schapp and phenomenology, see Gottlöber (2020). On the idea in Schapp, see also Michela Summa's paper in the present volume.

2 My translation of the title of Hering's essay differs from Hering 2021 in order to stay closer to the original German wording.

3 See Schapp's reference to Hering in Schapp 2012: 61 (footnote).

4 Hering himself wrote a very short review of Schapp's book, where he questions his former colleague's depiction of "classical phenomenology" (Hering 1954: 415).

5 Johannes Daubert writes that *SV* is "das Mittelglied, welches dasein muß, damit die Gedanken überhaupt an die Sachen hinkommen" (quoted in Schuhmann 2004: 202).

6 This claim is in line with what Husserl affirms in passing in the *Prolegomena*; see Husserl (1975: 128), (2001a: 81). See also my analyses in De Santis (2021: 45–46ff).

7 "The talk of state of affaire always also implies the talk of object" (Schapp 2016: 72).

8 Schapp himself refuses to speak of ontology in general: "The whole ontology sank into nothingness (*versank ins Nichts*) as soon as one took stories as the point of departure (*von Geschichte ausging*)" (Schapp 2017: 134).

9 "Individual stories are no objects" (Schapp 2015: 235). This being stressed, an ambiguity affecting the *SV-Geschichte* relation is to be pointed out. On some occasions, the *SV-Geschichte* relation is characterized in terms of "opposition," if not even exclusion: for instance, states of affairs are said to "chase" the stories "out" of the world (*hinausjagen*) (Schapp 2015: 234). States of affairs, he also writes, have *keinen Platz* in the stories (Schapp 2015: 254). On the other hand, recognizing the more original status of the stories, Schapp makes the case for considering *SV* as belonging to, and derived from, the *Geschichte* (Schapp 2016: 80–81). On this second view, stories are not reducible to *SV*s, but states of affairs and propositions exist only within this or that story. Of course, the two views do not necessarily exclude one another. One could claim that *SV*s exclude the stories because of the (wrong) way in which classical phenomenology has always conceived of their nature; yet once classical phenomenology and its (wrong) position on *SV*s have been left behind, one can finally make the case for regarding *SV* as belonging to the stories' domain.

10 This position is in line not only with Husserl, but also, for example, with the position of Johannes Daubert, who regards *SV* "als das Korrelat eines Urteils und das Urteil als einen Gedanken gegenüberstellt dem, was in dem Gedanken gefaßt wird"(Schuhmann 2004: 202). On Daubert, see also Schuhmann and Smith 1987.

11 I keep speaking of ontology because Schapp himself affirms that without entanglement, "it does not make any sense to speak of being" (Schapp 2012: 178). See bullet point *2* above.

12 On the histories of the notion of state of affairs, see Smith 1989, 1992; Milkov 2002.

13 This is in conformity with his definition of "object" as a subject of possible true predications (see §1 of this text).

14 "Content in the sense of 'matter' is a component of the concrete act-experience, which it may share with acts of quite different quality. [. . . .] To be alike in 'content,' while differing in act-quality has its visible grammatical expressions; the harmony of grammatical forms points the way to our analysis" (Husserl 1984: 426; Husserl 2001b: 120); "What do we mean by the 'same content'? Plainly the intentional objectivity of the various acts is the same. One and the same state of affairs is presented in the presentation, put as valid in the judgment, wished for in the wish, asked about in the question" (Husserl 1984: 426–427; Husserl 2001b: 120).

15 Here I am not considering Husserl's later, genetic approach to *SV*; see for example Husserl 2007: 284, where *SVs* are said to be "produced" (*erzeugt*) in a "*creative spontaneity*."

16 See also Dubois 1995: 24–25ff. In this respect, Reinach's view would be similar to Bolzano's. See Bolzano's letter to Exner from July 9, 1833, on the example, "That tree has exactly 101 apples" as independent of any actual or possible judgment referring to it (Bolzano 1935: 7–17, here: 9). On Husserl and Bolzano, see Künne (1987, 2013).

17 "But 'states of affairs' are there indifferently of which consciousness apprehends them, and of whether they are apprehended by any consciousness at all. In and for itself the a priori has not even the least thing to do with thinking and knowing" (Reinach 1989: 545). On the problem of the negative *SV* in Reinach, see Chrudzimski 2012: 117–120.

18 In his lectures of 1908 on the theory of meaning, Husserl will introduce the distinction between state of affairs and *Sachlage*. But such a distinction does not correspond to Conrad's. In fact, while Conrad is interested in the distinction between *SV* and non-propositional material (the amorphous matter), Husserl's distinction obtains within the domain of what is propositionally formed. The *Sachlage* means what different states of affairs have categorially in common, yet is apprehended differently: "The two states of affairs [a > b and b < a] [. . .] have the same *Sachlage* at their basis, which is only categorially grasped in different ways" (Husserl 1987: 29; see also Husserl's remarks in Husserl 2007, §59, where *SVs* are now said to "correspond" to *Sachlagen* which, in turn, are founded upon "objects").

19 I do not deny that *SV* could play also other roles and fulfill other functions. But for the sake of my discussion here, they can be easily disregarded (for a more comprehensive assessment, see Smith 1987).

20 Also Spiegelberg's position is worth being briefly recalled. Just like Pfänder, he speaks of *SV* as being "projected" by the judgment (the verb being *entwerfen*) (Spiegelberg 1935: 97-98); yet, just like Ingarden, he speaks of the coincidence "of the projected state of affairs with a factually obtaining state of affairs" (*Zusammenfallen des entworfenen mit einem tatsächlich bestehenden Sachverhalt*) (Spiegelberg 1935: 98). Unlike the former, the latter is "ontologically autarchic" (*seinsautark*) and independent of our cognitive acts (Spiegelberg 1935: 99).

21 Ingarden expresses his skepticism about Reinach's conception of negative *SV* in a still unpublished letter to Jean Hering (Ingarden 1958a: 1). It would be a mistake to believe that all phenomenologists without exception accepted the existence of *SV* (whether just positive or also negative ones). For example, Maximilian Beck argues extensively against *SV*s in Beck 1938: 139–143. Beck invests all his energies in denouncing the "absurdities" that follow from the introduction of a third domain in between "the logical sphere and the ontological one in the proper sense [of the term]" (Beck 1938: 141). Upon closer inspection, Beck's position turns out to be the opposite of Conrad's, who lays claim to the "*sphere of pure thought itself*, that of the content of thought we bring to expression in choosing understandable words and propositions by saying what our *meaning-intention* concerning a matter is—we are stating something *about* a matter and are not merely naming the matter. In this regard, the Göttingen Philosophical Society had already termed this conceptual sphere the sphere of meaning as something objective, in contrast to the subjective intending in the sense of the *verb* 'to mean' [. . .]. And throughout the entire Husserl School, this sphere was particularly significant for the elucidation of the essence of cognition: namely, the sphere of the 'state of affairs'" (Conrad 1954: 1–2, 3).

22 Spiegelberg seems to embrace an intermediate position. As he writes, states of affairs "exhibit" (*aufweisen*) the unity between the object and "a comportment (determination) pertaining to it (*zukommendes Verhalten (Bestimmtheit)*)." But the unity is such that the comportment is "subordinated" (*untergeordnet*) to the object (Spiegelberg 1935: 119–120).

23 I wish to thank Daniele Nuccilli for bringing these texts to my attention. See his remarks in Nuccilli (2024). I am also grateful to him for letting me consult his still unpublished PhD dissertation on Schapp (Nuccilli 2022), where the notion of state of affairs is extensively discussed in Ch. 3, §1.3.

24 Just as concepts result from an abstraction from their embeddedness in a proposition, so *SV*s are nothing prior to the stories to which they belong: they can be obtained only by making an abstraction from the total nexus of sense.

25 This work was supported by the Czech Science Foundation, financing the project "Rediscovering a German-Czech Member of Early Phenomenology: Intentionality, Consciousness and the Mind in the Philosophy of Maximilian Beck" (GAČR

24-10611S) and by the *Cooperatio* programme provided by Charles University (research field: philosophy), and implemented by the Faculty of Arts.

References

Beck, M. (1938), *Psychologie. Wesen und Wirklichkeit der Seele*, Leiden: Sijthoff.

Bolzano, B. (1935), *Der Briefwechsel B. Bolzanos mit F. Exner*, Prag: Königliche Böhmische Gesellschaft.

Chrudzimski, A. (2012), "Negative States of Affairs: Reinach versus Ingarden," *Symposium: The Canadian Journal of Continental Philosophy*, 16 (2): 106–27.

Conrad, Th. (1954), *Überblick über die im Wintersemester 1953/54 und Sommersemester 1954 in der "Münchener Philosophischen Gesellschaft" durchgeführten phänomenologischen Untersuchungen über das Wesen der phänomenologischen Methode als spezifischem Zugang zur Philosophie* (Bayerische Staatsbibliothek, Ana 378 V 2) (transcription by D. De Santis; English translation by E. A. Behnke), *The New Yearbook for Phenomenology and Phenomenological Philosophy*, vol. 22, 2024, 97–110.

Conrad-Martius, H. (1921), "Einleitung," in A. Reinach, *Gesammelte Schriften*, ed. by his students, Halle: Max Niemeyer: v–xxxvii.

Conrad-Martius, H. (1965), *Schriften zur Philosophie. Dritter Band*, München: Kösel Verlag.

De Santis, D. (2021), *Husserl and the A Priori: Phenomenology and Rationality*, Cham: Springer.

Dubois, J. M. (1995), *Judgment and Sachverhalt: An Introduction to Adolf Reinach's Phenomenological Realism*, Dordrecht: Kluwer Academic Publishers.

Gottlöber, S. (2020), "Phänomenologie," in K. Joisten, J. Schapp, and N. Thiemer (eds), *Die Rezeption der Geschichtenphilosophie Wilhelm Schapps. Kommentare und Fortsetzungen*, München: Karl Alber: 48–64.

Heinrich, E. (1910), *Untersuchungen zur Lehre vom Begriff*, Inaugural-Dissertation der Hohen Philosophischen Fakultät der Georg-August-Universität zu Göttingen, Göttingen: W. Fr. Kaestner.

Hering, J. (1921), "Bemerkungen über das Wesen, die Wesenheit und die Idee," *Jahrbuch für Philosophie und phänomenologische Forschung*, 4: 495–543.

Hering, J. (1954), "Wilhelm Schapp, *In Geschichten verstrickt. Zum Sein von Mensch und Ding*," *Revue d'histoire et de philosophie religieuses*, 34 (4): 414–15.

Hering, J. (2021), "Remarks Concerning Essence, Ideal Quality and Idea," trans. A. Szylewicz, *Phenomenological Investigations*, 1: 51–108.

Husserl, E. (1975), *Prolegomena zu einer reinen Logik*, Hua XVIII, ed. E. Holenstein, Den Haag: Martinus Nijhoff.

Husserl, E. (1976), *Ideen zu einer reinen Phänomenologie und phänomenologischen Philosophie. Band I*, Hua III/1, ed. K. Schuhmann, Den Haag: Martinus Nijhoff.

Husserl, E. (1984), *Logische Untersuchungen. Zweiter Band. Erster Teil*, Hua XIX/1, ed. U. Panzer, Den Haag: Martinus Nijhoff.
Husserl, E. (1987), *Über Bedeutungslehre. Sommersemester 1908*, Hua XXVI, ed. U. Panzer, Dordrecht: Martinus Nijhoff.
Husserl, E. (2001a), *Logical Investigations 1*, trans. J. N. Findlay, ed. D. Moran, London/ New York: Routledge.
Husserl, E. (2001b), *Logical Investigations 2*, trans. J. N. Findlay, ed. D. Moran, London/ New York: Routledge.
Husserl, E. (2007), *Erfahrung und Urteil*, Hamburg, Felix Meiner.
Husserl, E. (2014), *Ideas I*, trans. D. Dahlstrom, Indianapolis: Hackett.
Ingarden, R. (1925), "Essentiale Fragen. Ein Beitrag zu dem Wesensproblem," *Jahrbuch für Philosophie und phänomenologische Forschung*, 7: 125–304.
Ingarden, R. (1958a), "Brief an Jean Hering" (19.01.1958), Strasbourg: Fondation du Chapitre de Saint-Thomas (unpublished).
Ingarden, R. (1958b), "Brief an Jean Hering" (01.05.1958), Strasbourg: Fondation du Chapitre de Saint-Thomas (unpublished)
Ingarden, R. (1965), *Der Streit um die Existenz der Welt II/1. Formalontologie 1. Teil*, Tübingen: Max Niemeyer.
Künne, W. (1987), "The Intentionality of Thinking: The Difference between State of Affairs and Propositional Matter," in K. Mulligan (ed.), *Speech Act and Sachverhalt: Reinach and the Foundations of Realist Phenomenology*, 175–225, Dordrecht: Martinus Nijhoff.
Künne, W. (2013), "Intentionalität: Bolzano und Husserl," in S. Centrone (ed.), *Versuche über Husserl*, 97–144, Hamburg: Meiner.
Lübbe, H. (1954), "Das Ende des phänomenologischen Platonismus. Eine kritische Betrachtung aus Anlass eines neuen Buches," *Tijdschrift voor Philosophie*, 16 (4): 639–66.
Milkov, N. (2002), "Lotze's Concept of 'States of Affairs' and its Critics," *Prima philosophia*, 15: 437–50.
Mulligan, K. (2009), "Truth and Truth-Maker Principle in 1921," in E. J. Low and A. Rami (eds), *Truth and Truth-Making*, 39–58, Montreal: McGill-Queen's.
Nuccilli, D. (2020), "Species, Ideas, and Stories: Schapp between Phenomenological 'Platonism' and 'Anti-Platonism'," *Azimuth*, 15 (7): 61–75.
Nuccilli, D. (2022), *Wilhelm Schapp. Tra fenomenologia e filosofia delle storie*, tesi dottorale presentata e discussa all'Università di Roma "Tor Vergata".
Nuccilli, D. (2024), "70 Years of *In Geschichten verstrickt*: Context, Legacy, and Development," *The New Yearbook for Phenomenology and Phenomenological Philosophy*, 22, forthcoming.
Pfänder, A. (1963), *Logik*, Tübingen: Max Niemeyer.
Pfänder, A. (2009), *Logic*, Frankfurt: Ontos Verlag.

Reinach, A. (1982), "On the Theory of Negative Judgments," in B. Smith (ed.), *Parts and Moments: Studies in Logic and Formal Ontology*, 315–77, Munich/Vienna: Philosophia.

Reinach, A. (1989), *Sämtliche Werke 1*, München/Wien: Philosophia.

Schapp, W. (1951a), "Wieder Sachverhalt" (7.6.1951) (still unpublished typescript preserved at the Bavarian State Library, Ana 627).

Schapp, W. (1951b), "Geschichten" (13.7.1951) (still unpublished typescript preserved at the Bavarian State Library, Ana 627)

Schapp, W. (2012[1953]), *In Geschichten verstrickt*, Frankfurt am Main: Vittorio Klostermann.

Schapp, W. (2015[1959]), *Philosophie der Geschichten*, Frankfurt am Main: Vittorio Klostermann.

Schapp, W. (1959), "Erinnerungen an Husserl," in AA.VV., *Edmund Husserl 1859–1959*, 12–25, Den Haag: Martinus Nijhoff.

Schapp, W. (2016), *Philosophischer Nachlass. Teilband I: Auf dem Weg einer Philosophie der Geschichten*, ed. K. Joisten, J. Schapp, and N. Thiemer, Freiburg/München: Karl Alber.

Schapp, W. (2017), *Philosophischer Nachlass. Teilband II: Auf dem Weg einer Philosophie der Geschichten*, ed. K. Joisten, J. Schapp, and N. Thiemer, Freiburg/München: Karl Alber.

Schapp, W. (2025), "Recollections of Husserl," trans. E. A. Behnke, in D. De Santis and D. Nuccilli (eds), *The Philosophy of Wilhelm Schapp: From Phenomenology to Jurisprudence and the Hermeneutics of Stories*, 227–238, London: Bloomsbury.

Schuhmann, K. (2004), "Der Begriff des Sachverhalts bei Johannes Daubert," in his *Selected Papers on Phenomenology*, ed. C. Leijenhorst and P. Steenbakkers, 201–17, Dordrecht: Kluwer Academic Publishers.

Schuhmann, K. and Smith, B. (1987), "Questions: An Essay in Daubertian Phenomenology," *Philosophy and Phenomenological Research*, 47 (3): 353–84.

Smith, B. (1987), "On the Cognition of States of Affairs," in K. Mulligan (ed.), *Speech Act and Sachverhalt: Reinach and the Foundations of Realist Phenomenology*, 189–225, Dordrecht: Martinus Nijhoff.

Smith, B. (1989), "Logic and the *Sachverhalt*," *The Monist*, 72 (1): 52–69

Smith, B. (1992), "Sachverhalt: eine begriffsgeschichtliche Untersuchung," in J. Ritter and K. Gründer (eds), *Historisches Wörterbuch der Philosophie*, Vol. 8, 1102–113, Stuttgart/Basel: Schwabe.

Spiegelberg, H. (1935), *Gesetz und Sittengesetz. Strukturanalytische und historische Vorstudien zu einer gesetzfreien Ethik*, Zürich und Leipzig: Max Niehans Verlag.

Taieb, H. (2018), "Building Objective Thoughts: Stumpf, Twardowski and the Late Husserl on Psychic Products," *Archiv für Geschichte der Philosophie*, 100 (3): 336–70.

5

Perception and Stories

Schapp and Plato's *Theaetetus*

Alejandro G. Vigo

Wenn wir von den Geschichten und der Geschichte ausgehen, so ist unser Ausgangspunkt dem von Husserl diametral entgegengesetzt.

W. Schapp

1. Schapp, Platonism, and the Problem of Perception

As is well-known, Wilhelm Schapp's thought undergoes a profound change in the decades that separate his doctoral dissertation published in 1910 and his most original and best-known book, published in 1953, in which he presents his "philosophy of stories." The depth of the change would justify distinguishing between a "Schapp I" and a "Schapp II," as is often done with Heidegger.

In the first approximation, the path from Schapp I to Schapp II can be described as a distancing from Husserl, which leads Schapp to adopt a position that from the methodical point of view turns out to be the opposite of Husserl's. Schapp himself presents things this way when he claims that his own starting point in stories and history is diametrically opposed to Husserl's (Schapp 2012: 172). Husserl, Schapp assumes, takes perception as his point of departure. And Schapp himself also adopted the same methodical view in his doctoral dissertation, written under Husserl's supervision, in which he elaborates a phenomenological analysis of perception that in subtlety and detail easily approaches the achievements of his *Doktorvater*.[1] At first glance, the subsequent reversal of perspective might appear to be extrinsically motivated. But this is not the case. Rather, it is the result of a consistent radicalization of motives and impulses that are present, if only marginally, from the very beginning. Such a radicalization does not lead to an abandonment of phenomenology as such, but to a drastic reinterpretation of its true scope. In the framework of such a reinterpretation, what is explicitly abandoned is above all the Husserlian foundational claim to establish phenomenology as a strict science. Indeed, Schapp explains that he in no way intends to develop a scientific investigation that would become, so to speak, "armored" (*gepanzert*) by means of a system of concepts (Schapp 2012: 87).[2]

As far as perception is specifically concerned, once removed from its privileged place as a starting point, it becomes more of a *problem*—a problem whose adequate treatment poses significant methodical challenges.[3] But precisely as a problem, it also acquires a new centrality. In the book of 1953, the treatment of perception is strategically placed in the final chapter of the first part (chapter 10) and thus provides the transition between the analysis of "thing(s)-for. . ." (*Wozuding(e)*)[4] and the analysis of "entanglement in stories" (*Verstrickung / Verstricktsein in Geschichten*) that is developed in the second part of the work. One of the central objectives of this new treatment of perception is to draw attention to the almost insurmountable difficulty of establishing a field of investigation that properly corresponds to what is usually called perception, if there really is such a thing (Schapp 2012: 72). Schapp discusses each of the main paths through which access to the domain of perception was traditionally sought—(1) sensible qualities (*Sinnesqualitäten*) (Schapp 2012: 73–76), (2) imaginative representations (*Bildvorstellungen*) (Schapp 2012: 76–80), and (3) modifications of perception such as hallucinations, dreams, and phantasy representations (Schapp 2012: 80–82)—and he shows, on that basis, their irreparable methodical inadequacy.

This being the case, an important part of what needs to be explained here has to do with the reasons that account for the very fact that perception may have mistakenly been considered as something basic to be taken as a starting point. And that is what Schapp tries to do in different contexts of his work, especially when he discusses authors from the Western philosophical and literary tradition such as Plato, Descartes, and Kant on the one hand and Homer and Hesiod on the other (see especially Schapp 2015, Part II and III). Among these, Plato occupies a particularly important position. This is because Schapp assumes that there is a secret link between the starting point in perception and Platonism, as well as assuming that the Platonism dominant in the metaphysical tradition penetrated the philosophy of logic in the late nineteenth and early twentieth centuries and from there contaminated Husserlian phenomenology itself. This anti-Platonic motif plays a key role in the transition leading from Schapp I to Schapp II. A consideration of the way in which Schapp interprets Plato's *Theaetetus* may help to shed more light on this point (Section 3). But first (Section 2) it is worthwhile to draw attention, at least briefly, to the tension between Platonic and anti-Platonic elements that already surfaces—if only marginally—in the 1910 doctoral dissertation.

2. The Doctoral Dissertation: Between History and Idea

The phenomenological study of perception that Schapp elaborates in his 1910 doctoral dissertation should rightly be counted as one of the most distinctive contributions to phenomenological research made by the first generation of Husserl's disciples. Schapp's investigation in particular stands out for the exemplary way in which it attempts to accomplish the anti-reductionist ideal that animates every genuine phenomenological approach. In this sense, Schapp stresses that the phenomenologist must address perception "with a light hand" (*mit leichter Hand*), in an attitude characterized by an "unconditioned dedication" (*unbedingte Hingabe*) (Schapp 2013: 12), which aims to achieve a "deepening in the things themselves" (*Vertiefen in die Sachen selbst*) (Schapp 2013: 13). The analysis must be carried out in such a way that what is separated in it remains preserved at the same time, precisely as it is given (Schapp 2013: 12), since only what is originally seen (*geschaut*) belongs to phenomenology (Schapp 2013: 14). For the same reason, Schapp severely criticizes attempts to explain what is originally given by means of constructive theories such as, for example, the theory that assumes that things are made up of atoms: such a type of explanation can never replace recourse to lived experience itself, and its inclusion in phenomenological analysis can only cause obstruction or diversion (Schapp 2013: 19).

The description elaborated by Schapp contains, on the other hand, several aspects of detail that reveal a remarkable ability for the practice of phenomenological analysis. Its basic starting point is the question of the means by which the "world of things" (*Dingwelt*) is "presented" or "exhibited" (*darstellen*) (Schapp 2013: 10–55). What the phenomenological analysis of perception seeks to make explicit are the elements that belong a priori to the way in which such "presentation" or "exhibition" (*Darstellung*) takes place, through each of the senses and their corresponding objective correlates. In the initial and most general section of the treatment, Schapp analyzes color as the objective correlate of vision (Schapp 2013: 15–26), tone as the objective correlate of hearing

(Schapp 2013: 26–32), and taste (Schapp 2013: 32–36), in order to thematize the relationships between the different senses (Schapp 2013: 37–42) and on that basis to exhibit the space that belongs to the "world of things" (Schapp 2013: 42–55). Given that the entire analysis is guided by the intention of giving an account of the way in which the "world of things" is exhibited, color acquires a special relevance precisely because of the peculiarity of its exhibiting function. In the central section of the work, this exhibiting function receives a much more detailed analysis (Schapp 2013: 57–128). It is not possible to discuss here the remarkable analysis of color that Schapp elaborates.[5] But in general terms, it does not seem an overstatement to say that in differentiation and subtlety, it outperforms any other analysis elaborated within the phenomenological tradition.

In any case, Schapp's focus on the exhibiting function of sensuous qualities, and especially of color, produces some results that may seem surprising from the point of view of more traditional approaches. Schapp explains that space (*Raum*) does not possess an exhibiting function. Rather, it is on the side of what is represented or exhibited through colors and their arrangement. As for the figure (*Gestalt*), it also belongs to what is represented or exhibited, but in turn fulfills an exhibiting function with respect to the thing itself with its properties (*Eigenschaften*). However, it should not itself be seen as a form (*Form*) of the thing, but rather as something represented or exhibited, which in turn also fulfills the function of representing or exhibiting (Schapp 2013: 115). Ultimately, it is color that—without the mediation of space—exhibits the properties of the thing and its way of acting and being acted upon (*Verhalten*) (Schapp 2013: 116). From the fact that space lacks an exhibiting function it follows, for Schapp, that if one abstracts from the properties exhibited through color, nothing remains of the thing itself—nothing that can still be regarded as spatial (Schapp 2013: 116). From this perspective, the thing itself cannot be thought in the Cartesian way, for it cannot be reduced to spatial extension. Deprived of its properties, the thing itself disappears. The identity of the individual thing is thus indissolubly linked to its properties, just as these are represented or exhibited through color and its arrangement.

It is this line of thought that leads Schapp to hit upon a motif that in the context of the doctoral dissertation does not receive further development, but will become central later, namely, what is presented to us in perception is always something individual that possesses its own "history/story" (*Geschichte*), a history that has always left its "traces" (*Spuren*) in it:

> These traces sometimes appear like "scars" (*Narben*), which we know how to "read." We immediately see what has happened to the individual thing that becomes present in perception. We see how the wood is cut and thus see how it behaves under the saw; we see the fine scratches of a golden clock and thus also see the softness of gold. Every thing we see always shows in its contingent configuration what it has already gone through and thus also its history, its own character (*Eigenart*), and the way it has withstood its destiny (*Schiksal*). This also occurs where we see something for the first time: things never appear as if they came out of a box, but always bear the traces of their destiny. Even when they leave the factory, they already show how they have been made. (Schapp 2013: 117)

Schapp's claim that individual things in the world have their own history must be seen as strictly phenomenological. As such, and contrary to what is sometimes assumed, it does not exclusively concern things produced by human beings, but also things and products of nature. The opposition between what is produced by nature and what is produced by human beings usually plays a key role in traditional metaphysical conceptions that rely on the notion of cause as a guiding thread. But this is not the case with the phenomenological approach that Schapp develops.

However, the path toward a radical historicization that is foreshadowed in this passage is not followed in the further development of the doctoral dissertation. On the contrary, the last section of the work (Schapp 2013: 129–57), dedicated to the question of the role played in perception by what Schapp calls "the Idea" (*die Idee*), clearly aims at reinforcing the alignment with Husserl, and does so through recourse to a traditional Platonic motif. The eidetic turn that Schapp's analysis undergoes here is somewhat striking, since at least at first glance, it does not seem to be internally motivated.[6] Schapp takes the Platonic notion of the Idea in a very traditional sense, as equivalent to "essence" (*Wesen*) or even "concept" (*Begriff*), and asks how it can be found in perception (Schapp 2013: 130). Accordingly, his analysis aims to highlight the function of the Idea as a principle of unity and limitation operating on the aesthetic level, and not as a principle of conceptual classification or categorization in the sense of the traditional logic of genus and species. What operates at the aesthetic level, Schapp explains, is the "individual Idea" (*Einzelidee*), which is not to be confused with the "genus" (*Gattung*) under which the thing falls. Nor is it identical with the form, and in general, it adds nothing to the thing itself. Rather, it is the "light" (*Licht*) that spreads over the thing in perception (Schapp 2013: 133ff.).

In explaining the way in which the Idea operates in perception itself, Schapp strives to avoid any misinterpretation that would assimilate the function of the Idea to the most common forms of conceptualization. Like everything that belongs to perception and forms part of its constitution, the Idea is in some way employed in perceptual observation, but without being itself thematized or objectified (Schapp 2013: 136). For the same reason, its function has nothing to do with the usual cases in which something is subsumed under a concept. The determination (*Bestimmung*) of the object by means of the Idea, as it takes place in perception itself, has an immediate character. It is carried out without recourse to experience and excludes any kind of reflective mediation (Schapp 2013: 136ff.). But it is the operative presence of the Idea that accounts for a certain "law" (*Gesetz*) to which all perception is subject—namely, when we see something univocally (*eindeutig*), what we see appears as univocally determined, that is, it unveils itself (*enthüllt sich*) to us and thus reveals its essence to us (Schapp 2013: 139). In this sense, the Idea accounts, Schapp thinks, for the principle of univocity (*Eindeutigkeit*) and determination (*Bestimmung*) that regulatively governs all perception, that is, serves as the telos to be reached by all perception that is not deficient (Schapp 2013: 140ff.). The Idea, Schapp explains, is not itself something sensible, but belongs to a non-sensible sphere and has its own independence (*selbstständig*) there. But it is through it that the sensible world becomes, for the first time, a "world" (*Welt*), a "cosmos" (*Kosmos*), something univocally determined, and not "chaos" (*Chaos*) such as occurs in the darkness, in the distance, or in the twilight, when everything turns indeterminate (*unbestimmt*) and multivocal (*vieldeutig*) (Schapp 2013: 140ff.). The Idea has, then, a fundamental function with respect to the sensible world, for it is the Idea that endows it with meaning (*Sinn*). Thus, as regulatively governed by the principle of univocity and determination, perception is always perception of something *as something*. This explains why Schapp resorts here to the notion of understanding (*Verstehen*) (Schapp 2013: 143–149). What the Idea makes possible is ultimately the specific mode of understanding that takes place in perception, at least where it has reached its goal (*Ziel*) (Schapp 2013: 146). Schapp suggests that the specific notion of understanding introduced here could be brought into connection with what Husserl calls "ideal meaning" (*ideale Bedeutung*), provided it is taken in a weak sense that does not make it the objective correlate of an act of thematic grasping (Schapp 2013: 146). The understanding that takes place in perception is not the result of a previous process of elaboration, but occurs "all at once" (*mit einem Schlage*), "suddenly" (*plötzlich*), without our knowing where it is coming from (Schapp 2013: 147).

Perception suddenly becomes "meaningful" (*sinnvoll*) (Schapp 2013: 148). It is a sort of "revelation" (*Offenbarung*) or "illumination" (*Erleuchtung*) that occurs in contact with the Idea, and this in the traditional Platonic-Augustinian sense that refers to the intelligible as a source of light radiating on the sensible (Schapp 2013: 147). In this sense, understanding manifests itself as "light" (*Licht*) (Schapp 2013: 148).

However, despite the decidedly Platonic character of the eidetic turn that Schapp carries out here, it should be emphasized that his concern not to give rise to conceptualist derivations of a constructive nature is also evident in the treatment of the function of the Idea. We have already seen that Schapp insists on the need to avoid assimilating the Idea to the genus or approaching the question of its function in perception from the perspective of the logic of genus and species. What Schapp puts in the center of attention from the very beginning is instead the relationship of the Idea and the sensible. Clarifying this relationship is accordingly the task of the last part of his investigation, where he discusses the notion of boundary (*Grenze*) (Schapp 2013: 149–57). Here Schapp provides a variety of remarkable phenomenological hints,[7] but the essential point of his elaboration consists in making it clear that it is the Idea, as strict unity (*strenge Einheit*) unrelated to anything else, that makes possible the delimitation of the thing as it is given in adequate perception: of each thing there is an Idea, and it is the Idea that delimits the thing when we see it in its essence (Schapp 2013: 156). In this way, the boundary that the thing "has" is just a "function" or even a "product" of the Idea (Schapp 2013: 157). What we have here, in the case of the limit, is only a particular example of a specific type of "objectivity" (*Gegenständlichkeit*), which is constituted on the basis of the relationship between the Idea and sensibility. A new field of investigation opens up here, the study of which would give rise, Schapp thinks, to a new table of categories (Schapp 2013: 157).

3. Plato on Perception: Schapp's Reading of the *Theaetetus*

As has already been said, in the 1953 book, perception has lost its privileged place as a starting point—the place it held, following Husserl, in the doctoral dissertation. With this, any trace of Platonism has also disappeared. In fact, Plato's name is not even mentioned in the work. But a look at the *Nachlass* shows that in the same year, Schapp began to deal intensively with Plato and continued to do so in the following years.

A set of notes dated between August 1953 and January 1956 contains thoughts inspired by the (re)reading of Platonic dialogues, particularly the *Cratylus* and the *Sophist* (Schapp 2016: 39–51). Schapp's interest focuses on the Platonic treatment of language and proposition (*Satz*). But what he is looking for there are above all correspondences with classical phenomenology—more precisely, "vestiges" (*Spuren*) of what Husserl later understood under meaning (*Bedeutung*) and concept (*Begriff*) (Schapp 2016: 39). His aim is thus avowedly deconstructive: it is to pursue to its most remote historical source the conception of meaning and language from which Schapp has distanced himself, that is, the classical phenomenological conception elaborated by Husserl (Schapp 2016: 41). This is why in his reading of the Platonic text, Schapp especially emphasizes those aspects that could have served as starting points for the development of a different conception, aligned with the one he himself presents in the 1953 book. His effort aims above all to show that the characteristic multidimensionality of Platonic thought opens possibilities of appropriation that deviate from the historical path followed by, so to speak, "really existing Platonism," which ultimately leads to Husserl. For instance, the way in which Plato speaks of history and knowledge in the *Cratylus* certainly seems to aim at emphasizing the moment of permanence subtracted from change, which is the motif later taken up by the traditional theory of meaning (Schapp 2016: 39). Nevertheless, the treatment of language and logos in the *Sophist* seems to be closer to a pragmatic theory of discourse (*Rede*), based on everyday speech, than to a theory of proposition in the style of logic and theory of meaning (Schapp 2016: 41ff.). A second set of notes from the same years contains reflections on the *Theaetetus*, the dialogue that presents the most extensive discussion of perception contained in the Platonic *corpus* (Schapp 2016: 89–107). Again, Schapp's main intention is to go back to the ultimate source of a way of conceiving perception from which he has distanced himself. And here too, Schapp tries to highlight aspects or motifs that could have given rise to different developments, more akin to the position he himself has adopted in the 1953 monograph.

As is well-known, these elaborations contained in the *Nachlass* are just preliminary work for the chapter on Plato included in the 1959 book (Schapp 2015: 167–87). As such, they are rather provisional, and at times, somewhat disorganized. It should be noted, however, that the treatment sequence *Cratylus—Sophist—Theaetetus* remains intact in the 1959 book, since it is motivated by both methodical and thematic concerns. Indeed, in the first part of the 1953 book, the analysis of the world starts with the "things-for" and only reaches "perception" in the last step, after having gone through "genus" (*Gattung*) and "universal proposition" (*allgemeiner Satz*), a sequence of treatment that corresponds to the new starting point adopted by Schapp after distancing himself from Husserl. The discussion of Plato in the years following the publication of the 1953 book basically displays the same sequence: it starts from the problem of names and meaning (*Cratylus*), passes through the treatment of propositions (*Sophist*), and finally ends in the discussion of perception (*Theaetetus*). By this time, perception, as already mentioned, has fundamentally become a problem, to the point that it is no longer known for sure whether there is such a thing (at least in the way it is taken for granted in traditional approaches). The reading of the way in which Plato treats perception in the *Theaetetus* is therefore inserted from the very beginning into this general interpretative framework and aims to underpin it from the historical point of view. From a more general point of view, it can be said that what Schapp offers here, through his reading of Plato, is part of a story about the history of the philosophical problem of perception. This story—which should be seen instead as a "meta-story"—aims to tell how in the history of philosophy, understood fundamentally as the history of Platonism, the link between perception and stories was increasingly lost from view. Plato, of course, plays a key role in this context. Let us now consider, from this angle, the most salient aspects in Schapp's reading of the *Theaetetus*.

In a completely unorthodox way, Schapp begins with the passage 209c–209d, included in the last section of the dialogue, where the characterization of knowledge as true belief accompanied by explanation or justification is discussed. Socrates refers there to the representation he possesses of Theaetetus, whom he has seen many times and knows well. Schapp is interested in the passage precisely because it concerns the relationship between perception and "representation" (*Vorstellung*), taken in a broad sense that is not limited to the realm of imagination (Schapp 2015: 177). Plato seems to be thinking, Schapp explains, of imaginative representations combined with conceptual representations of characteristics (*Merkmale*) that—without being themselves completely individual—allow one thing to be distinguished from different things (Schapp 2015: 177). The example of such a characteristic is Theaetetus's crooked nose. According to Schapp, Plato here approaches the relationship of perception to representation from the point of view of the possibility of recognizing representation in perception itself, that is, of identifying it with perception: when representation provides a sufficient basis for such identification, it follows that it must possess a peculiar character of "rightness" (*Richtigkeit*), something that seems to be essential for knowledge (Schapp 2015: 177ff.). To the example of Theaetetus and his crooked nose, Schapp immediately adds the example, taken from Hesiod, of the "chariot of one hundred pieces of wood," which had been mentioned earlier in 207a–c. This approach to the text, focusing on two examples, may seem surprising at first glance. But it is part of a hermeneutical strategy that Schapp consciously opts for, as the *Nachlass* shows (Schapp 2016: 90f.). The point that Schapp is interested in highlighting concerns an asymmetry in the way Plato deals with both cases: in the case of the human being Plato starts from the individual, while in the case of the artifact he starts instead from the genus or concept (Schapp 2015: 178; see also Schapp 2016: 92).[8] From this, Schapp derives some decisive consequences for his interpretation.

First, concerning the chariot, Schapp points out that in order to explain how a right representation can be obtained, recourse to a generic characterization or even a definite description is not enough: the hundred pieces of wood referred to by Hesiod provide only a beginning for the task of achieving a right representation of the chariot (Schapp 2015: 178). In addition, it would be necessary to place the chariot in a complete historical series that traces the evolution from the first and most primitive chariot to the chariot still in use in the times of Hesiod or Socrates. Seen in this light, the chariot is a "piece of the history of human culture" (*ein Stück Kulturgeschichte der Menschheit*), which it is only possible to understand within the framework of the history of culture as a whole and proceeding from the human being (*vom Menschen aus*). This approach, Schapp thinks, might allow us to arrive at a new understanding of Protagoras's "*homo mensura*" principle. But even then, we would not get to the heart of the question as to what is to be understood by right representation and knowledge (Schapp 2015: 179).

Second, as far as Theaetetus as an individual human being is concerned, Schapp claims that the best way to get a right representation is to turn to the stories in which he has been or is entangled: Theaetetus is, in effect, the one entangled in his own stories, either on his own or with others. But furthermore, Schapp explains, it is only through the mediation of stories connected to individual human beings like Theaetetus (or anyone else) that we can achieve full access to things like the chariot and the other "things-for" that appear in such stories (Schapp 2015: 179; see also Schapp 2016: 93ff.).

With this, Schapp has presented a two-level model to account for the possibility of cognitive access to the individual *qua* individual. In all cases, such access takes place through the mediation of certain stories, but these primarily involve individual human beings, that is, persons, and only through them do the stories also involve things of the world, as "things-for." This model, he thinks, provides the basis from which the question can be raised as to whether we have arrived at some knowledge (*zu einem Wissen*) or form of cognition (*zu einer Art Erkenntnis*), and what it is (Schapp 2015: 179). It is at this point, and based on the perspective thus reached, that Schapp turns to the discussion of perception that Plato offers in the first part of the *Theaetetus*. This retrospective reading of the Platonic text reflects Schapp's basic methodical claim that perception cannot serve as a starting point, nor can it be understood on the basis of itself: perception, if there is such a thing, is reached proceeding from stories, and not the other way around.

On this basis, Schapp's interpretative strategy consists of highlighting the fact that in his discussion of perception, Plato is guided by a preconceived idea of Being according to which true, real Being is that which is permanent and stable, without any variation or change. Plato, Schapp explains, does not properly ask what perception is. Rather, he considers perception from the side of that which would be its objective correlate. The fact that perception does not offer access to anything permanent is what makes it necessary to conclude that it cannot be identified with knowledge. It is in the context of this consideration that Plato appeals to Heraclitus's supposed doctrine that "everything flows" (Schapp 2015: 180ff.). What Schapp is mainly interested in is the way in which Plato proceeds in approaching the problem of perception, that is, his method. The aim is to establish what knowledge is. The possibility that it is identical with perception is then examined. Yet a certain conception of knowledge is tacitly presupposed from the very beginning. This conception assumes that what is most characteristic of knowledge is its reference to truth, as opposed to falsity; this is what leads to perception, since it claims to provide access to what is true or real. However, once it is established that perception can offer nothing that is real or true, nothing that can count as Being in the proper sense, its (hypothetically assumed) identification with knowledge is definitively discarded. What is not discarded, though, is the underlying assumption that the search for Truth and Being is itself legitimate and needs no justification, as if assuming the contrary would imply depriving philosophy of any possible foundation (Schapp 2015: 181). This is certainly the basic conviction that animates all possible Platonism.

That all perception is relative, subjective, uncertain, and deceptive is, Schapp explains, a view that was already old in Plato's time (Schapp 2015: 181). Nor is the recourse to constructive explanations based on the theory of sensible qualities originally Platonic. Schapp thinks that such an approach to perception represents instead a "foreign body" (*Fremdkörper*) in the framework of Plato's thought (Schapp 2015: 182ff.). It is, moreover, phenomenologically inadequate, even if it has been able to survive (with the changes forced by the development of science) to our day—it does not do justice to our experience of the world of life, which always appears to us as already given, and not as the result of a construction from simple elements arrived at by abstraction (Schapp 2015: 183). For this very reason, what Plato reaches through the analysis of sensible qualities is not perception as such, nor could it be: by starting from sensible qualities, the dialogue goes down the wrong path (Schapp 2015: 183).

There is, however, a second way in which Plato tries to approach perception, namely, in contrast with dream (*Traum*), madness (*Wahnsinn*), and hallucination (*Sinestäuschung*). Schapp refers to the discussion in 157d–162b, where Plato compares perception with the "representations" that occur in dreaming, madness, and hallucination. The comparison leads to the conclusion that there is no difference between them that would make it possible to say with certainty which of them should count as true (Schapp 2015: 183ff.). Here again, the notion of perception remains hopelessly underdetermined, which also has a negative impact on the contrast that is to be established. Certainly, Plato is living in a time and culture in which the privilege of perception and wakefulness over dreaming, madness, and hallucination is assumed to be self-evident. Schapp points out, however, that this is not the case in other cultural contexts, in which dream or delirium (*Rausch*) is privileged, and refers as an example to the times depicted in the Gilgamesh poem (Schapp 2015: 185). In any case, the most important point to which Schapp wishes to draw attention relates to what he calls Plato's "fundamental presupposition" (*Grundvoraussetzung*), namely, that there is something like Being, which could perhaps be known by means of perception, as a cognitive act. At first, Plato looks for this Being in perception, which, according to Schapp, allows the suspicion (*Verdacht*) that it would be something like the "material Being" (*stoffliches Sein*) that pre-Socratic physiologists were searching for (Schapp 2015: 185).

Naturally, Schapp is not unaware that even in the *Theaetetus*, Plato places Being among the common things accessed by thought, and not through any of the senses (Schapp 2015: 184, with reference to 186a). But his point is probably that the same basic presupposition, which identifies true Being with the permanent and changeless, operates at both levels of consideration, that is, both in the analysis of the sensible world accessed through perception and in the manner of representing the intelligible order, which would be accessed through thought considered as the "eye of the soul." If this is the case, an idea of Being that has its remote origin in pre-Socratic philosophy is transposed by Plato to the realm of the intelligible as well.

Whatever the case may be, Schapp's final verdict is categorical, what Plato lacks is the relationship to stories (*das Verhältnis zu den Geschichten*). The way in which he seeks to contrast perception with dreaming, madness, and hallucination is burdened by his one-sided orientation toward objects, which leaves no room for the attempt to elucidate the relevant differences proceeding from stories (Schapp 2015: 186). Even Plato is a child of his age. The enlightened ideal of his time aims to leave behind the misty darkness of archaic times. Attachment to sensible reality is a key element of the conception of rationality that characterizes such an enlightened ideal. But as Schapp explains, from the peculiar self-understanding of a given epoch, it does not follow that this epoch achieves a greater closeness to Being than other past and future epochs. When Plato finally turns against the Enlightenment of his time and denies ultimate reality to the world of things and the sensible world, he remains in a peculiar relationship with this same Enlightenment, which maintains its validity—at least by providing that which he himself opposes. With his projection of an ideal order, which would represent something like a superior totality or system of the world (*Weltganzes, Weltsystem*), Plato runs the risk, in his attempt to refute the Enlightenment, of moving away from reality as much as the Enlightenment itself does (Schapp 2015: 187).

4. By Way of Conclusion

In his penetrating critical review of the 1953 book, which Schapp himself recognizes as apt (Schapp 2015: 120 n. 13), Hermann Lübbe characterizes the position reached by Schapp, with its attack on Husserl's conception of the "general object," as "the declared end of phenomenological Platonism" (Lübbe 1954: 650). This characterization touches the very heart of the matter, provided it is understood in its true sense. The distancing from Husserl, even if radical, does not represent for Schapp an abandonment of phenomenology itself, but merely of what might be called its Platonizing distortion. Strictly speaking, the only way to persist in a phenomenology that does justice to what it claims to be—namely, a radical project of self-transparency—is to remove from it everything that cannot be justified in light of its own demands. At times, attempts have been made to shed light on Schapp's turn to history and stories by resorting to the link with the tradition of German historicism, along the lines of Dilthey, as is also often done in the case of Heidegger.[9] However, what might be true in this interpretation, at least from the historical point of view, could at the same time be misleading if one does not pay due attention to the internal motivation that animates the evolution of Schapp's thought in the transition from Schapp I to Schapp II. This internal motivation is nothing other than that which comes from an inalterable fidelity to what phenomenology itself is called from the very beginning to be.

It is in this framework that Schapp's interest in Plato, and particularly in the way in which the latter attempts to elucidate perception, is also inscribed. As we have seen, Schapp's engagement with Plato is driven by the detection of the secret link that bonds the starting point in perception with Platonism. And it is from here that Schapp derives the critique of Husserl and Husserlian-style phenomenology, which is also, and above all, an austere exercise in self-criticism. Within this framework, Plato is certainly seen as the true founder of the historical Platonism from which Schapp seeks to distance himself. This has nothing to do with a vulgar disqualification of the philosopher par excellence. Rather, it should be seen as an attempt to do justice to the story in which he himself became entangled. After all, without reference to that particular story, his incomparable greatness could never be adequately appreciated.

Notes

1 In his preface to the fourth edition of 2004, Thomas Rolf points to the resonance that Schapp's dissertation had in phenomenological circles in the 1910s: the work was read as a kind of commentary on Husserl's *Logische Untersuchungen*, helping to clarify obscure passages in the Husserlian text. See Rolf (2013: vi ff).

2 For a good discussion of Schapp's abandonment of the Husserlian program in favor of a narrativist conception and its consequences for the idea of phenomenology, see Liebsch (2010). Schapp never understood his distancing from Husserl as an abandonment of phenomenology itself, but rather as a radicalization that allowed him to expand and purify it. Schapp points out that thanks to his progressive liberation from Husserl, a new immense field of work opened up "within the framework of phenomenology, with countless individual investigations and with possibilities of investigating prior philosophies with regard to their phenomenological content and freeing them from constructions" (see Schapp 1959, as quoted in Joisten 2015: 5ff., Schapp 2025: 232).

3 In the 1950s Schapp goes so far as to declare his uncertainty as to whether there is truly a field of research delimited by the term "perception." Instead, he mentions A. Reinach as a follower of Husserl's view. See Schapp (2015: 182); see also 122f.

4 The expression *Wozuding(e)*, coined by Schapp, alludes to the fact that the things that appear (with)in the world are for this very reason inscribed in broader

connections of significance of a purposive nature, which ultimately refer to the interweaving of different stories. In her English translation of an important book by the Italian philosopher Tonino Griffero where Schapp is mentioned, Sarah De Sanctis offers the alternative version "thing(s)-towards-which." See Griffero (2017: 10).

5 For a brief overview, see Vigo (2012: 159ff).

6 Rolf suggests that the final section of the dissertation may have been the fruit of an attempt to meet Husserl's expectations in terms of establishing a connection with the history of *Erkenntnistheorie*. See Rolf (2004: x).

7 For a discussion that explores implications of greater philosophical interest, see Sepp (2010).

8 Schapp acutely observes that between the two examples, Plato places as a transition the example of the sun, characterized as the brightest celestial body (see *Theaetetus* 208d): the indication of that characteristic seems to suffice here for identification (Schapp 2015: 178). The point does not seem to be simply that a defined description suffices to perform the function of identification. Rather, it happens that within the horizon of understanding in which Greek astronomy operates, the sun represents the case in which individual and species seem to coincide (as is also the case with the moon), since it is assumed that there is only one individual of such a species. On this point, see Aristotle, *Metaphysics* VII 15, 1040a27–33.

9 For instance, see Rosen (1960).

References

Griffero, T. (2017), *Quasi-Things: The Paradigm of Atmospheres*, trans. S. De Sanctis, Albany: State University of New York Press.

Joisten, K. (2015), "Wilhelm Schapps *Philosophie der Geschichten*. Ein Zugang," in: Schapp (2015): 5–11.

Liebsch, B. (2010), "Die Idee der Phänomenologie im Lichte ihrer narrativistischen Verabschiedung im Werk Wilhelm Schapps," in K. Joisten (ed.), *Das Denken Wilhelm Schapps. Perspektiven für unsere Zeit*, 22–48, Freiburg i. Br.: Karl Alber.

Lübbe, H. (1954), "Das Ende des phänomenologischen Platonismus. Eine kritische Betrachtung aus Anlass eines neuen Buches," *Tijdschrift voor Philosophie*, 16 (4): 639–66.

Rolf, T. (2013), "Wilhelm Schapps *Beiträge zur Phänomenologie der Wahrnehmung*," in: Schapp (2013): v–xii

Rosen, S. (1960), "Philosophy and Historicity," *Review of Metaphysics*, 14 (1): 110–33.

Schapp, W. (1959), "Erinnerungen an Husserl," in AA.VV., *Edmund Husserl 1859–1959*, 12–25, Den Haag: Martinus Nijhoff.

Schapp, W. (2012[1953]), *In Geschichten verstrickt*, Frankfurt a. M.: Vittorio Klostermann.

Schapp, W. (2013 [1910]), *Beiträge zur Phänomenologie der Wahrnehmung*, Frankfurt a. M.: Vittorio Klostermann.

Schapp, W. (2015[1959]), *Philosophie der Geschichten*, Frankfurt a. M.: Vittorio Klostermann.

Schapp, W. (2016), *Philosophischer Nachlass. Teilband I: Auf dem Weg einer Philosophie der Geschichten*, ed. K. Joisten, J. Schapp, and N. Thiemer, Freiburg, München: Karl Alber.

Schapp, W. (2025), "Recollections of Husserl," trans. E. A. Behnke, in D. De Santis and D. Nuccilli (eds), *The Philosophy of Wilhelm Schapp: From Phenomenology to Jurisprudence and the Hermeneutics of Stories*, 227–238, London: Bloomsbury.

Sepp, H. R. (2010), "Welt und Grenze. Wilhelm Schapps Philosophie der Geschichten," in: K. Joisten (ed.), *Das Denken Wilhelm Schapps. Perspektiven für unsere Zeit*, 49–64, Freiburg i. Br.: Karl Alber.

Vigo. A. G. (2012), "Colores verdaderos: Una panorámica fenomenológica," in L. X. López Farjeat (ed.), *Reflexiones filosóficas sobre el color*, *Euphyía* (Aguas Calientes, México) 6 (10): 153–223.

Part II

Philosophy of Values and Law

6

The Character of Things: *Ding*, *Werk*, and *Wozuding*

A Path in Wilhelm Schapp's Thought

Daniele Nuccilli

0. Preliminary Remarks

The thought journey of the German philosopher and jurist Wilhelm Schapp is characterized by three moments. The first moment, the one that could be defined as strictly phenomenological, pertains to his experience of the early phenomenological circles and can be traced back to his doctoral dissertation under Husserl in 1909, published in 1910 with the title *Beiträge zur Phänomenologie der Wahrnehmung*. The second moment, which could be defined as that of the "phenomenology of values," comprises the two volumes of *Die neue Wissenschaft vom Recht* (1930, 1932), along with a book from 1937 entitled *Zur Metaphysik des Muttertums,* which was published posthumously in 1965. Finally, the third phase is the most famous and is represented by the so-called "philosophy of stories," a trilogy of works: *In Geschichten verstrickt* (1953), *Philosophie der Geschichten* (1959), and *Metaphysik der Naturwissenschaft* (1965). In this trilogy, Schapp develops a radical critique of Husserl's phenomenology through the basic concept of the entanglement of humans in stories. On the argumentative level of Schapp's philosophy of stories, the deconstruction of certain classical assumptions of phenomenology and the construction of a new theoretical model of a hermeneutic-narratological character are closely interconnected, and one of the main cornerstones of this argumentative framework involves the internal evolution of the concept of "thing" (*Ding*). Indeed, each investigation of the thing corresponds to a different conception of humans and of the cognitive model that characterizes their understanding of things and of the world. In the phenomenology of perception, the thing (*Ding*) is seen as the primary reference for perception and knowledge of the external world; the corresponding anthropological figure is, therefore, that of the theoretical human being as observer. In the philosophy of law, the thing is seen, first and foremost, as a work (*Werk*) and as a value (*Wert*); the human being is therefore seen as the creator of the thing, and the anthropological model is that of the practical human being. Finally, in the philosophy of stories, humans are seen as entangled in stories. They are in a foundational co-implication with the external world since they find themselves in a network of relationships through the production and use of so-called things-for (*Wozudinge*), which are in turn embedded in the stories of the persons who have or have had to do with them—thus representing the occasion for the encounter of the stories of different humans, even if they are far away in time and space. Through the stories in which the world is framed and mediated, the anthropological figure of reference is first and foremost that of the storyteller, although for Schapp, human beings are only a vehicle for the story's self-narration rather than being the tellers of the story (cf. Habermas 1981: 224; Ricoeur 1992: 161).

The analysis of the thing thus represents one of the fundamental conceptual junctures in Schapp's philosophical production as a whole. As I have already indicated, this is true for two reasons: (1) the discussion of the thing in its different meanings (*Ding*, *Werk*, *Wozuding*) appears at the nerve center of each of the writings that characterize the three fundamental periods of his philosophical works; and (2) the revolution in Schapp's thought from the phenomenology of perception to the philosophy of stories centers on these different conceptions of the thing. In this chapter, I will briefly attempt to explain how this happens.

1. *Das Ding selbst*: Characteristics of Things, Observing Perception, and History

The investigation of the thing (*Ding*) constitutes the central thematic core of the second section of *Beiträge*, which culminates in a dense section entitled *Das Ding selbst* (The thing itself) in which Schapp brings to fulfillment the long analysis of the presentation of the thing in perception through perceptually presenting materials, such as colors, sounds, and tactile sensations. Here, three aspects are useful in attempting to grasp the central importance of the analysis of the thing, both with regard to the phenomenological tradition on which it rests (i.e., the Husserlian phenomenology of the thing) and in relation to how it prepares the field for the subsequent evolution of Schapp's philosophy beyond—

and in contrast to—the central assumptions of the early phenomenological circles. The first aspect (A) pertains to the presentation of the thing in the fullness of all its structural and manifestational characteristics, in its character of "reality." The second aspect (B) concerns an "observing" perception, a specific attitude of consciousness that enables the thing to configure itself as that unitary manifestational pole on which other forms of knowledge of the external world, especially those of a physical-mathematical character, are then built. The third aspect (C) concerns the wholly peculiar Schappian conception that real things are not traceable to perceptual schemes that are reducible to constitutive processes of perception but rather are always located in the lifeworld, thus in a unique and unrepeatable texture of events that already manifests itself in the very perception of the thing—in its individuality—through its history.

Before addressing these three points, however, we must try to understand what Schapp means by "thing" in *Beiträge*. In this work, the thing is not understood in the extended meaning of the *Sache* from the well-known phenomenological dictum *zu den Sachen selbst* (to the things or matters themselves) in the *Logical Investigations*, where the purpose of phenomenology is to document all of the matters that present themselves to consciousness in their diverse modes of intuitive givenness (cf. Husserl 2001: 101, 168; see Moran 2001: xxiv). Rather, Schapp's concept of thing is *Ding*, and is thus reduced to the objects of the external world (both objects of use and natural objects) that present themselves to perception as a unity—the things of everyday experience that Husserl addresses in the lectures *Thing and Space* (cf. Husserl 1997: 1ff.; see Rojcewicz 1997: xii). Even though the two approaches are at some points very far apart and not assimilable, Schapp does take up Husserl's essential distinction between *res materialis* and *res extensa*, using the criteria of material and spatial qualities to develop his concept of a thing (at least as far as the problem of presentation and that of pregivenness are concerned).

A. The Character of Things: Material Nature and Form

In his investigation of the thing, Schapp transposes the Husserlian problem of presentation by contiguity into a different key. He aims to show how "despite the fact that sight 'authentically' (*eigentlich*) perceives only colors and the ear only sounds" (Schapp 2013: 38), even in the visual perception of a single thing, "properties such as elasticity and shine become so highly representable (*vorstellig*) that we have them before us in the flesh (*leibhaftig vor uns haben*)" and so faithfully that "there is no point in asking whether they can be perceived more directly" (Schapp 2012: 21). The division of the qualities of the thing between presenting and presented is not only connected to the problem of the materiality of the thing, but as a function of this, it is also linked with the problem of the spatial patterns of perception, especially visual perception and its relation to the real form of objects. These two elements characterize both the way Schapp understands the thing cognitively and his methodological approach. Indeed, for Schapp, it is not as important as it is for the Husserl of the Göttingen lectures (cf. Husserl 2004: 26ff.) to ask why—despite the fact that only one side of the thing perceptually presents itself to us—we can understand it in its entirety by filling in the gaps of sensible intuition with empty intentions. Instead, the key is to try to grasp the intuitive aspect of the thing presenting itself as something that transcends its merely spatial configuration of colors, surfaces, and angles and instead offers its most peculiar and individual characteristics. Schapp's investigation unfolds in this direction by passing through a whole series of perceptual examples that show how the different aspects of the thing that are not immediately ascribable to sensible contents nevertheless come to full manifestation in simple observation. For Schapp, the best way to draw on the materiality of things is to see how they behave in the lifeworld and how they react to human action:

> And without referring to other senses [. . .], we see the properties of things more clearly when we see how they behave in different situations [. . .]; when we look at how red-hot iron twists, bends under the blacksmith's hammer, and how it takes on different shapes, and at the same time we see that if the iron were dark [i.e., cold], it would break rather than allowing itself to be shaped; when we see how the hard, sharp iron of the planer makes the shavings fly away from the softer wood; in short, when we go to the various craftsmen and observe how things are worked. (Schapp 2013: 25)

This example of the practical experience of working with things is also relevant to the experience of touch. According to the author, when we are talking about the sense of touch, two different attitudes toward things when they are worked on should be distinguished: the attitude of the human being "at work" (*werktätiges Mensch*) and the attitude of the theorizing human being (*theoretisches Mensch*). As already sketched, the first attitude is that of humans handling a certain thing when dealing with it to fulfill certain purposes of everyday life. The second attitude, on the other hand, is that of those investigating the thing, forgetting its use and purposes and focusing instead on its properties (see Schapp 2013: 33). Only in the latter case can one speak in the strict sense of the perception of the object. If following Schapp, we return to the example of the craftsmen, we note that the only moment when they "perceive" the properties of materials is when they ascertain their quality, for example, checking whether that particular material is suitable for the purpose. From that moment on, however, one is completely turned toward the production of the object, and while working with the material, one no longer perceives it in its peculiarities but shapes it to make an object for use. Once it is ready, it will not be "perceived"—investigated in its constituent aspects—by those who will use it, except precisely to assess its quality and manufacture. An observer watching the production will therefore perceive, simply by observing, those characteristics of the object better than the craftsman can.

The last point represents one of the axes around which Schapp's turn toward the philosophy of stories revolves: the person at work will become the basic figure on which the theory of entanglement in stories rests. In *Beiträge*, however, he continues with the formal investigation of perceptual processes, and thus retains the central anthropological figure of the theorizing human being. This is the theoretical direction that Schapp takes in investigating the concept of form. For Schapp, in addition to colors and matter, form is not something that delimits the perimeters of the space occupied by the thing, but is a structural feature of the thing itself in all its factuality. According to the author, if one considers the form only in geometric terms, one is precluded from gaining access to the manifestational dimension that allows one to reach the intimate reality of things. If one stays with the itself-giving of things without giving way to abstract and mathematizing instincts, we can see that the form a thing takes is not entirely random but already displays an immediate relation to the material of which it is made: "just as crystals, whether large or small, always have the same form, in the same way every matter has its own form" (Schapp 2013: 23). He then adds several more examples. The handkerchief on the table makes folds because it is soft, and some handkerchiefs are more prone to making folds than others—cotton ones, for example, are more resistant to pressure than linen ones. One can also mold a piece of tin and give it the shape of a linen handkerchief. However, this will not make it soft to sight; rather, one will notice that that material has been forced to take that shape. On closer examination, then, such characteristics will always manifest themselves to sight as not belonging to the very essence of that material. Even the form a thing takes, and the way it takes this form, thus allows immediate access to the structural qualities of the thing—softness for linen, hardness for a brass apple (cf. Schapp 2013: 23–4).

B. Observing Perception: The Clarity and Givenness of Things

The form and the matter of the thing are the two fundamental components that configure the thing's "character of reality" (*Realitätscharakter*) (Schapp 2013: 54) beyond the manifestational filter given by colors, tactile sensations, and sounds. They represent, so to speak, *a parte obiecti*, the thing offering itself to perception. For the full manifestation of the thing, however, there is a need for another fundamental element, *a parte subiecti*, which enables consciousness to channel and order the presenting of things in the external world into a unified pole of manifestation. Schapp calls this cognitive element "observing perception" (*beobachtende Wahrnehmung*) (Schapp 2013: 65). "Observing perception" is "that peculiar kind of perception that seeks above all to overcome the impediments and obstacles placed before it [. . .], which is not satisfied with what is offered to it (*das Gebotenen*), with what shows itself, but wants to know how what is observed is in truth and not how it seems [. . .]" (Schapp 2013: 66). Thus, the observing perception actively operates within what is offered in perception to deliver the presented itself. This is done in the first instance by recognizing and isolating the presented in relation to the other elements present in the perceptual field, and in the second instance by moving beyond the mere presenting aspect of the thing to its more structural elements. It is only by distinguishing observing perception from perception in the broad sense, from being aware of something—from that particular type of visual perception that moves voluntarily in search of a focal point in the perceptual complex of elements offering themselves to view—that one can arrive at the actual manifestation of the thing, which is therefore configured in this sense as a correlate of a specific perceptual function of observing (see Schapp 2013: 70). Such a perceptual procedure is accompanied by, and culminates in, a cognitive act that Schapp calls "picking out with intention" (*herausgreifend meinen*):

> We see a series of tin plates placed in the cupboard [. . .] and notice that we are mainly occupied with one plate, observing it by picking it out with intention while the other objects remain to the side ("*daneben*" *stehen*). In this "picking out with intention" (*herausgreifend meinen*), one must distinguish between grasping (*das Anpacken*) at one point, as when one grasps the plate from the side or center, and intending in a broad sense, which addresses the object as a whole. Since in grasping the whole object is brought to us even if it is grasped at only one point, we can always determine which object is in this privileged position with respect to us and from where we grasp it. The plates that are close to the one we privilege are co-intended (*mit gemeint*); they too are highlighted from the background, but without our action. (Schapp 2013: 68)

The example of the plates in the cupboard forms the basis of a new conceptual reworking of mass-produced objects—one that prescribes the route we can trace between the critique of universals and the later formulation of the thing-for that we find in *In Geschichten verstrickt*. Nevertheless, here it serves to show the dual perceptual plane on which "observing perception" works. Indeed, Schapp specifies that "in observing perception, the thing stands before us as a whole" and that "the highlighted part of the thing is not highlighted as the thing in relation to other things" (Schapp 2013: 69). The perceptual plane thus lies on a kind of ideal boundary represented by the thing, a boundary beyond which there is the external world and within which there is the thing with its parts, and especially with its properties. The thing as the correlate of the cognitive act internal to the peculiar kind of perception here termed observing perception thus represents the ideal limit for knowledge of the world, and also represents a form of pregivenness in the Husserlian sense.[1] Indeed, it is that from which every further cognitive approach, from the practical experience of everyday life to the praxis of scientific research, takes its point of departure. This evaluation is very important to Schapp. He is convinced that every form of technical aid to scientific research has the ultimate goal of bringing the things investigated to the same perceptual limit as the objects of everyday life. When microorganisms are investigated with the microscope, for example, they are brought by the lens to a perceptual level that makes them observable as if they were things, or at least as if they were living organisms of a size suitable to be seen with the naked eye like things we might encounter in everyday situations. After a certain number of enlargements, the amoeba, for example, appears under the microscope in much the same way as a jellyfish appears to the naked eye. Obviously, the starting point in the investigation of microorganisms is not an everyday experience—it takes, in fact, a wealth of theoretical assumptions and technological development to get to the point of discovering and visualizing them—but once they are brought into view, they are configured in perception as things. This means that the scientist inherits this form of perceptual conception from everyday life. Schapp calls this form of knowledge "clarity" (*Deutlichkeit*), that is, the clear and distinct manifestation of the thing to observing perception. He can thus say that the manner of the thing's giving itself can be ascribed precisely to this latter peculiar kind of perception, which traverses the phenomenon by aiming at the thing until it assumes a sharpness that prevents the gaze from going beyond it. It is because of this aiming at things and their clear and distinct presentation, then, that observing perception stands apart from other forms of intuition, especially from aesthetic perception, and is the only one that truly aims at theoretical knowledge of things (cf. Schapp 2013: 75–6).

C. The History and Individuality of Things

The configuration of the thing facing consciousness as a unitary pole of manifestation—both of its most intrinsic characteristics (matter and form) and of its location in a context of relations given by the external world and the lifeworld—provides the preparatory thematic framework for the analysis of the thing itself. In paragraph VII of the second section entitled *Das Ding selbst*, Schapp ties up the threads of the examples that had emerged so far in his investigation and links them inextricably to one of the cornerstones of his present and future thought: the concept of history/story.[2] Aiming to show how our knowledge of the material characteristics of things is not limited to the experience we have of them through manipulation (whether this takes place with productive or simply cognitive intentions), Schapp writes as follows in what is perhaps the most speculatively incisive passage of *Beiträge*:

> it is as if everything has its own history and this history leaves traces behind it. These traces sometimes appear to us as scars that we can interpret; immediately we see what becomes of the thing. From the way wood is cut we see it "behaving" (*verhalten*) in relation to the knife; from the fine scratch on a gold watch we see the fineness of gold. Each thing in its contingent form (*Gestalt*) always shows what it has gone through, and with that, its history, its specific manner and the way in which it has survived its destiny. When we see things, they are certainly not as taken from the box, but they have their own destiny and carry with them the traces of this destiny. Even if they have just come from the factory, they show us the way in which they have been made. (Schapp 2013: 117)

The excerpt quoted above may seem entirely out of context, both with respect to the Platonizing tendency of the phenomenology of perception in the Munich and Göttingen circles and with respect to Schapp's approach in the third section of *Beiträge*. It is no coincidence, then, that the concept of history/story provides the element on which the critique of the phenomenological Platonism of the philosophy of stories will later be based.[3] In my view, this dystonia can be explained through a cultural hybridization that takes place in *Beiträge*. If we want to understand the relevance of this theoretical step in the treatment first of the concept of work and later of that of the thing-for, we have to refer to Theodor Lipps, and in particular, to the concept of work in his *Ästhetik*. The perceived thing, such as the work (of art or manufacture) in Lipps's aesthetics, does not allow itself to be reduced to its barest materiality, yet its materiality does display traces of this particular object's individual path in the world. There are perceptible aspects in the work that refer, on the one hand, to human action, and on the other, to the series of unique and unrepeatable events that have marked that work's path in the world (see Lipps 1903: 206f., 1920: 483–585). In this regard, Lipps speaks of "fangs of time" (*Zahn der Zeit*) to express the signs of wear on an object that allow us to understand the specificity of its composition (Lipps 1920: 558).[4] In order to express the uniqueness and unrepeatability of an object's perceptual appearance and the reference to its passage through the world, Schapp states that things "are certainly not as taken from the box" (Schapp 2013: 117). This seems radically different from Husserl's metaphor in *The Idea of Phenomenology* for which the immanent data are not "in" consciousness in the sense in which things are "in" a box (see Husserl 1964: 56). Schapp's concept of history is thus quite different from the concept of history that will soon make its appearance in Husserl. By the "destiny" of the thing, Schapp does not mean the "constitutive" history of the object, that is, the intentional path it takes within consciousness, which can be traced back to the hyletic-immanent level and thus to its genesis in original time-consciousness (cf. Husserl 1966: 345, and see Biceaga 2010: xv; Zahavi 2003: 94). Rather, what is meant is the unique perceptual aspect of the thing and the occurrence in it of traces of events (whether related to human action or not) that mark the fundamental moments of its existence, from its production to its encounter with our sight. History is thus always the manifestation in the thing of the world's eventuality and facticity. Through the concept of history in *Beiträge*, Schapp breaks free from a view of reality that is reduced to its mere mechanical phenomena and reverses the relationship between the thing and space/matter. The thing is not merely reduced to the space it occupies and to its matter but "has its own character that shows us new aspects every day" (Schapp 2013: 117). In this way, then, the thing's priority over matter and space is also established ontologically, since the material form that a thing takes can certainly reveal something of the thing's character. But as Schapp points out, one should not confuse the presenting with the presented; on the side of the presented, "The thing retains only its individuality, not its space in relation to other things. It lives among the others according to its character" (Schapp 2013: 122). It is at the heart of the individualistic and historical conception of the thing that one finds the first hint of Schapp's possible escape from any form of abstract and schematic understanding of perceptual phenomena. And in the description of the concept of work, the framework will change still further, leading to questioning the very principles of the phenomenological method.

2. *Werk*: Production, Value, World, and History

The concept of *Werk* (work) represents a fundamental milestone in the internal evolutionary path of Schapp's thought that leads from the thing to the thing-for. (see J. Schapp 2010: 68ff.). With a few rare exceptions, there is a tendency in the secondary literature to frame the thing-for completely within the new perspective that Heidegger opened in phenomenological research with his concept of *Zuhandenheit*—the basic characteristic of objects of use being "ready-to-hand"—laid out in *Being and Time*.[5] In addition to this obvious conceptual influence and interaction, however, one cannot forget that the thing-for has a whole other set of specific characterizations vis-à-vis the Heideggerian "ready-to-hand," most of which are derivatives of the insights that take shape in the investigations into the pre-legal relationship between humans and produced things that Schapp sets forth in his philosophy of law (see J. Schapp 2013: 62ff.). Indeed, it is through the analysis of those things in the world that can be called "works" and of their relation to the sphere of value that the Aurich philosopher finds a way out of the static and neutral understanding of the thing that took shape in *Beiträge* and that, in part, also marked Husserl's phenomenology of the thing.

Schapp addresses the notion of work within the investigation of the constitution of property as a pregivenness of positive law that he sets out in the first section of the second volume of *Die neue Wissenschaft vom Recht*.[6] Taking a rudimentary example, Schapp identifies the core of the pre-legal dimension of property in the production of the thing. He states, "In the situation in which someone produces a stone axe or carves a bow and arrows, property already finds its place" (Schapp 1932: 34). Having extended the application of this concept to all objects produced from the Stone Age to contemporary times—with the only difference that in the case of contemporary objects that are assembled in several parts, a more complex production process must be considered, thus involving multiple actors—he then points out the difficulties that can be faced in applying the phenomenological method to such an investigation:

> If the reader now sets the book aside and tries to ascertain for himself something essential about this simple process, he will understand the difficulty of the

> investigation that follows and the ambiguities necessarily connected with it [. . .]. If we now approach this process from the outside, and try to imagine Stone Age man removing sliver by sliver and shaping the rough stone, this image still tells us nothing about the inner connections of the creation of the stone axe. (Schapp 1932: 34)

Compared to the description of the emergence of properties of things within the context of production as treated in *Beiträge*—where "we see the properties of things more clearly when we see how they behave in different situations [. . .], when we go to the various craftsmen and observe how things are worked" (Schapp 2013: 25)—what we see in *Die neue Wissenschaft II* is a shift of perspective. By simply observing from the outside, one cannot grasp the essential dimension of the relationship between humans and materials in workmanship. Instead, to understand the internal connections of this phenomenon properly, one should transpose oneself into the meaning-context in which it is produced. Those who work with the thing may be enslaved or free, may produce the object for a religious rite or for more profane purposes, may produce it for themselves or for others. These conditions are not secondary to understanding the object. Rather, it is these conditions that define, according to Schapp, the pregiven relation that production has with property.

These evaluations lead to both a methodological- and an ontological-value consequence. From a methodological point of view, the investigation can no longer be a search for the essence of the material constitution of the thing, since the thing as a work is now placed in a meaning-context involving sociocultural aspects, which cannot be reduced to mere perception. In fact, the method Schapp suggests is the "comparative method" that will consist of comparing the process of producing the stone axe production with similar processes (see Schapp 1932: 34). From an ontological-value point of view, on the other hand, the thing is only conceivable as a work when there is a creator (*Schöpfer*), someone who releases it from the stone, and in so doing, excludes it from the world of natural objects, inserting it instead into the world of human-made objects and then of objects with a specific value. In this regard, Schapp firmly states that "There is no work without a creator" (Schapp 1932: 36), establishing an immediate relationship between the thing and the human being—one that he defines as an *Ich-Werk-Beziehung* (I-work-relationship). Any cognitive evaluation of the thing and its composition must therefore be immediately referred to the productive context and the human being who produced it (cf. Schapp 1932: 36ff.).

According to Schapp, through the evaluation of the thing-work, we are drawn back not only to human beings in the flesh (even if they lived thousands of years ago), but also to their activity, to the tools and gestures that they used and that left marks of their "will" on the work and therefore manifest a part of each creator's ego through the work.[7] Compared to the thing, the work is distinguished, then, by two orders of reasons: (1) it is a corporeal entity that is detached from other, merely natural entities as a result of workmanship, and this gives the concept of matter a whole other meaning; and (2) it is an entity that is inextricably bound up with the will of an "I" that produced it. For Schapp, however, these two aspects still do not fully exhaust the "character of the work" (*Werkcharakter*). In order to understand the character of the work of the thing fully, one must also recognize the meaning that governs the production, and this can only happen if "we transpose ourselves into what the creator had in mind with the work" (Schapp 1932: 38). The work thus becomes intelligible only if one understands the reason that runs through the production and the purpose that guided the creator to bring it into being. It is precisely at this point that Schapp accordingly extends the question of the role of understanding in perception to the dimension of the everyday practice of the use of the thing, without yet accomplishing the complete revolution that we find in the thing-for of the philosophy of stories.

To demonstrate the inadequacy of mere perception in understanding objects of use, he takes the example of a pincer-shaped object found on a smoking table. If we observe this object, we immediately recognize that it is in some way a work, and probably a tool. However, "we only understand the work in its fullest sense when the smoker uses it to bring the cigarette to his mouth, thus avoiding soiling his fingers with nicotine" (Schapp 1932: 38). It is only through the interpretation of the circle of relations established between idea, planning, production, and use that the character of the work of the thing that presents itself to perception can truly be understood. "A phenomenology of creation (*Schaffen*)" must, therefore, be inaugurated in order to comprehend this value dimension (Schapp 1932: 39; cf. Schapp 1930: 176). The scope of such a phenomenological analysis takes place in *Die neue Wissenschaft II* and explores the entire breadth of the concept of the work, ranging from everyday objects to artistic and spiritual productions to mathematics, geometry, and all the a priori sciences. This new phenomenological perspective aims at the construction of an all-encompassing value system that includes every aspect of human activity. And here, I think it is important to highlight the emergence of two perspectives regarding the way the work is framed, perspectives that will later constitute the ground of the critique of phenomenology that Schapp sets out in *In Geschichten verstrickt*.

The first perspective is that of the lifeworld. According to Schapp, the context of productive significance is not limited to the close relationship between human beings and the material to be shaped, nor even to the social condition and cultural context in which the workmanship takes place, but already implies the manifestation of a broader dimension of meaning involving other aspects of the world, aspects that constitute the premises on which all productive human action is based. According to Schapp, "If we want to understand the stone axe as a work, we have to think about the fact that it serves to cut wood and that a house can be built with wood and that the house serves to shelter from the wind and rain and the heat of the sun during the day" (Schapp 1932: 40). Beginning with the axe, then, a series of references radiates out, opening a window to the world that also involves a semiotic rearticulation of some of its aspects, from stone to the sun. To understand any object of use, one must therefore already have in the background not only a plan that requires finding suitable materials and developing an appropriate technique, but also an awareness of its context of use and its placement within a chain of purposes of which it is only the means. And it is on the basis of this "horizontal" opening that Schapp later inserts the discourse of the manifestation of the world as a whole through the prism of the thing-for that we find in *In Geschichten verstrickt* (see Schapp 2012: 33ff.). The second perspective, which intersects with the first, could be called "historical," and Schapp explores this in a chapter in which he is concerned with identifying the very essence of the work. In pursuit of this goal, the author begins with a universally popular object, a shoe, and proceeds with a meticulous description of each of its components. He writes,

> If we consider the shoe from the outside, we immediately recognize the single parts: the sole, the toe box, the upper, and the heel. In this subdivision, each part takes on its own meaning. The division between sole and heel allows for greater support of the metatarsal; the division between sole and upper facilitates repair. Each part of the shoe refers us back to someone who first discovered its meaning. It dissolves before our eyes into multiple paths, each of which can be traced back to a discovery. These discoveries have their temporal locus, that is, a place in historical time. (Schapp 1932: 47)

Each component of the shoe points back to the individual human who conceived it. Embedded in any assessment of the essence of the work is a projection back into the past, even hundreds of years, in search of the value- and meaning-context in which the idea or plan led that individual to perfect an object already in use or to create a new one. In relation to this search, what is important is to immerse oneself in the "idea"—in the spiritual attitude in which the different humans who contributed to the improvements of the thing "shoe" were situated. In this way, the person who observes the shoe and its components is somehow immersed in the same value context as those different humans, and can thereby get in touch with a fragment of their spiritual story. In assessing the essential predicates of the shoe as a work, one can thus no longer be satisfied with isolating the characteristic aspects that make it the thing we know as a shoe; instead, one must place it in an evolutionary dynamic of productions and discoveries that characterizes the micro-history of shoe production within the macro-history of humankind's evolution. In some very dense lines, Schapp writes,

> The history of humankind is the history of its works. The relations we have identified between self, work, value, and production are fundamental relations for history; they represent the a priori of historical science. In this sense, a bottle of Moselle wine, a shoe, a car, a horse, the color and smell of a rose all have their own histories. (Schapp 1932: 67)

And in this precise stance, one finds already *in nuce* all of the elements that make up the treatment of the thing-for, from the entanglement of humans in stories to the resulting deconstruction of phenomenological Platonism, which is one of the central axes of the critique of "classical phenomenology" in the philosophy of stories.[8] The critique of the concept of essence set forth therein can therefore be traced back to, or at least presupposes, the semantic shift undergone by the concept of essence with regard to what pertains to the work, as opposed to that which instead characterized the thing, and the consequent need to formulate the inquiry into what essentially defines the work in different terms.[9]

The above exposition of what is at stake in the second volume of *Die neue Wissenschaft vom Recht* does not accomplish either a fully developed way of questioning the phenomenological method or an explicit formulation of a theory of stories. The historicist and hermeneutic sensibility with which Schapp approaches the problem of the phenomenological description of the work—including the identification of the inseparable relationship between the history of each individual object and the history of those who produce it, and on a broader level, between the history of production and the history of the evolution of humankind and its way of inhabiting the world—nevertheless represents a decisive and fundamental step toward the treatment of the thing-for that he deepens in *In Geschichten verstrickt*. Indeed, as I explain in the next section, in the thing-for there is a recomposition of the historical-value level of the work and the perceptual-material level of the thing-for, now placed within the new perspective of entanglement and stories, a perspective he acquired in the late 1940s and early 1950s (see Nuccilli 2024).

3. *Wozu-Dinge*: Entanglement, Story, and the External World

> We humans are always entangled (*verstrickt*) in stories (*Geschichten*). To every story there belongs someone who is entangled (*Verstrickter*). Story and being-entangled-in-stories (*In-Geschichte-verstrickt-sein*) belong together so closely that they cannot be separated from each other, probably even in thought. The greatest works of mankind have as their object stories and being-entangled (*Verstricktsein*) in stories. (Schapp 2012: 1)

This is the opening of *In Geschichten verstrickt*, the work that inaugurates and demarcates the crucial points of Schapp's philosophy of stories. As we can see, from the point of view of the hermeneutic paradigm through which we understand human beings, the perspective has been completely transformed. Humans are now neither observers (phenomenology of perception) nor creators (phenomenology of law), but simply "entangled in stories." This implies that their experience is no longer centered on a strong and autonomous egological structure, as with Husserl's theory of intentionality, but is structurally hetero-constituted—not only immersed in the history of humanity and in other humans' stories, but also already characterized, at its core, by taking part in these stories. This paradigm shift also entails a reversal of perspectives concerning knowledge of the world and the self. The starting point for any form of knowledge is no longer a kind of experience that is as neutral as possible and is hidden behind the phenomenon and the manifestation of things (see Lübbe 1972: 108ff.). Instead, it is a kind of experience that, on the one hand, is already narratively informed (Marquard 2004: 57), and on the other hand, implies an already oriented and inescapable view of the world—the precise view of being entangled in one's own stories (*Eigengeschichten*) (see Schapp 2012: 120ff.). Every aspect of the world and the self thus presents itself to us in the experiential milieu and hermeneutic filter of our stories (see Nuccilli 2018: 38ff.).

The story is thus, the privileged place for the emergence of every aspect of reality. Other humans, animals, plants, and even the external world appear in it, as well as everything that belongs to the universe of abstraction and fantasy (see Schapp 2012: 2–3). And it is precisely in referring to the problem of how the external world as it is itself can be manifested that Schapp introduces the concept of thing-for. In a well-known passage, he states, "Here there seems to be a subtle thread that establishes an intimate relationship and reveals an internal connection between the stories and the external world. We see the juncture between stories and the external world in the formations (*Gebilde*) that we name things-for (*Wozudinge*)" (Schapp 2012: 3). At the problematic intersection between thing, story, and the external world, the examples that emerged in the analysis of the work in the phenomenology of law are incorporated into the new argumentative framework provided by the concept of entanglement. After identifying things-for as "things created by humans: tables, chairs, cups, houses, palaces (the works of humans)," Schapp specifies that the relationship to the story can be attributed to the fact that each thing-for "is planned by a single person with a purpose, in a meaning-context." Therefore, to assert that a thing-for has a story means—first and foremost—that he integrates the discourse he undertook in *Beiträge* and deepened in *Die neue Wissenschaft vom Recht* into the analysis of the thing-for, insisting "that it is embedded in the story of a single human being" (Schapp 2012: 3). The thing-for accordingly represents, on the one hand, the visual angle from which one can phenomenologically frame the entangled human being, and on the other hand, the place where a whole series of horizons open that allow for the emergence of the story, from its planning, and of the world, from its production. With respect to this cornerstone function, it can be said that the production of the thing-for opens a horizon into the external world that is established on the plan and purposes of the producer. It is in this sense that Schapp asserts the primacy of stories over the external world, and it is in this way that he encloses the experiential horizon of the world within the experiential horizon of the story.

The first fundamental point in the account of the thing-for is the description of the characteristics that distinguish it from natural things. In addition to those characteristics concerning use and production, which hearken back to the sociocultural dimension of the thing and its "destiny" in the world (and thus its story), what distinguishes a thing-for from a natural object, according to Schapp, is having a "from-what" (*Auswas*). By "from-what" he means that every "thing-for refers back to a matter of which it is composed" (Schapp 2012: 11). However, the relationship between thing-for and matter is not to be understood simply as a static relationship between matter and form; rather, matter itself receives its own specific position in what Schapp calls the "overall image of the world" (*ganze Weltbild*) (Schapp 2012: 11) through the thing-for, or rather, through the production of the thing-for. Compared to the investigations of *Beiträge*, the character of the thing is no longer restricted to the physical properties that enable it to interact with the external world; there are, in fact, things-for that can be made of different materials. For example, a drinking glass can be made of wood, iron, gold, or porcelain, but this does not affect its purpose and has nothing to do with its use. It is for this reason that, according to Schapp, there is a difference—not only in the conceptual but also in the objectual domain—between matter and thing-for. Indeed, from the phenomenological point of view, when one focuses on the "what" of an object of use, whether it is a cup, a table, or a chair, what emerges before the spiritual gaze is the concept that grasps the meaning of the thing-for and the meaning-context in which it is embedded, beyond the matter of which it is composed. The same thing, however, cannot be said for materials. What emerges before the spiritual gaze when thinking about the "what" of a particular material such as gold, silver, or wood is the composition of the material itself (cf. Schapp 2012: 16).

The relationship between the perceptual corporeality of the thing and the ideality of the concept applied to it in *Beiträge* (see Schapp 2013: 122ff.) is articulated here around the pole of manifestation of the "character-for" (*Wozucharakter*) of the thing and the story of its production, which allows the matter to take on a specific meaning and a precise position within the story of the thing—and thus of the humans who had to do with it (see Schapp 2012: 17).

This is connected with the discussion of how certain structural characteristics of things such as rigidity, hardness, and elasticity occur in perception. In *Beiträge*, it was assumed that these properties could already come to full givenness through sight, simply by observing the craftsman at work (see above, 1.A). However, in the first paragraphs of *In Geschichten verstrickt*, he explains (without citing his 1910 writing, but evidently reworking some of the passages there) that this "emerging" (*auftauchen*) of matter through colors is nothing more than a secondary way of emerging, which is closely related to another way that is instead the primary one (cf. Schapp 2012: 19) and which concerns

> the workmanship of things, the craftsman's commitment to things and their material, the sawing, the drilling, the hammering [. . .] the dragging, the pulling, the pushing, and everything else that goes in that direction. While in facing the chromatic world the sensation may prevail that it is a matter of inspecting, of contemplating, here we are faced with the man at work (*tätige Mensch*). One has at first the impression that the man at work is working a found material, a matter already found. We think, however [. . .] that matter emerges primarily in and with activity and that the determinations of matter become comprehensible only from this activity. (Schapp 2012: 20)

In *In Geschichten verstrickt*, as far as the manifestational horizon of the external world is concerned, an inversion between *theoresis* and *poiesis* takes place. This inversion is certainly a consequence of Heidegger's hermeneutic turn, but nevertheless fits into the groove already marked by *Beiträge* and the openness to the lifeworld that emerged there. However, here it is not simply a matter of reversing the direction of what had been sketched out in *Beiträge*, and thus returning from the phenomenological breakthrough achieved through intuitive contemplation of things (see above, 1.B) to a more ordinary commerce with them. Rather, it is a matter of projecting oneself into the circle that envelops humans, not only when they test the qualities of the material, but in their "being at work," when they are the dynamic center of a series of actions and reactions in which the "will" to produce encounters the properties of matter (see Schapp 2012: 21). It is only by beginning with the circle of relations that is generated around the one working on the thing-for that qualities such as rigidity, heaviness, and other properties of matter come to primary manifestation. Upon this primary form of manifestation is then founded the secondary mode of emergence, the perceptual one (cf. Schapp 2012: 22–3).

In addition to the material character that links it to production (and from there unveils a worldly horizon), the thing-for has a whole other set of characteristics that make it a "formation of stories" instead, and thus open its historical-narrative horizon. Such characteristics are beyond the scope of any consideration of the thing that does not already contemplate it as being embedded in a context of use and in a series of cross-references that leads backward, toward the creator's design and plan—in the direction of the arche, so to speak—and forward, toward its being a means prepared for a purpose, having a telos, an aim, and a destiny in the human story. Picking up again on a Lippsian theme (see above, note 4), Schapp claims that the thing-for is presented to us, first and foremost, with an age (*Alter*) (see Schapp 2012: 13) that is more or less determined and determinable, that is, the thing-for may have just been made, or it may have been produced a long time ago. This peculiar character points back to production and thus to the creator's plan. Regarding this plan, the thing-for can be realized or unfulfilled, that is, the creator's intentions may have been carried out or left pending for some reason. The thing-for may also be in an unusable condition, but this does not in any way downgrade it from its status as a thing-for, since the very fact that it is not functional for the purpose(s) for which it was intended places it in the series of objects that can be used by humans for a certain purpose, along with the other "fulfilled" things-for of the same kind. In addition to this, things-for may have a whole multiplicity of characteristics related to time and wear and tear—

"the knife and the plow may be rusty; the wooden cabinet moth-eaten, broken, have a crack or lose parts" (Schapp 2012: 13)—and characteristics that define its state, for example, "expressions such as dirty, neglected, painted, stained, sanded, glazed, planed, exposed, solid, carved, patinaed, modern, antiquated, old, new, used" (Schapp 2012: 13). All these adjectives denote the thing-for and make sense only as determinations of the thing-for. For this reason, the thing-for cannot be reduced to its punctual manifestation, to Husserl's *hier und jetzt*, since with each of its determinations a glimpse of its past also emerges. Such determinations are variously related to the historical and cultural situatedness of the thing-for, its use, its functionality, and its being immersed in a context of present and already past relations. Thus together with presence, a horizon is articulated that reveals a part (or the entirety) of the thing-for's story.

The description of the determinations related to the story of the thing-for is the fulcrum of Schapp's shift from analyses of perception to analyses of entanglement. Indeed, at the very center of this description, we find an example that demonstrates how the focus on the manifestational aspect of the thing must now be placed in the broader meaning-context pertaining to the thing-for. At the end of the paragraph devoted to the horizons of the thing-for, Schapp writes, "The cup from which I drink daily has a crack in it. Yesterday this crack was not yet there. On the horizon now appears the question of how this crack was caused. With this, there is formed, so to speak, an island within in the always available horizon" (Schapp 2012: 17). Within the immersive perceptual experience of the thing, a window is thereby opened to the concatenation of events that led to the modification of the thing. For Schapp, such a window represents an overview of the concept of entanglement. It is from there that the horizon of the story of the thing-for in relation to its origins is unveiled, at the depths of which we find the producers with their plans and the sociohistorical context in they live: "with that, even if for the moment only remotely, through the thing-for we already encounter something of the 'essence human,' to which all our efforts are ultimately directed," as Schapp states in a crucial passage of *In Geschichten verstrickt* (Schapp 2012: 17).

It is precisely because—as Schapp shows—things are situated in a broader hermeneutic horizon that the story of the thing-for is not reduced to its discernible perceptual traces, which point back to past events concerning it; rather, the perception is itself modulated and directed from within by the story. To support this thesis, Schapp goes through the problem of the relative size of things. Things-for of the same size appear smaller to perception as their distance from the observer increases. This, however, does not mean that qualities such as big and small are solely perceptual functions of distance (cf. Schapp 2012: 34). Rather, big and small are also intrinsic properties of the character-for of the thing. If we think, for example, of the thing-for "cup," it can have different sizes depending on its purpose: it can be an espresso cup or a coffee cup. However, "if it becomes smaller than an espresso cup, it is no longer a cup, and similarly, it is no longer a cup even if it becomes as big as the room" (Schapp 2012: 34). The discussion of size makes sense, then, only in reference to the context in which the thing-for is found and the uses to which it is devoted. A huge cup outside at a café, for example, loses its function as an object that one can easily bring to one's mouth in order to drink something, which changes its character as a thing-for: "from an object-of-use, 'cup' becomes a showpiece, the thing-for 'cup for advertising'" (Schapp 2012: 34). Concepts such as "big and small" are thus to be understood, according to Schapp, only from the context or from the story of the thing-for. With such concepts, moreover, he no longer means a corporeal size, but is referring to determinations of the thing-for itself: "The cup is big and small or too big or too small in the same sense that it is dirty, clean, split, without a handle, with a handle, and perhaps even too empty or too full. These are all determinations of the same level, determinations of the thing-for that are not attributable without any 'character-for'" (Schapp 2012: 35). It is the character-for, then, that allows the thing to maintain its size even as it gets farther away. Taking the example of the house at the end of the valley in *Beiträge* (see Schapp 2013: 67), he says that it "maintains itself at a constant size as long as we see it or recognize it as a house, as long as it emerges as such. As soon as, at a great distance, it becomes something whose meaning can no longer be discerned, this something loses with this its determination of size as well" (Schapp 2012: 37). When considerations concerning the relative size of a thing take place, then, a translation to the plane of the meaning-context given by the story of the *deutlich-undeutlich* (clear-unclear) dichotomy of the phenomenology of perception (see above, 1.B) occurs. Indeed, a certain phenomenon can be said to bring the thing-for to givenness only as long as it is intelligible in the context in which it is situated, and thus in its story.

The latter aspect plays a crucial role in *In Geschichten verstrickt*, for it allows the investigations of perception in *Beiträge* to be fully incorporated within the story of the thing-for and the horizons to which it refers. This happens in two directions: in a horizontal direction, along the worldly horizon of production at the center of which is the human at work, and in a vertical direction, along the story that entangles and co-entangles the person in the stories of the humans who have had, have, or will have to do with that thing-for. Regarding these two directions, the analysis of the concept of work that one finds in *Die neue Wissenschaft vom Recht II* plays a key role.

4. Conclusions

In this chapter, the goal was to show how within the evolution of Schapp's thought from the phenomenology of perception to the philosophy of stories, one of the main topics was the evolution of the concept of a thing. As I have shown, the analysis of the concept of a thing is built around a new conception of humans and a different perspective on their way of relating to and knowing the external world. In the phenomenology of perception, the thing is seen as the core manifestation of different aspects of the external world. In the philosophy of law, on the other hand, the thing is considered as a work, and thus the gaze is no longer focused on its constituent aspects, but on its value and on the meaning-context in which it is planned and realized. This allows a first glimpse into the ego that conceived it and the egos that promoted its development, as well as those using it in everyday life. The work thus allows us to reconstruct insights into human history from the history of its discoveries. With the thing-for, however, this insight into the ego and the external world is placed in a new perspective given by production and use. The thing-for not only exhibits all the characteristics of the work—and thus its own history in the historicist sense and its own position within the history of humanity—but it is first and foremost characterized as a place for the emergence of the external world from the experience of the production and use of the individual humans, and thus becomes the occasion for the emergence and interconnection of the stories of humans. It is for this very reason that it represents one of the generative loci for entanglement and co-entanglement. In this sense, the concept of *Geschichte* that one finds in *Beiträge* and later in *Die neue Wissenschaft II* undergoes, precisely in the proximity of the thing-for, a shift of meaning from "history" into "story." This happens because in the philosophy of stories, it is no longer just a question of reconstructing the events of the individual thing and the evolutionary history of the kind of thing of which its history is a part, but of grasping from that angle the story of the individual human as well as of the way in which the thing-for enables the story of other entangled human beings to emerge. The history of the thing-for emerges in the stories of humans, where story is understood in an extended sense, from a mythological narrative to the Little Red Riding Hood fairy tale, as a central place for understanding the other and oneself through stories and entanglement in stories.[10]

Notes

1 "That a thing stands there and presents itself bodily as this or that is nothing but a title for the pregivenness (*Vorgegebenheiten*) that must precede every theory about things and perceptions of things" (Schapp 2013: 37). In his personal copy of *Beiträge*, Husserl added the letter H at the end of this sentence, as if to claim authorship of that statement (see Vongehr and Giuliani 2004: xlvii).

2 As already mentioned in the introduction to the present volume, the German term *Geschichte* used by Schapp beginning with *Beiträge* can refer either to a succession of events or to the narration of these events. For this reason, in some cases the English term "histories" should be preferred, in others the English term "stories." For a more detailed discussion of the problem from a semantic point of view, see Nuccilli (2023). In the conclusion of this chapter, I will briefly show how Schapp's works move from a conception of *Geschichte* as history to a conception of *Geschichte* as story.

3 However, as I have shown in Nuccilli (2020), the critique of the concept of species included in *Beiträge* already contains *in nuce* an initial escape route from the phenomenology of Husserl and other members of the phenomenological circles.

4 Lipps also speaks of the *Alter* (age) of works of art (Lipps 1920: 558), a recurring concept and terminology in *In Geschichten verstrickt* used to describe the perceptually primary characteristic of things-for.

5 Views on this issue are divided. The following speak against a direct influence of Heidegger on Schapp's thought: Lübbe (2012: ix), J. Schapp (2004: 19), and Schollenberger (2004: 242), while those speaking in favor of it include Fellmann (2015: 166–168), Greisch, (2010: 193), Marquard (2004: 48), and Rolf (2004: 107).

6 Schapp's argument deepens what he had already sketched in the conclusion of the first volume. See Schapp 1930: 176f. For an assessment of the importance of the pre-legal dimension of truth as a function of thing-for, see J. Schapp (1968: 55–74).

7 "If we take a closer look at this relationship to a human being, we first come across a physical activity in the case of physical works—the hammer, for example, which is governed by an arm, or the saw, the drill, the chisel, which are handled by the human being, and which have left their traces in the work. And if we advance further, we come upon the human being as an 'I' from whom the work proceeds—coming, we can say first of all, upon the human being with the will for the work" (Schapp 1932: 38). The terminology and thematic framework of this passage demonstrate two things. The first is the continuity of the problem of work and workmanship with Lipps's aesthetics, as I attempt to show above in 1.C. The second, on the other hand, concerns the foundational character of the investigations of the work for the subsequent treatment of the thing-for; the reference to the saw, the

hammer, and the drill are in fact references that one also finds, as I describe below, in the production of the thing-for.

8 For a more in-depth analysis of how the critique of the phenomenological concept of essence is intertwined in Schapp with an aversion to phenomenological Platonism, see Nuccilli (2020).

9 Schapp remains firmly convinced that the proper way to delve into the relationship between the work and the creator is to investigate the relations of essence (*Wesenszusammenhänge*) (see Schapp 1930: 48) that structure it a priori. Thus, he remains firmly anchored in the methodic principles of phenomenology. However, he believes that these laws do not lead to the intuition of ideal entities, nor can they lead us back to a unitary essence that applies to each individual shoe, since they refer us precisely to the historical nature of the work, consistent with what was outlined in *Beiträge* (see Schapp 2013: 131ff.); therefore, he takes a critical stance against a certain static and eidetic view of objects of use.

10 This work was supported by the European Regional Development Fund project "MSCA Fellowships CZ – UK2" (reg. no.: CZ.02.01.01/00/22_010/0008115).

References

Biceaga, V. (2010), *The Concept of Passivity in Husserl's Phenomenology*, Dordrecht: Springer.

Fellmann, F. (2015), *Phänomenologie zur Einführung*, Hamburg: Junius Verlag.

Greisch, J. (2010), "Phänomenologie als Philosophie der Geschichten: eine vierte, stille Revolution der philosophischen Denkungsart?" in K. Joisten (ed.), *Das Denken Wilhelm Schapps. Perspektiven für unsere Zeit*, 190–214, Freiburg/München: Alber.

Habermas J. (1981), *Theorie des kommunikativen Handelns. Zur Kritik der funktionalistischen Vernunft*, Vol. 2, Frankfurt am Main: Suhrkamp.

Husserl, E. (1964), *The Idea of Phenomenology*, trans. W. P. Alston and G. Nakhnikian, The Hague: Martinus Nijhoff.

Husserl, E. (1966), *Analysen zur passiven Synthesis. Aus Vorlesungs- und Forschungsmanuskripten 1918–1926*, Hua XI, ed. M. Fleischer, Den Haag: Martinus Nijhoff.

Husserl, E. (1997), *Thing and Space: Lectures of 1907*, trans. R. Rojcewicz, Dordrecht: Kluwer Academic Publishers.

Husserl, E. (2001), *Logical Investigations 1*, trans. J. N. Findlay, ed. D. Moran, London/New York: Routledge.

Husserl, E. (2004), *Wahrnehmung und Aufmerksamkeit. Texte aus dem Nachlass (1893–1912)*, Hua XXXVIII, eds. T. Vongehr and R. Giuliani, Dordrecht: Springer.

Lipps, Th. (1903), *Ästhetik. Psychologie des Schönen und der Kunst: Grundlegung der Ästhetik*, Leipzig: Verlag von Leopold Voss.

Lipps, Th. (1920), *Ästhetik*, 2nd edn, Leipzig: Verlag von Leopold Voss.

Lübbe, H. (1972), *Bewusstsein in Geschichten. Studien zur Phänomenologie der Subjektivität: Mach-Husserl-Schapp-Wittgenstein*, Freiburg: Rombach

Lübbe, H. (2012), "Vorwort zur zweiten Auflage," in W. Schapp (ed.), *In Geschichten verstrickt. Zum Sein vom Mensch und Ding*, v–xi, Frankfurt am Main: Vittorio Klostermann.

Marquard, O. (2004), "Die Philosophie der Geschichten und die Zukunft des Erzählens," in K.-H. Lembeck (ed.), *Geschichte und Geschichten. Studien zur Geschichtenphänomenologie Wilhelm Schapps*, 45–56, Würzburg: Königshausen & Neumann.

Moran, D. (2001), "Introduction," in E. Husserl (2001), *Logical Investigations 1*, trans. J. N. Findlay, ed. D. Moran, xxi–lxxii, London/New York: Routledge.

Nuccilli, D. (2018), "History and Stories: Schapp's Ontological Conception of the Entanglement," *Kritika & Kontext* 22: 27–43.

Nuccilli, D. (2020), "Species, Ideas, and Stories: Schapp between Phenomenological 'Platonism' and 'Anti-Platonism'," *Azimuth* 15 (7): 61–75.

Nuccilli, D. (2023), "Wilhelm Schapp on the Narratological Structure of Intersubjectivity," in A. Božič (ed.), *Thinking Togetherness: Phenomenology and Sociality*, 143–55, Ljubljana: Institute Nova Revija for the Humanities.

Nuccilli, D. (2024), "70 Years of *In Geschichten verstrickt*: Context, Legacy, and Development," *The New Yearbook for Phenomenology and Phenomenological Philosophy*, 22 (forthcoming).

Ricœur, P. (1992), *Oneself as Another*, trans. Kathleen Blamey, Chicago: The University of Chicago Press.

Rojcewicz, R. (1997), "Translator's Introduction," in E. Husserl (1997), *Thing and Space: Lectures of 1907*, xi–xvi, Dordrecht: Kluwer Academic Publishers.

Rolf, T. (2004), "Der dichtende Gegenstand," in K.-H. Lembeck (ed.), *Geschichte und Geschichten. Studien zur Geschichtenphänomenologie Wilhelm Schapps*, 87–114, Würzburg: Königshausen & Neumann.

Schapp, J. (1968), *Sein und Ort der Rechtsgebilde. Eine Untersuchung über Eigentum und Vertrag*, Den Haag: Martinus Nijhoff.

Schapp, J. (2004), "Erinnerungen an Wilhelm Schapp," in K.-H. Lembeck (ed.), *Geschichte und Geschichten. Studien zur Geschichtenphänomenologie Wilhelm Schapps*, 13–25, Würzburg: Königshausen & Neumann.

Schapp, J. (2010), "Geschichtenphilosophie und Recht," in K. Joisten (ed.), *Das Denken Wilhelm Schapps. Perspektiven für unsere Zeit*, 65–85, Freiburg/München.

Schapp, J. (2013), "Sprache, Gesetz und Recht," *Zeitschrift für Rechtsphilosophie*, 1: 60–76.

Schapp, W. (1930), *Die neue Wissenschaft vom Recht,* Vol. 1, *Eine phänomenologische Untersuchung. Der Vertrag als Vorgegebenheit*, Berlin/Grunewald: Rotschild.

Schapp, W. (1932), *Die neue Wissenschaft vom Recht,* Vol. 2, *Eine phänomenologische Untersuchung. Wert, Werk und Eigentum*, Berlin/Grunewald: Rotschild.

Schapp, W. (2012 [1953]), *In Geschichten verstrickt. Zum Sein von Mensch und Ding*, 5th edn, Frankfurt am Main: Vittorio Klostermann.

Schapp, W. (2013 [1910]), *Beiträge zur Phänomenologie der Wahrnehmung*, Frankfurt am Main: Vittorio Klostermann.

Schollenberger, A. (2004), "Jenseits der Aufklärung," in J. Heil (ed.), *Dimensionen praktischer Philosophie*, 235–56, London: Turnshare.

Vongehr, T. and Giuliani, R. (2004), "Einleitung," in E. Husserl (2004), *Wahrnehmung und Aufmerksamkeit. Texte aus dem Nachlass (1893–1912)*, Hua XXXVIII, ed. T. Vongehr and R. Giuliani, xiii–lii, Dordrecht: Springer.

Zahavi, D. (2003), *Husserl's Phenomenology*, Stanford: Stanford University Press.

7

Wilhelm Schapp's *The New Science of Law*[1]

Sophie Loidolt

With his double qualification in philosophy and jurisprudence, Wilhelm Schapp can be counted among the first interdisciplinary representatives of phenomenological research. He belongs to the important contributors of early legal phenomenology. Schapp studied with several renowned professors in both subjects: he heard lectures by Heinrich Rickert, Wilhelm Dilthey, Georg Simmel, and Alexander Pfänder in Freiburg, Berlin, and Munich. Later he continued his studies in Göttingen with Edmund Husserl, where he graduated as a Doctor of Philosophy in 1909. Directly after his studies, Schapp decided to work as a lawyer and notary. In the First World War, he served and survived. After this, he returned to university and pursued another doctorate in jurisprudence, under the supervision of Julius Binder, a famous neo-Hegelian philosopher of law in Göttingen.

Schapp shares his double qualification and interdisciplinary interest with Adolf Reinach who, in 1913, was the first one to develop a phenomenological approach to questions of law in his book *The Apriori Foundations of Civil Law*. Reinach's ideas proved to be enormously influential on Schapp. As Spiegelberg recalls: "Independently of each other, the Göttingen students of phenomenology like Wilhelm Schapp, Dietrich von Hildebrand, Alexandre Koyré and Edith Stein, in their accounts of this period refer to Reinach, not to Husserl, as their real teacher in phenomenology" (Spiegelberg 1982: 191–2). Tragically, Reinach was not so lucky as Schapp to survive the First World War. His early death in 1917 left his friends and students bereaved and some important philosophical work undone. By taking up the project of a *New Science of Law* in 1930, Schapp revives the Reinachian project and gives it a new twist. In this chapter, I will provide a brief introduction to some of the main themes of this work and contextualize it with the legal phenomenology of Reinach's preceding study (for further aspects, see also Purnhagen 2009).

1. Adolf Reinach's Groundbreaking Study

> We ourselves are closest to Reinach in our investigations. We have had more from Reinach than from anyone else. (Schapp 1930: 182)[2]

This quote nicely illustrates the extent to which Wilhelm Schapp follows Reinach's legal phenomenology in his *Die neue Wissenschaft vom Recht* (1930). Adolf Reinach indeed must be acknowledged as the founder of phenomenology of law (cf. Theunissen 1977: 401). His 1913 publication *The Apriori Foundations of Civil Law* remains the paradigmatic representative of this strand of research which, however, differentiated into many diverse approaches throughout the twentieth century.[3] Reinach's main research question concerned the origin and status of "legal entities." One of his central theses was that the basic legal concepts of "claim" and "obligation" were not just conventions but originated as an own form of being in the "social act" of promising. A social act, for Reinach, is an act that is not only directed at another person but also "*is in need of being heard (vernehmungsbedürftig)*" (Reinach 1983: 28). This means that social acts like asking, commanding, promising etc. can—in contrast to other-directed acts like admiration or forgiving—only be performed successfully together with another person. Now, through the performative act of the promise, if it is heard and not explicitly rejected, "something new enters the world" (Reinach 1983: 9). This is to say that in the successful act of promising, claim and obligation emerge as a specific kind of "entities" (*Gebilde*): they are not real entities like trees or chairs, but ideal ones; but unlike mathematical and logical ideal entities, they originate at a certain point in time and disappear again when they are fulfilled. This way, Reinach could bring together phenomenological research on social acts and their correlates with an inquiry into basic concepts founding the legal sphere.

The elaboration of the promise as a "social act" consequently operates at the heart of *The Apriori Foundations of Civil Law*: if person A makes a promise to person B, which the latter takes up, then this social act, by itself alone, gives rise to a claim on the part of B to fulfill the promise, as well as to an equal obligation in A to fulfill the promise. This is Reinach's basic line of thought, by which he opens up a sphere of its own in which one can speak of law not as a positively set norm, or norm of nature or reason but as a sphere of being ("legal entities") that possesses a certain "essence" or eidetic structure (*Wesen*) (Reinach 1983: 4–6). In this way, he establishes an a priori doctrine of law (*Recht*) that aims at articulating and discerning basic lawful relations between these entities and the social acts founding them or being directed at them. For example: "a claim to have something done dissolves as soon as the thing is done" (Reinach 1983: 9). One could also call this a *deontic logic* which, essentially, is independent of positive law in its being and validity. Hence, in defiance of all the juridical and juridico-philosophical considerations of his time, Reinach claims that the basic legal concepts are grounded in a *being* (of legal entities) and not in an *ought*. He calls his investigations a "material" eidetic since their subject goes beyond only formal ontological laws. A material eidetic is determined by the a priori structure of its matter. It is one of Husserl's basic claims that also sensual matters, such as colors, emotions, etc. have an eidetic structure, and not just formal logical or categorial laws. Consider, for example, the eidetic insight that of three different tones, one must be the highest and one the lowest one, or that color and surface must always go together. Accordingly, Reinach looks for eidetic laws in the region of claim and obligation, and further, of all a priori legal concepts which eventually root in the person and her legal capacity or power (*rechtliches Können*) (Reinach 1983: 34).

Reinach's primary legal-philosophical orientation can thus be called "eidetic-realistic." The legal essences are "found" or "discovered" by positive law which, more often than not, takes them up and integrates them in its basic concepts and propositions. Yet, positive law is also free to contradict these essential laws, since it originates by itself from a social act, namely that of enactment (*Bestimmung*) (cf. Reinach 1983: 102–18). What is essential for Reinach (1983: 4) is that positive law does not *create* these entities, be it by normative positionings, prescriptions, or interpretations, but as has been said, only *discovers* them. This makes him a "realist" in terms of the origin and status of legal entities, and an essentialist in terms of the validity foundation of legal concepts and propositions.

2. Schapp's Uptake, Continuation, and Modification of Reinach's Legal Phenomenological Approach

Schapp follows on from this and goes beyond it in his analyses of the *contract*, mainly by including the world of *values*. Wilhelm Schapp is not the only one who continues Reinach's project. Earlier on, Edith Stein (1925/2006) had investigated the material eidetics of the state (and thus public law) in a similar vein, whereas, the Japanese legal philosopher, Tomoo Otaka (1932/2023) concentrated on questions of "social associations" (*sozialer Verband*) (and thus public and international law). Schapp, in contrast, continues to focus on civil law, which Reinach had originally worked on. His project seeks to place the legal concepts of contract, claim, and property in a larger pre-legal context of meaning and value: he hence deals with the subject of "legal pregivenness (*rechtlichen Vorgegebenheiten*) for every civil law" (Schapp 1932: III).

Schapp's *The New Science of Law* comes in two volumes: (1) "A Phenomenological Investigation" (*Eine phänomenologische Untersuchung*) (1930); and (2) "Value, Work, and Property" (*Wert, Werk und Eigentum*) (1932). In essence, Schapp adopts Reinach's doctrine of social acts and theory of promise, as also Theunissen (1977: 401) observes: "Although in the first volume of his work, he considers a legal phenomenon excluded by Reinach [. . .], namely the contract, we find everything there again that was of importance in the 'a priori foundations.'" Yet, the distinctive feature of Schapp's theory is that he pays more attention to the basis in values and valuing attitudes, presenting them as the "substructure" of the contract, while calling the conclusion of the contract itself the "superstructure." In the following quote, we can see how Schapp takes up Reinach with a slight implicit criticism that points into the direction of his own investigations:

> Reinach's strength lies in the study of acts and in their neat delineation from one another and in the establishment of a relation between acts and legal relations. The resistance Reinach has encountered is probably due to the fact that he begins his investigation with the abstract acts, that he overlooks or at least does not treat the foundation of these acts in the bases of value. (Schapp 1930: 182)

This "underpinning," which Schapp now wishes to elaborate, consists in the fact that "a fixed series of considerations must have preceded in the minds of the contracting parties" (Schapp 1930: 2) before they enter into a contract. And these considerations, according to Schapp, take place in the realm of valuing.

> Resolutions are made on the basis of the evaluations. The resolutions lead to the stage in which the issuing of declarations of will comes into question. However, these declarations of will are not arbitrary declarations of will, but social acts. They are psychic and interpsychic processes, i.e., processes that take place simultaneously in the soul and between souls, such as promising, permitting, commanding. (Schapp 1930: 56)

Thus, the conclusion of the contract itself (the "superstructure") corresponds precisely to Reinach's social act of promising: through the promise issued in a contract, claim and obligation arise in each of the two parties involved, independently of positive law. Like Reinach, Schapp conceives of positive law as an "enactment" (*Bestimmung*) that can circumvent the "pregivenness" (*Vorgegebenheiten*) of eidetic relations, though without being able to change anything in their essence.[4] "[P]ositive law finds these formulas and selects those which seem expedient to it and gives them an increased significance" (Schapp 1930: 36). Schapp's theoretical intentions go beyond this. Therefore, *The New Science of Law* does not coincide with "jurisprudence" (as a science of positive law), but wants to be a separate, new science of the pregivens of legal structures and their relation to positive law (cf. Schapp 1930: III).

In the first volume of his work, Schapp outlines the essence of the "legal figure" (*Rechtsfigur*) of the contract (Schapp 1930: 62–5), including its preset structures in the domain of values and evaluation. In the second part, he takes a similar approach to the subject of property, which is acquired with respect to the "valuable work" in the sense of a privilege (*Vorrecht*) (Schapp 1932: 1). In general, it can be said that Schapp, especially in presentation, style, and language, is less theoretically oriented than Reinach; he gives plenty of examples, especially from literature and history, and also responds more concretely to the understanding of practicing lawyers. Yet, his goal echoes his background: "I hope that my investigation will give some an opportunity to pick up Reinach again" (Schapp 1930: 182). The following division of the subchapters is roughly based on Schapp's table of contents of the first volume of *Die neue Wissenschaft vom Recht*. At the end of the chapter, I will give a brief preview of the second volume.

3. The Reasonable Contract as a Pregiven (*Vorgegebenheit*)

Schapp places the contract at the center of his investigations. He sees it as the "main field of the jurist" (Schapp 1930: 6). However, as he muses, it is not so easy to say what a contract really is. An easier task is to stipulate what a reasonable contract is. In this case, a fixed series of considerations in the minds of the contracting parties have preceded the transaction of goods or services (cf. Schapp 1930: 2). Schapp tries to work out an a priori of these fixed series of considerations and hence an a priori of the reasonable contract. This goes beyond the "a priori of social intercourse" (*sozialer Verkehr*) (Reinach 1983: 6), in that, it takes into account value perceptions and valuing (*Wertnehmen*) beyond social acts.

> In all [contracts] the substructure consists in the assessment of the values to be realized and the superstructure in enunciations which bring about this realization. (Schapp 1930: 34)

The considerations that precede the contract lead into the world of values: "Value is somehow an emphasis (*Akzent*) of the valuable objectivity. It is not itself, however, the object in theoretical consideration, but in a peculiar way something objectifiable (*Gegenständliches*) about the valuable, which is experienced in enjoyment (*Genuss*)" (Schapp 1930: 7). This indicates that Schapp concords with the phenomenological theory of values, as developed by Husserl (1988, 2004), Scheler (1913/1973), Stein, Reinach, von Hildebrandt, and others. Like Scheler, Schapp compares the particular manifestation of values with colors. In an analogy to blindness, he describes value blindness as the inability to perceive the value in an object (whereby it is not a matter of "perception" in the strict sense, but rather the value is opened up through feeling, a "value (re)ception" or "value-taking" (*wertnehmen*)). According to Schapp, it is above all this realm of value (*Wertwelt*) that occupies an essential position in human existence: "The world of values and unvalues is the actual world in which we live" (Schapp 1930: 11). This is also significant for jurisprudence: the procuring of values, the protection of the world of values assigned to a person, the enrichment of another world of values through my action is one main field of jurisprudence—and is at the same time a pregiven for jurisprudence: "In a cosmos that contained no values, jurisprudence would lose most of its meaning, if not all meaning" (Schapp 1930: 22).

Schapp's concern, then, is to show that even positive law remains related to a substructure to which it "answers" as a pregiven in a specific way. Jurisprudence would thus, not be a science of mere legal constructs that have been freely invented but a realm of abstraction that, however, refers to a concrete reality. This reality can, in turn, be grasped in a priori structures constituting the regional ontologies of social reality and value reality: "The remarkable thing here is not that some artificial structure, which the jurist calls 'purchase,' contains artificial parts, but that a natural structure, of which legislation has only taken possession, contains natural parts" (Schapp 1930: 5).

The connection between a reasonable mutual contract and the world of values consists in the fact that everyone who consciously enters into a contract, evaluates beforehand how the transaction could present itself as an increase of his or her "world of values." Schapp gives a multitude of colorful examples; let me only mention the first one here, in which a watch collector exchanges a duplicate for another watch of the watch seller. "That this relation has remained unnoticed for so long probably stems primarily from the fact that, normally, it is not intrinsic values (*Eigenwerte*) that are directly transacted in reasonable mutual contracts, but instead mainly mediated values (*Mittelwerte*) [money, S.L.], or mediated values for intrinsic values" (Schapp 1930: 26).

How does Schapp then sketch out the a priori structure preceding a contract? First, he claims that to "every soul" pertains a "world of value" (*Wertwelt*) (cf. Schapp 1930: 21). This world is of the greatest variety in itself, from the sunrise which I like to look at, up to the highest value according to Schapp, the self-value of another human being. When we conclude a contract, considerations related to such worlds of value always play a decisive role. By considering worlds of value, Schapp tries to go beyond the limits of speaking only of sales contracts, but intends to open up a much wider area, such as the contract of marriage, or the idea of a contract with God.

> The reasonable mutual contract now consists in the fact that something is transplanted from the value world of one into the value world of the other and vice versa. Without this relation to a world of value, the mutual contract would be meaningless. This relation can be completely hidden from third parties. But for the contracting parties the relation must be present. (Schapp 1930: 27)

This concerns the substructure of the reasonable contract. Its superstructure is, as already mentioned, fully modeled on Reinach's promise: claim and obligation arise essentially from the social act of promising in concluding a contract, without needing the sphere of positive law (cf. Schapp 1930: 40ff.). The superstructure and substructure together finally result in the idea of the "legal figure" (*Rechtsfigur*), which Schapp illustrates with the case of the purchase (cf. Schapp 1930: 62ff.): "This whole thing, which takes place in the mutual contract arising from the first evaluation up until the fulfillment, and which indeed takes place on the most diverse levels, we call a legal figure" (Schapp 1930: 63). How evaluations can emerge, which resolutions must arise in the contracting parties, how it finally comes to the act of concluding the contract and to its legal consequence—all of this constitutes the *Rechtsfigur*.

In addition to the exemplary case of the mutual contract, Schapp examines two other particular forms of contract and their basis of value. He compares this "eidetics of legal figures" to the approach of the mathematician who distinguishes, say, the circle, the triangle, the quadrilateral, and derives rules from them, but always in the awareness that there are an infinite number of figures of this kind with an infinite number of intermediate levels. Schapp thus, wants to take into account fixed unities on the one hand, and a certain fluidity on the other, which constitutes legal figures as eidetic forms of practical legal life. From this, results a first structuring of eidetic forms of contract or different types of legal figures: (1) the mutual contract; (2) the gift contract, and (3) the social contract (as an association of several participants for one purpose, e.g., the building of a bridge). On the basis of these types, the "reasonable contract" as such can now be characterized eidetically in broad strokes: it turns out to be primarily a mutual contract. Schapp contrasts it with the "reasonless" (*vernunftlos*) contract as a unilateral contract, which plays a major role in positive law, namely, as a unilateral obligation without a counterpart, but which "in reality is a nothing" (Schapp 1930: 73). Examples of unilateral obligations would be: "I promise you 100, I transfer to you this property, this thing, I order you a usufruct, I waive my claim" (Schapp 1930: 70). From this we can see that, interestingly, the act of the promise does not suffice to constitute a reasonable contract, since it is only unilateral. This is not a contradiction to Reinach but just shows that a contract is something different than a promise or a waiver. Schapp argues that unilateral obligations lack the three basic components necessary for a reasonable contract: the valuation basis, the execution of the acts, and the emergence of the claims. Therefore, unilateral obligations as contracts would always need the "cement" of positive law, which sets the obligation through an "enactment" (*Bestimmung*)—otherwise it would not exist "by itself."

4. The Enactment (*Bestimmung*) as a Pregiven

According to Schapp's approach, he also needs to understand enactments themselves also as a pregivenness for positive law, in order to conceive of positive law as coming into reality through a special social act of enactment: "An enactment corresponds to the attitude of sic volo sic iubeo." (Schapp 1930: 97) Not any enactment is yet positive law. It can refer to one's own affairs or be an enactment over others—then it is a social act that must be heard, etc. Positive law is enactment over others, behind which there must also be a power of enactment: "The enactment exercises a legal effect in the sense of being a pregivenness only if there is power of enactment" (Schapp 1930: 104). The act of submission to the power of enactment is necessary for a legally effective obligation (this, again, is identical with Reinach's claim, cf. Reinach 1983: 110).

> If such submission occurs, the power of enactment of the state to which one has submitted oneself is thereby phenomenologically insightfully established. There is then an ontological connection in the sense of a legal figure between submission, power of enactment, enactment, and legal effect of the enactment. (Schapp 1930: 105)

In this sense, one can speak of a pre-givenness of enactment that is intimately related to the act of submission. If this submission should describe an actual social reality qua eidetic law, or if it rather reminds of legitimation figures of social contract theories, remains as open as in Reinach.

The question of morally correct or "right" law is also touched upon by Schapp, but he answers it only by referring to the world of values: for only by taking a stance on the world of values can one speak of the correctness of law at all. A communist state, for example, must have a different law than a state that rates the value of private property more highly. Laws and the world of values of a state can thus be reciprocally derived from each other. The question of the correct law must consequently boil down to whether the legislator was not "mistaken in the world of values" (Schapp 1930: 122). Can something similar be said for customary law and for custom as such (Schapp cites, for example, the custom of dueling in officer circles or the position of women)? This is a difficult question, Schapp suggests, which cannot be solved here. For if one were to apply the standard of correctness to custom and customary law, one would have to say—in the case of a negative judgment—that not only the legislator but all have erred in the world of values (cf. Schapp 1930: 121–3).

Positive law, Schapp argues, stands in an undeniable relationship to pregivenness. But so do religion, morality, and custom, in that they formulate codes and rules that refer to pregivens and thus can, in part, compete with positive law (cf. Schapp 1930: 124). Among other pregivens besides the contract, Schapp includes "property" and "prohibited action" (*unerlaubte Handlung*). On the latter, he develops some brief considerations in connection with the world of value (cf. Schapp 1930, 168–74). Property is the central topic of the second volume of *The New Science of Law* in the contexts of work and value (Schapp 1932). There, Schapp explores the concept of value, the I-work relation (*Ich-Werk-Beziehung*) (creating, making, etc.), and finally, the concepts of property and possession in positive law.

5. Conclusion

Some instructive remarks on Schapp's realist-phenomenological understanding of law can be found at the end of the first volume under the heading: "How does one learn jurisprudence?":

> The young lawyer brings everything to the study of jurisprudence in the same sense that the mathematician brings everything to his science. In the same way

> that Socrates quizzes the slave on the Pythagorean theorem, the teacher of law could quiz the student of law on every legal institute. The only prerequisite is that the student knows or feels what is valuing, what is enjoyment and value, what is promise, enactment, command, what is a claim, what is creation. But the student can never learn this if he does not bring it with him. The teacher can only deepen the differences and neatly delineate the realities. These pregivens and their relation to each other constitute jurisprudence par excellence. Positive law, as an enactment, is just as much a pregiven as the other pregivens. The interventions of positive law into the level of pregivens can also only occur according to the rules that ground in the essence of the enactment. The structure of law, including its basis in valuation, is as transparent as a mathematical structure. (Schapp 1930: 179)

This longer quotation shows that within the framework of realist phenomenology, law is conceived as a structured whole of relational determinations of Platonic character. These eidetic relations emerge on the basis of pregivens that manifest themselves, for example, in social acts. Schapp's insight that such pregivens are essentially determined by values, value attitudes, and worlds of value is an important contribution to phenomenology of law. One point of critique might be that, in spite of this strong emphasis on values, he does not position himself unequivocally with regard to a possible material axiology and its possible objectivity (cf. communist state vs. state protecting private property). Rather, he remains as formalistic and relational as one would expect this from a legal scholar, in the sense that he does not determine one material world of values as the "right" one but just claims that certain laws would relate to certain values. If one consistently follows the theory presented, however, then such an objective world of value would have to be just as attainable as the legal relations corresponding to it. Another point of critique might be that by referring to pregivens and eidetic relations, certain legal and customary concepts might come to be naturalized instead of historically explained and thereby deconstructed. Ernst Bloch (1987: 144) already criticized this heavily with regard to Reinach's notion of property.[5]

Finally, Wilhelm Schapp's theoretical elaboration of a social reality of valuing, interacting persons, in which Reinach's "social acts" must always already be embedded, undertakes a first turn toward a legal phenomenology of the lifeworld. In this respect, Schapp can be considered a representative of phenomenology of law who links the eidetic and the lifeworld spheres, especially with regard to his later philosophy of an "entanglement in stories" (Schapp 1953 and 1959).[6]

Notes

1 This article is a reworked English version of the chapter on Wilhelm Schapp in my book *Einführung in die Rechtsphänomenologie* (*Introduction to Phenomenology of Law*) (cf. Loidolt 2010: 123–8).
2 All translations of German works without an official translation are mine.
3 Cf. my *Einführung in die Rechtsphänomenologie*, in which I propose a classification of classical legal phenomenology into three different strands: eidetic-realistic, logical-positivistic, and lifeworldly-socio-ontological phenomenology of law (Loidolt 2010: 76–200).
4 Another difference between the sphere of a priori and positive law is that there can be no compulsion in the former: if a claim is not fulfilled, it remains in essence as a violated claim.
5 "The blindness of phenomenology to the economic-historical production and genesis of 'essential contents' has the effect of letting capitalist patterns of thought flow unimpeded and uncontrolled into the 'intrinsically obvious nature of the matter'" (Bloch 1987: 144).
6 Wilhelm Schapp's son, the civil lawyer and legal philosopher, Jan Schapp, explicitly took up his father's legal phenomenological approach, especially in an early publication, and combined it with his "philosophy of stories" Cf. Schapp, J. (1968, 2009).

References

Bloch, E. (1987), *Natural Law and Human Dignity*, trans. Dennis J. Schmidt, Cambridge, MA and London: MIT Press.

Husserl, E. (1988), *Vorlesungen über Ethik und Wertlehre, 1908–1914*, Ullrich Melle (Hrsg.), Dordrecht: Kluwe.

Husserl, E. (2004), *Einleitung in die Ethik: Vorlesungen Sommersemester 1920/1924*, ed. Henning Peucker, Dordrecht: Kluwer.

Loidolt, S. (2010), *Einführung in die Rechtsphänomenologie. Eine historisch-systematische Darstellung*, Tübingen: Mohr Siebeck.

Otaka, T. (1932/2023), *Grundlegung der Lehre vom sozialen Verband*, Wien/Berlin: Springer. Translated as: *Foundation of a Theory of Social Association,* Derek Robbins (ed. and trans.), Berlin et al.: Peter Lang.

Purnhagen, K. (2009), "Grundlagen der Rechtsphänomenologie. Eine kritische Darstellung der Rechtsphänomenologie von Adolf Reinach und Wilhelm Schapp zu den apriorischen Grundlagen des Privatrechts," *JURA Juristische Ausbildung*, 31 (9): 661–8.

Reinach, A. (1983), "The Apriori Foundations of the Civil Law," J. F. Crosby (trans.), *Aletheia* 3: 1–142.
Schapp, J. (1968), *Sein und Ort der Rechtsgebilde,* Den Haag: Nijhoff.
Schapp, J. (2009), "Phänomenologie und Recht," in Id., *Methodenlehre und System des Rechts. Aufsätze 1992–2007,*245–55, Tübingen: Mohr Siebeck.
Schapp, W. (1930), *Die neue Wissenschaft vom Recht. Band 1: Eine phänomenologische Untersuchung,* Berlin/Grunewald: Rothschild.
Schapp, W. (1932), *Die neue Wissenschaft vom Recht. Band 2: Wert, Werk und Eigentum,*Berlin/Grunewald: Rothschild.
Schapp, W. (1953), *In Geschichten verstrickt. Zum Sein von Mensch und Ding,* Hamburg: Meiner.
Schapp, W. (1959), *Philosophie der Geschichten,* Leer: Rautenberg.
Scheler, M. (1913/1973), *Der Formalismus in der Ethik und die materiale Wertethik,* Jahrbuch für Philosophie und phänomenologische Forschung 1&2. Translated as *Formalism in Ethics and Non-Formal Ethics of Values: A New Attempt toward the Foundation of an Ethical Personalism,* Manfred S. Frings and Roger L. Funk (trans.), Evanston, IL: Northwestern University Press, 1973.
Spiegelberg, H. (1982), *The Phenomenological Movement. A Historical Introduction,* Haag: M. Nijhoff
Stein, E. (1925/2006), *Eine Untersuchung über den Staat.* Jahrbuch für philosophische und phänomenologische Forschung 7. Translated as *An Investigation Concerning the State,* Marianne Sawicki (trans.), CWES, Vol. 10, ICS Publications.
Theunissen, M. (1977), *Der Andere. Studien zur Sozialontologie der Gegenwart,* Berlin/New York: de Gruyter.

8

Wilhelm Schapp's Qualitative Social Ontology

The Role of Values for the Law

Francesca De Vecchi

1. What Is Qualitative Social Ontology?

What am I talking about when I talk of qualitative social ontology? I am talking about a social ontology that has an existential gaze, so to speak, and accounts for our being, living, and acting as personal subjects in the world. Indeed, it is a social ontology that is intrinsically connected with an ontology of the person and focuses on the relation between the personal and the social. It describes the social world as a lifeworld, as the world that we experience daily as persons who in that world live and act together with other persons, and it dwells on the being of the persons in the social world as a personal world. The qualitative social ontology I am accounting for is a phenomenologically inspired and oriented social ontology, which is grounded in classic phenomenology, which develops in the first three decades of the last century. I mean the phenomenology that focuses on topics such as personal identity, the common surrounding world, and lifeworld as the world seen by a personalistic attitude, phenomenology of intersubjectivity, collectives and social acts, phenomenology of the law and values. These are topics that we find in the works of Edmund Husserl (1984, 1950, 1994, 1973, 1976), Edith Stein (1922, 1925, 2008), Max Scheler (1954, 1973), Adolf Reinach (2012), and Wilhelm Schapp (1930). Indeed, these phenomenologists, among others, are all fundamental references for the personally embedded qualitative social ontology I am presenting here. They deal with social ontology extensively, and it is not by chance that the first occurrence of the expression "social ontology" is in Husserl's work (1973: 99-104). I am convinced that classic phenomenology offers a precious perspective in social ontology, precisely because it is about the essential connection between the ontology of the person and the ontology of society. Therefore, with the expression "qualitative social ontology," I propose a new line of research in social ontology that, in addressing the connection between the personal and the social, opens a different research track with respect to the mainstream social ontology in the tradition of analytic philosophy, that of John Searle (1995, 2010) and Margaret Gilbert (1989, 2014), for instance, which is instead characterized by a "*lacuna* on the qualitative," so to speak. I already focused on Husserl's, Stein's, and Reinach's contributions to social ontology as a qualitative one in previous works of mine. In this chapter, I concentrate on Schapp's phenomenology of law and aim to show how and why it justly belongs to the tradition of phenomenologically embedded qualitative social ontology.[1]

1.1 The Novelty of Qualitative Social Ontology: The Individualizing Role of Values

The novelty of qualitative social ontology reveals itself plainly: as persons, we do not experience the things of the world as bare things but as things that are qualitatively characterized. This means that we experience things not merely as physical objects, as only spatio-temporally situated and mathematically measurable—the famous primary and objective qualities of the Galilean tradition—nor merely as sensory-perceived objects—colors, flavors, smells, etc., the famous secondary and subjective qualities—rather, we experience things also, and most importantly, as identified by value-qualities, which may be positive or negative.[2]

Here are some examples: this chair I am sitting on is uncomfortable, my grandmother's kitchen knife is blunt, my place is cozy, the town I am living in is chaotic, the dress you are wearing is elegant, my promise to you is sincere, the air this morning is stale and stifling, that seawater is inviting me to swim in it, the person who is speaking with me is gentle, etc.

The qualitative social ontology I am presenting here deals with *the good life of things*-that which is their own, simply in virtue of the value-qualities that identify everything for the thing/what it is: the delicacy of the caress, the sharpness of the knife, the justice of the judge, the lightness of the gymnast, the economical utility of the enterprise, the courage of the warrior, the sweetness of a musical adagio, etc. This does not mean that every knife we deal with is sharp, that every judge is just, that every enterprise is economically productive, and so on. Nevertheless, it does mean that each one of these things, be they natural or artifactual, cultural, institutional, in order to be the thing, it is, has to realize, more or less adequately, the value-qualities that are essential to it. Only if things satisfy this condition can they then be good exemplars of their type, and realize their *ontological paradigm*. Of course, the world is full of knives that do not cut, of enterprises that are not economically productive, of judges who are not just, etc. Nevertheless, this does not imply that to be a good judge, the judge ought not to be just; that to be a good knife, the knife ought not to be sharp; that to be a good enterprise, the enterprise ought not to be economically productive; etc. This perspective, of course, introduces an *ontological gradualism* with respect to the being of things: each thing may be a good or bad exemplar of the type of thing it is; that is, it may have a good or bad life, so to speak, according to its ontological paradigm that everything realizes in its own way and degree.

1.2 An Ontology of the Person and Society

Let us now look more closely at the connection between the personally embedded social ontology and the good life of things—between an ontology of the person applied to social ontology and a qualitative ontology of things. This is a very close connection. Personally embedded qualitative social ontology accounts for the qualitative richness of the things of the world since they are the things we experience personally, in our living and acting as personal subjects, as subjects of personhood.

A personally embedded qualitative social ontology suggests a new form of correlation between subject and object: between a subject who is a person, the persons living together in various forms of collectives (persons embodied in a living body and centers of personal acts: of decisions, value-qualities perception, emotions as affective responses, etc.), and objects that are things perceived as valuable (or valueless) things, as goods (or ills) of various kinds. Indeed, our personal lives develop in position-takings toward things as goods (or ills) of different kinds, and in doing that we become the subject of a motivational life and unfold our personhood. Briefly put, we experience things as valuable things only from a "personal attitude" toward them and the world that contains them.[3] So, my point is that things in the world, be they natural or artifactual, cultural, institutional, are all rich in value-qualities that constitute and identify their being, without value-qualities, things are not the things they are for us. In the natural, spontaneous attitude that we have as personal subjects, we grasp the being of things as an essentially qualitative being.

Each thing we experience in the world is a good (or ill) of some sorts, and our world is full of all kinds of goods (and ills). Each of them is identified by specific value fields; that is, useful value-qualities make useful goods such as artifacts (knives, chairs, cars, computers), vital value-qualities make vital goods (covid vaccines, medical units, the air we breathe and the water we drink), cultural value-qualities make cultural goods (philosophical theories, universities, schools), artistic and aesthetical value-qualities make artistic and aesthetical goods (Matisse's paintings, Jane Austin's novels, the Arese Borromeo Palace and park), moral and juridical values make moral and juridical goods (the Universal Declaration of Human Rights, the Constitution of the Italian State, the law against homotransphobia crimes which in Italy has not yet been promulgated), holy values make holy goods (Mount Olympus, the holy bread, the Torah), etc.[4]

1.3 A New Ontological Paradigm: The Unitary Foundation versus the "Powdered-Sugar Cake" Ontological Paradigm

If value-qualities are constitutive parts of things and are even what makes a thing the thing it is, that is, a valuable thing, a good of a certain kind, then the classical ontological paradigm, let us call it the "powdered-sugar cake ontological paradigm," reveals itself as inadequate to account for the qualitative being of the things. Indeed, the classical ontological paradigm is composed of an existentially independent basic layer, or substratum, which is physical and natural, and by a supervenient layer that is qualitative: it is conceived as an accidental, decorative frill (like the powdered-sugar on the cake) and is existentially dependent on the physical-natural layer, as classically Aristotle (2002) argues for (*Categories*). Under this ontological paradigm, the physical-natural layer is the only one that has the ontological status of reality.

Another new ontological paradigm is needed: the powdered-sugar cake ontological paradigm is unable to explain the compenetrating way in which value-qualities belong to things and individualize them. Things are "unitary foundations" (Husserl 1984, *Third Logic Investigation*, §21), wholes constituted by parts, among which there are also valuable parts, and are characterized by several directions of dependency relations: bottom up, among the parts and from the parts to the whole, and top down, from the whole to the parts—and the parts are not only physical and material but also qualitative parts.[5]

Together with the ontological powdered-sugar cake paradigm, the classical separation between brute or physical and natural facts, on the one hand, and social and cultural facts, on the other hand, also reveals itself to be unjustified: it no longer has its raison d'être. The same occurs with the separation between the natural world and the social world. Indeed, these separations are founded on the powdered-sugar cake paradigm: the social facts are nothing else but a qualitative layer, a "status function" (Searle, 1995, 2010) attributed, conventionally, to things as natural facts: the natural and physical layer of things are the real being of things.

The social world is nothing else but a world that is not natural, so it is not objectively real. All the qualitative is not objectively real: it is just a subjective projection, a mere attribution of the subject on the real things, just some powdered-sugar on a cake that already exists as such. As is well-known, Searle's attempt to give social reality a foundation is as follows: social facts are ontologically subjective but are epistemically objective, that is, intersubjectively recognized and shared. Therefore, the social fact that Joe Biden is the US president is not a private and individual fact, but a social one (Searle 2010).

On the contrary, the personally embedded qualitative social ontology I am outlining, and that I retrace in the phenomenological tradition, goes beyond the separation between natural facts and social facts, and suggests that "social" is everything that has a personal salience for us, and it therefore concerns our unfolding as subjects of personal acts: "social" are even natural entities such as the strawberry plants, when I plant them together with my kids in the garden, and they become a good for our family life—and "social" is not only the kids' enrollment in the swimming course.

1.4 The Personalist and Correlative Claim

Moreover, personally embedded qualitative social ontology shows that what we gain at the level of qualitative ontology, that is, concerning the being of things, also has deep repercussions for the ontology of the person. Indeed, things, as valuable things, are the things we deal with daily in our life as personal subjects. An ontology that accounts for the qualitative being of things also implies a gain on the level of the ontology of the persons who together deal with those valuable things in the world.

Indeed, if things were no longer goods, if their value-qualities were not some of their constitutive parts, if things were just bare things, then we also would cease to exist as personal subjects who experience things as valuable things and would exist simply as psychophysical individuals. I have to clarify this point in addressing the relationship between us as personal subjects and things as valuable things.

Things are valuable things, goods for us who are personal subjects who experience them. As persons, we are subjects of value-perception acts; we live in a world that is not only physical-natural, we live personally in the world we share with others (Husserl 1994, Third Section on the Constitution of the Spiritual Word).[6] The philosophical challenge of the personally qualitative social ontology is accounting for the qualitative being of things as correlates of the qualitative being of ourselves as personal subjects. *A parte subjecti*, things are valuable things for us who experience them. However, our experience is not a sufficient condition but just a necessary one for them to be qualitative things. *A parte objecti*, there is another necessary condition for the qualitative being of things: their ontological structure as unitary foundation. This means that the qualitative being of things is neither a subjective attribution to things nor a being of the thing that is absolutely independent from the relationship with the personal subjects who experience it. Rather, there is a mutual correlation and existentially mutual dependency between the qualitative being of things and the personal being of the subjects.

2. Schapp's Qualitative Social Ontology

Schapp's phenomenology of law belongs to the phenomenological tradition in which qualitative social ontology is embedded—this is one of the main claims of my chapter. Indeed, Schapp's phenomenology of law focuses on the relation between law and values, and more precisely on the foundation of the law in the evaluation of values. It contains an analysis of the ontological status of values, of the sociality of values, and of the sharing of values that undoubtedly involves a new ontological paradigm: values are constitutive qualities of the being of things and persons. In other terms, there is no trace in Schapp of the powdered-sugar cake ontological paradigm; on the contrary, there is a qualitative ontological paradigm in which values are constitutive of the being of things and persons and have an essential role for their existence and individuation. Moreover, Schapp develops an account of the "existential relation," so to speak, between law and values that represents one of the most original ways in which Schapp contributes to qualitative social ontology. Indeed, Schapp's account of the law opens a quite fruitful perspective on the *existential foundation* of the law: the law is grounded on the essential tendency of persons to "enjoy values" (*genießen Werte*), and to "savor values to the full" (*auskosten des Wertes bis zum Letzten*) (Schapp 1930: 12). Persons need to enjoy values in order to have a meaningful existence, and also values need to be enjoyed by persons in order to reach their fullest vitality. This is Schapp's interesting development of the theme of the correlation between persons and valuable things that is, as I have shown, one of the fundamental topics of qualitative social ontology.

More in detail, according to Schapp, the law, and precisely its "pre-givennesses" (*Vorgegebenheit*) or a priori structures such as the "*rational* and *mutual contract*" (*vernünftiger, gegenseitiger Vertrag*) are founded on the existential relation between values and persons, the law arises and develops as the normative tool that allows persons to share values and intensify their enjoyment of values. Therefore, Schapp claims, the "*world of values*" (*Welt der Werte*) constitutes the "*infrastructure*" (*Unterbau*) of the "*rational* and *mutual contract*," that is, of the law.[7] The character of "rational," attributed by Schapp to the contract as "pre-givenness of the law," is based on the fact that the conclusion of the contract by the counterparts is preceded by an evaluation process of values: the contracting parties take the decisions to exchange and share values, in order to enrich their own world of values, after an attentive evaluation of the values in play. Indeed, Schapp points out that there is an essential connection between persons' social and legal acts of mutual promising that perform contracts, and persons' evaluations of the value of things, which make things goods of various types.

In my chapter, I focus on one of the main claims of Schapp's phenomenology of law, which can be summarized in the following way: there are values (both individual and collective values) and they are salient in the everyday life of persons, in which they enjoy values that essentially characterize the being of things and make them a certain type of good (or ill); values are the foundation of the "rational contract," which is a "pre-givenness," that is, an a priori structure, of civil law; so, *values are the "infrastructure" of an a priori structure of the law*; more in general, *values are necessary for law to exist: there is no law if there are no values*.

Moreover, I inquire into the nature of the ground of the relation between values and law in Schapp: I show why this ground is an *existential* one, as it is deeply embedded in the quality of the existence of both persons and things of the world as essentially constituted by values. This existential perspective of Schapp's work on values represents a great contribution for qualitative social ontology and its filling the "qualitative *lacuna*" that characterizes mainstream social ontology.

I concentrate on the first part of Schapp's book, which is devoted to the "The rational contract as pre-givenness" (*Der vernünftige Vertrag als Vorgegebenheit*) (Schapp 1930: 1-67). It is in this part of his work that Schapp develops his original account on the relation between values and the a priori of the law. Within this account, he takes up Reinach's analysis of the essence of social acts (Reinach

1912), in particular the act of promising in its variation of the "mutual promising contract", and he places his phenomenology of law on the trail of Reinach's.

2.1. The Main Thesis on the Essential Relation between Values and Law

The structure of Schapp's main thesis and arguments on the relation between values and law is as follows:

(i) From the viewpoint of the values: there are values; persons enjoy values, evaluate values in their everyday life, and constitute their "world of values" (*Weltwert*); values are the quintessence of the life persons live everyday; persons exchange and share their world of values with other persons, and the "rational-mutual contract" comes into play in this sharing: "the mutual contract consists in the fact that, from the world of values of one, something is transplanted into the world of values of the other and *vice versa*."[8]

(ii) From the viewpoint of the law: there are "pre-givennesses," a priori *structures of the law*, among which, the rational contract; in the rational contract, and, more precisely, in its paradigmatic case of the mutual contract, values are the objects of "evaluations" and "reflections" by the persons who are the part and the counterpart of the contract; then, the contracting parties decide to share their world of values, to take on in their world of values some values of the world of values of the other, in order to enrich them; values and processes of reflection on values are the "infrastructure" of the rational-mutual contract as "pre-givenness" of the law.

Thus, the fundamental elements of Schapp's thesis and arguments are: the crucial role of the existence of values in persons' everyday life, in their enjoyment and evaluation of values, and persons' decision to exchange or share values. These elements together constitute the ground on which the rational-mutual contract takes place as a pre-givenness of the law; more concisely, the rational-mutual contract as a priori structure of the law is grounded in the values and in the reflection processes of persons on values.

As already mentioned above, it is necessary to highlight that, accordingly with such thesis and arguments, Schapp's foundation of the law in values, which are considered the quintessence of persons' everyday life, has the character of an *existential foundation*.[9] The law is rooted in something that deeply characterizes the existence of human persons and makes of it a meaningful existence, that is, values. This is a perspective of correlation in a double direction. Indeed, one correlation is that between persons and their personal attitude to enjoy values, on the one hand, and values as ontologically constitutive of the things of the world, on the other; the other correlation is that between persons and their need to exchange and share values in order to savor them to the full, on the one hand, and the law that in its constitutive form of rational contract is founded on values and valuable things that persons share and exchange, on the other. This is an extremely original perspective on the foundations of the law that manifestly provides a great contribution to the phenomenologically embedded qualitative social ontology.

2.2 The Ontological Status of Values

However, it should be noted that there is an intrinsic problem in Schapp's account of the foundation of law on values. This is Schapp's *confusion between values and goods*, that is, between values and valuable things, the things which are the bearers of values. Such confusion is a critical point in Schapp's theory of values and the a priori of the law: ultimately, is it goods or, rather, values which constitute the foundation of the law? Is it the sharing of values or rather the sharing of goods (which are the bearers of values) that has to be normed by the rational-mutual contract?

Schapp does not develop a theory of values comparable to the very extended, fine-grained, and exhaustive theory of values presented by Max Scheler in his masterpiece, *Formalism in Ethics and Non-formal Ethics of Values* (1954).[10] Schapp just outlines an account of values as grounds of the rational-mutual contract and of the positive law in general. Thus, Schapp's theoretical contribution on values is partial, in the sense that his main focus is on the law and not on values: values play the role of counterpart of the law within the frame of Schapp's theory of the law (it is no coincidence that the title of Schapp's work is *The New Science of Law* and that "*Values*" does not occur in the title).

Thus, let us focus on the ontological status of values in Schapp's phenomenology of law.

The following quotation presents some of the main claims characterizing Schapp's idea of values:

> Was unter Wert zu verstehen ist, ist leichter zu fühlen, als begrifflich zu umgrenzen. Der Wert ist irgendwie ein Akzent der wertvollen Gegenständlichkeit. Er ist selbst

> aber nicht der Gegenstand theoretischer Betrachtung, sondern in eigenartiger Weise etwas Gegenständliches an dem Wertvollen, welches im Genuß erfahren wird. Dies „Genießen" ist etwas ganz anderes, als sich theoretisch mit einem Gegenstand beschäftigen. (Schapp 1930: 7)

2.2.1. *Values are Qualities of the Valuable Objectivity That Are Experienced in Enjoyment and Known in Savoring*

Values are "an accent of the valuable objectuality," and, therefore, are not to be identified with valuable objectivity. In other words, *values must be distinguished from their bearers*, from goods that are valuable objectivities.

The distinction between values and goods is very important for preserving a transcendence of the type of the value with respect to its instantiations in goods: without such distinction, a value, for instance, friendship, would be identified with a certain instantiation of friendship in a certain bearer.[11] Unfortunately Schapp is not sufficiently rigorous with regard to this claim. As already said, he often seems to confuse values and goods and to speak of goods instead of values. For instance, he speaks of people dear to one's heart as values or of a cathedral as a value: they are, of course, bearers of values, goods in which values such as love, friendship, and religiousness, are embedded but they are not values themselves (Schapp 1930: 13, 20).

A value "is experienced in enjoyment." In effect, values are not the object of a theoretical consideration: enjoying values is very different from focusing on objects theoretically. Thus, the intentional mode of grasping values is an affective mode. Values are enjoyed through the "capacity of enjoying" (*Genußfähigkeit*) that belongs to the field of feeling and not to the field of cognizing and that, as a capacity, can be adequate or inadequate, and can be increased or decreased.[12] Values are grasped by *enjoying* and are objectified, "known" (in a very different sense of theoretical knowledge), by *savoring*. Schapp states two axioms about the enjoying and savoring of values: "Without enjoyment, values cannot be grasped by persons" and "without savoring (*Kosten*), any value can be objectified" (Schapp 1930: 9).

2.2.2. *There Are Values but Also Disvalues*

Besides values, there are also *disvalues* (*Unwerte*). Disvalues are not enjoyed. Rather, they are borne. For instance, "we bear a pain. Pain as quality has the character of a disvalue" (Schapp 1930: 10)[13] that is, pain is a disvalue.

There is a broad parallel between values and disvalues and between "valuable objectuality" (*wertvollere Gegenständlichkeit*) and "disvaluable objectuality" (*unwertvollere Gegenständlichkeit*) (Schapp 1930: 9-10).[14] "The world of values and disvalues is the actual world we live in," it is the quintessence of our life. "Without values, the world would be just a scheme, something purely mathematical which has no interest for us" (Schapp 1930: 11).[15] Our personal life is marked by our relationship with values and disvalues: we do not experience things as mere physical things, individuated solely, according to the Galilean tradition, by so-called primary, objective qualities, which are the objects of physics and mathematics, or as mere sensory things identified by so-called secondary qualities, the ones correlated to our sensory perception. On the contrary, we always experience things also as (positively or negatively) valuable things. This is a strong claim by Schapp that indubitably places his account on values in the frame of qualitative social ontology (see *supra*, §1.1), and recalls the claims of Scheler (1973), Husserl (1994, 2002), and Stein (1922) on the qualitative being of the things in our lifeworld.

2.2.3. *Values Exist Independently of Persons' Enjoyment, but Their Meaningful Existence Depends on Persons' Enjoyment*

According to Schapp, *the existence of values is independent of persons' enjoyment of the values*, just as the existence of objects is independent of whether or not they are perceived by persons (see Schapp 1930: 12).[16] However, the *meaningful existence of values is dependent on persons' enjoyment of them*: "values that are not enjoyed fail to achieve their purpose in relation to human beings" (Schapp 1930: 11).[17] Thus, very interestingly, Schapp distinguishes between the *existence of values*, on the one hand, and the *meaningful existence of values*, on the other. Schapp's argument for this claim is that our enjoyment of values can be more or less complete, that is, more or less adequate. So, there are degrees in enjoying values–just as there are degrees in knowing objects (see Schapp 1930: 11).[18] The crucial point is that values achieve their "fullest vitality" (*vollste Lebendigkeit*) only when they are savored to the full by persons (see Schapp 1930: 12).[19] So, *values exist fully only on condition they are savored to the full.*

Schapp's claim regarding the meaningful existence of values extends the concept of existence and of existential dependence to the idea of "quality of existence." Values that are not savored to the full do not have a satisfactory and vital existence. The consideration of the quality of the existence of an entity—and not only of its mere existence or inexistence—is a fundamental topic of qualitative social ontology, a topic which is unfortunately neglected in the mainstream social ontology of the analytic philosophy tradition.[20] Indeed, even one of the most complete social ontological theories, that of Searle, neglects this point. Searle intends to explain how social and institutional reality is created and maintained in existence, but he does not address the issue of the quality of that existence (see Searle 1995, 2010).

Moreover, Schapp's idea of the meaningful existence of values as depending on a person's enjoyment is also a very original and fruitful way in which Schapp elaborates on the qualitative social ontology's fundamental issue of the essential correlation between values and persons' experience of values. Values exist independently of a person's enjoyment, but they exist fully only when they are adequately enjoyed by persons, and the other way around. Let us explore Schapp's idea of such correlation in greater depth.

2.2.4. The Interdependence between the Quality of Existence of Values and Persons

Schapp suggests that the greatest importance of enjoying values for human persons is that "from this enjoyment flows a force for the rest of human life in the most varied directions" (Schapp 1930: 12).[21] "The *enjoyment of values seems to be the actual source of life*, which supports life and by which life creates the strength and the courage to live on" (Schapp 1930: 13).[22] In other words, through enjoying values, the existence of human persons gains fullness and vital energy: Schapp points out the interdependence between the *quality of the existence of values* that are enjoyed to the full, and the *quality of the existence of persons* who savor values to the full; savoring values to the full brings forth both the fullest aliveness of values and the fullest life force of persons.[23]

Schapp's account of the ontological status of values is both a *realistic and existential* one. It is *realistic* because values are considered as real entities that inhabit our lifeworld and that we experience as value-qualities of the things of the world. It is also an *existential* account because the *quality of the existence of both values and human persons depends the one on the other*: in order to have a meaningful existence, values need to be savored to the full, and correlatively human persons need to savor values to the full; only if this condition is satisfied can both values and human persons reach their fullest vitality, that is, have a *good life*. Indeed, this issue of the "fullest vitality" (*vollste Lebendigkeit*) of values and persons is the original way in which Schapp declines the qualitative social ontology issue of the *good life* of things and persons (see *supra*, §1.1.). I will show soon how this qualitative-existential character of the being of values and persons is essentially connected with the existential character of the law in Schapp's account (see *infra*, §2.4.).

2.3. The Sociality of Values

To sum up: I have dwelt upon the ontological *status* of values and highlighted the need of values to be savored to the full, and the need of human persons to savor values to the full, a mutual need on which Schapp insists strongly: only if this need is satisfied, can the existence of the persons and things of the world as valuable things, that is, as things ontologically constituted by values, reach its fullest vitality, that is, can be a real good life. I now address the correlated issue of the sociality of values: Schapp highlights the pervasiveness of values in the existence of both singular individuals and collectives: without values, social life would not be possible; among values, there are specifically "collective values" and values which can be shared and exchanged.

2.3.1. Values and Persons' Social Life

Where are values? Where do we enjoy values? According to Schapp, values are firstly in the human persons we deal with and live with. Persons are *valuable individuals*. Schapp means both the single individual and multiple collective forms which persons give rise to and in which they live together: environment, town, country, etc (see Schapp 1930: 13).[24]

Besides values, Schapp also focuses on *value relations* (*Wertbeziehungen*), which take place in and with all these kinds of collective forms and are constitutive of peoples' *social life*: "value relations, which of course are mutual relations, are the social life indeed. Without value relations, it would not make sense to speak of social life" (Schapp 1930: 13).[25] Without the value relations of social life, peoples' lives would be very meager: "it is enough to consider what the life of a single individual would lose, if in his/her life there were no more playing children, no more women and men we care about" (Schapp 1930: 13).[26] Schapp's claim is true: without social life's value relations, grounded in intersubjective and interpersonal relations, our lives would be very meager indeed. Values pervade our existence, and the persons we deal with and live with are themselves bearers of values.

It needs to be pointed out that the examples of the value relations of social life presented by Schapp are still characterized by Schapp's confusion between values and goods: the "playing children" and the "women and men we care about" are neither examples of values nor of value relations as such; rather, they are examples of goods that realize values or value relations. The problem is that Schapp does not distinguish between the *value* as such and the *bearer* of the value that is a *valuable objectuality*, a *good*. So, coming back to Schapp's examples, he does not distinguish between *love* as a value and my wife as a bearer of love, as a good in which the value *love* is embodied, and, moreover, he does not distinguish between *love* as the type of the value *love* and *love* as the token of the value love, which is embodied in my wife. Similarly, he does not distinguish between *vital energy* as a value and my playing children as bearers of such vitality, that is, as a good in which the value *vitality* is embodied.

2.3.2. Collective Values as a Specific Class of Values

Nevertheless, Schapp's analysis of values is very precious and insightful, he addresses the issue of *collective values* as values that can be *enjoyed only collectively* and that cannot be enjoyed by a single individual. He points out that there are *values that are essentially collective*: values that can be enjoyed only by a community of individuals together. Examples of collective values are a town's cathedral (see Schapp 1930: 20),[27] and more generally, values connected to the state: the state itself is a collective value. According to Schapp, cathedrals and states are examples of collective values because they require the "converging of many individuals" (*Zusammengehen von vielen*) (for instance, the religious community, in the case of the cathedral, or the citizens) to be adequately enjoyed. Thus, *collective values need to be enjoyed collectively* in order to be enjoyed adequately, that is, in order to be fully savored and to reach their fullest vitality. Collective values have to be distinguished from *values that can be enjoyed by more than one individual, but that do not need to be enjoyed collectively*. For instance, the sunset may be a value for many individuals, but everyone can enjoy this value individually, solitarily, without sharing anything with others (see Schapp: 25).[28]

Schapp's distinction between collective values that need to be enjoyed collectively, and values that can be enjoyed both individually and collectively, is a very perspicuous and original insight for social ontology. However, a question is not answered by Schapp, a question typically addressed by philosophers interested in the topic of collective intentionality: in the case of collective values, who, ultimately, is the subject of collective intentionality? Who is the subject who enjoys collective values? Is that subject the individuals within the community or rather the community itself? More in general: Is there a genuine collective-we or only the sum of individual-Is (see Schapp 1930: 20)?[29]

Moreover, we should point out that Schapp continues to confuse values and goods. He does not distinguish between religiousness as value and the cathedral as the bearer of the community's religiousness, as good in which the religiousness is embedded, and he does not even distinguish between religiousness as a value-type, and religiousness as a value-token that is embodied in the cathedral.

2.3.3. Sharing Values

It is in virtue of the possibility of exchanging, transferring, and sharing values that there can be collective values. Schapp tackles the problem of the collective intentional modes by which values can be shared by persons and transferred from one person to another. This is a crucial point of Schapp's account of the foundation of the law in values.

According to Schapp, each person has their own world of values, and that world of values is characterized by a great variety (see Schapp 1930: 21):[30] the sunrise in my birthplace, the people I love to meet, and an infinity of other things (see Schapp 1930: 21).[31] Now, the point is that the *world of values of the one can be shared with and enriched by the world of values of the other*: the values of a person can be exchanged with, transferred to, and shared with the values of another person. "There is the possibility to supply certain values to others, to transfer values to others [. . .]. I can in some way facilitate others in accessing the values. I can point out to others the values which they have chanced upon without having assumed them into their world of values."[32]

Schapp very interestingly claims that the sharing of values does not imply a diminishment of the values for the person who is sharing her world of values with another person. *Shared values* are not decreased values; rather, they are *increased values*: "*a shared joy is a doubled joy*" (Schapp 1930: 23).[33] Indeed, under Schapp's perspective, a shared joy is no longer only the joy I feel or the joy you feel, singularly, the shared joy is the joy we feel together that is therefore a doubled joy since it is no longer one single joy. It is the joy that is personally felt by me and the joy that is personally felt by you, but on the contrary, it is the joy felt by me with respect to you and the joy felt by you with respect to me. Actually, Schapp does not dwell on this in order to clarify exactly how it can happen, but we know from phenomenological analyses on empathy that empathy and reflexive empathy are some of the principal ways in which individual feelings may become collective feelings (Stein 2008, section on "The essence of acts of empathy," shows this very well).

Moreover, Schapp points out that persons can share their world of values in a very strong sense of sharing that brings forth a unitary world of values which is enjoyed by more than one person at a time. For instance, the worlds of values belonging to a husband and a wife build together a "unitary world of values" that the two individuals "enjoy as a unity."[34] Here Schapp mentions, without analyzing it, a very important feature of the sharing of values: sharing values creates social unity. This is a crucial issue for a social ontology that inquires into the problem of the stability and solidity of collectives: sharing values makes collectives stable and solid.[35] However, Schapp does not inquire into the problem of *what it really means to share values*. What does it mean to share a "unitary world of values" and to enjoy it "as a unity"? Can all kinds of values be shared? The neglect of these problems is also due to the fact that Schapp is still confusing values and goods, and now even values and feelings. Schapp speaks of sharing one's own world of values with the world of values of another individual, but in his examples, what is shared seems to be more like the bearers of values (goods) or feelings, than values themselves—for instance, the cathedral, the sunrise, the people I love to meet, etc., and joy. Fortunately, Scheler's axiology can help us to outline an answer to these issues. Indeed, it includes not only a very accurate distinction of values and goods but also a very precise analysis of what kinds of values can be shared and what not. According to Scheler, there are sharable values, such as cultural, moral, aesthetical values (values of the person) and the values of the holy, on the one hand, and values that are not sharable and that can only be divided, such as "values of the sensibly agreeable" and economic values. The former can be shared without any diminution of their being, and their sharing even increases social unity among the persons who share them: in this sense, the sharing of these values constitutes an intensification, a doubling in Schapp's perspective, of the experience of values. On the contrary, the latter can only be divided, and their division involves a diminution of the values and creates conflict of interest and social divisions between the persons who want to divide them. Thus, by applying Scheler's insights to Schapp's account, the collective experience of divisible values could not involve an augmentation of the value's experience: no doubling of value, but, on the contrary, its diminution (Scheler 1954: 111-112;).[36]

Nevertheless, both the points Schapp makes, that is, the one on the sharing of values as implying an increase of the enjoyed values, and the other on enjoying two different worlds of values as "a unitary world of values," are very important and original points of Schapp's qualitative social ontology, and they play a crucial role for Schapp's argument for the foundations of the law on values. It is because shared values are doubly enjoyed values, and it is because persons are able to acquire values from one another (in sharing and exchanging them), to enjoy the acquired values as their own values and build a unitary world of values, which is enjoyed as a unity, that persons who need to savor values to the full in order to achieve a meaningful existence, tend essentially to share and exchange values with other persons, and therefore, they perform mutual contracts.

2.4. The Passage from Values to Law

I have addressed the issues of the ontological status of values and of the sociality of values in Schapp's account of values. As I have just pointed out, these two issues constitute the two necessary steps for Schapp's foundation of the law in values. I deal now with the issue of the relation between values and the law, between the "world of values" and the "rational mutual contract" (Schapp 1930: 26), that is with the decisive passage from values to law.

2.4.1. The Creation and Enrichment of Worlds of Values, and the Foundation of the Law

> Dies Verschaffen von Werten, die Bereicherung einer anderen Wertwelt durch meine Handlung, ist ein Hauptgebiet der Jurisprudenz. Daß diese Möglichkeit besteht, ist eine Vorgegebenheit für die Jurisprudenz. Zwei große Gebiete der Wertwelt, in welchen diese gegenseitige Bereicherung möglich ist, haben die Römer kurz mit ihren Ausdrücken *jus commercii* und *jus connubii* angedeutet. Ein anderes Hauptgebiet der Jurisprudenz ist der Schutz der dem Ich zugeordneten Wertwelt gegen Beeinträchtigung, das Recht der unerlaubten Handlung. Die enge Beziehung dieses Teils der Jurisprudenz zur Moral leuchtet von selbst ein. *In einem Kosmos, der keine Werte enthielte, würde die Jurisprudenz den größten teil ihrer Bedeutung, wenn nicht alle Bedeutung verlieren.* (Schapp 1930: 22)

The above quotation encapsulates the main claims advanced by Schapp on the relation between the creation and enrichment of the world of values, and on the foundation of the law in its pre-givennesses, which are rooted in the essential relation between qualitative existence of values and persons.

Schapp's general claim is on the *dependence of the law on values: without values, jurisprudence would not make sense*: "the creation of values and the enrichment of the world of values of the one through the activity of the other is the main field of jurisprudence." This possibility of "mutual enrichment" of one's own world of values is a "pre-givenness for jurisprudence."

More in detail, Shapp also advances a historical claim: the ancient Romans used the legal expressions *jus commerci* and *jus connubi* for two great domains of mutual enrichment of the world of values. Moreover, he affirms that there are other pre-givennesses of the law, like the pre-givenness that norms "the protection of the world of values belonging to a person against damage": "the law of the forbidden action," that is, penal law. Finally, he advances a strong claim on the relation between law and morals: he suggests that the law is grounded in morality. The foundation of the law in values is ultimately a foundation of law in moral values, at least as regards the domain of law concerning the protection of the world of values, that is, the "law of the forbidden action": "The close relation of this aspect of jurisprudence with the Moral is manifest." Unfortunately, Schapp's account of values and his analysis of the different kinds of values we enjoy—be they moral, aesthetical, religious values, etc.—is not sufficient for providing an adequate justification of his claim on the foundation of the law in morality. One could easily object that the law may even be grounded in moral disvalues, as some positive laws of the human history show.

In general, it should be noted that Schapp's claims here are weakened in their credibility by the same problem I have already pointed out several times: Is Schapp actually speaking of values, or rather of goods? When he speaks of *jus commerci* and *jus connubi*, is he not rather talking about goods that are exchanged and shared? These goods are, of course, bearers of values, and their exchange or sharing may constitute the creation of a new world of values or the enrichment of preexisting worlds of values, but they are primarily goods, and not values.

2.4.2. From the Worlds of Values to the Rational-Mutual Contract: "Infrastructure," "Superstructure" and a Priori Structures of the Law

Let us now examine in more detail the passage from the worlds of values of two persons to the mutual contract between them: "The rational-mutual contract consists in the fact that from the world of values of the one something is transplanted into the world of values of the other, and the converse." The worlds of values and the exchange between the worlds of values constitute the ground for the rational-mutual contract: "without relation to a world of value, the mutual contract makes no sense" (Schapp 1930: 27).[37] Now, the question to address is how that exchange between the worlds of values can take place. Schapp's answer is that *the exchange between worlds of values takes place through the law*: the law norms the practice of the exchange of values (see Schapp 1930: 27).[38]

> If two pieces of two worlds of values are to be exchanged, the one with the other, then *the question is how that exchange happens*. According to the ignorant, nothing is easier than this. *From that exchange, the jurist has made a science, which is treated in rather developed laws in thousands of paragraphs*. For the

> jurist, the way of the exchange is the *mutual contract*. [. . .] The requirement for the mutual contract is the particular relation of two worlds of values, in which a piece of the one urges to be exchanged with a piece of the other. We define this requirement as the *infrastructure* of the mutual contract, while the exchange itself represents the *superstructure*. (Schapp 1930: 28)[39]

According to Schapp, the legal figure that regulates the exchange between two different worlds of values is the rational-mutual contract. The worlds of values and the relation between two worlds of values that are about to exchange something constitute the motivational requirement for the mutual contract: indeed, they are the ground or the "*infrastructure* of the mutual contract," while "the exchange itself represents the *superstructure*" of the mutual contract.

Schapp describes very concretely the process that flows from the world of values of (at least) two persons into the conclusion of the mutual contract.

Firstly, "in the mind of the individuals who are involved in the performance of the mutual contract, a series of reflections (*Überlegungen*) take place": these reflections are "evaluations" (*Wertungen* or *Abschätzungen*) of the values in play (Schapp 1930: 2). The persons involved in the contract evaluate whether and how the exchange of values can enrich their own world of values.

Secondly, based on those evaluations, some decisions (*Entschlüsse*) are taken. These decisions lead to the will-declarations (*Willenserklärungen*).

Third, the will-declarations represent the moment in which the evaluations of values and the following decisions on the values to exchange are made known by the contracting parties to each other. The moment of the declaration and of the making known represents the superstructure of the contract: "in any contract, the infrastructure (*Unterbau*) consists in the evaluations (*Abschätzungen*) of the values to exchange (*umsetzen*), and the superstructure (*Oberbau*) consists in the making known (*Kundgeben*) which produces that exchange (*Umsetzung*)" (Schapp 1930: 34).[40]

Schapp points out that "the *will-declarations*," in which the superstructure of the contract consists, "are not, in fact, just any will-declarations; rather, they are *social acts* (*soziale Akte*)" (Schapp 1930: 40),[41] and that the *mutual contract* is precisely a variation of the social act of promising: it is a *mutual act of promising*. Thus, just as promising produces an *obligation* and a *claim*, so also the mutual promising-contract (*gegenseitiger Versprechensvertrag*) brings forth a *claim* and an *obligation* that arise in the parts involved in the contract, independently from any positive law.[42]

According to Schapp, all the forms that the mutual contract can assume, as for instance, the "buying contract" and the wedding contract, are not dependent on positive law and "are not obtained through universalization of the known positive laws." Rather, these forms constitute "the foundations of any positive law": "the positive law finds these forms and chooses the forms which seems to it appropriate and gives to such forms a more important meaning" (Schapp 1930: 356).[43] In other words, all the typical forms of the mutual contract are a priorilegal forms.

Finally, Schapp identifies the *Rechtsfigur* of any kind of mutual contract: this would be a *whole* (*Ganze*) whose parts (*Teile*) are the *infrastructure* (worlds of values, evaluations of the values, the urge to exchange values, decisions to exchange values) and the *superstructure* (utterances of decisions and declarations of will) of the rational-mutual contract that brings forth *obligations and claims* (see Schapp 1930: 63-64).

2.4.3. The Existential Character of the Law and the Essential Tendency of Human Persons to Savor Values to the Full

It is in *values' need to be savored to the full* and in *human persons' need to savor values to the full* that Schapp lays the *foundations of the law in values*: it is because the meaningful existence of values and that of human persons are so interconnected and interdependent upon each other, that the law and, even more so, the "pre-givennesses" of the law exist. It is in virtue of the mutual dependence of the quality of existence of values and of the quality of existence of human persons that the law, whose raison d'être is to regulate the relation between values and human persons, is characterized by pre-givenness, that is, a priori structures that precede and are independent of the institution of any positive law.

The need of values to be savored to the full and the need of human persons to savor values to the full, on which Schapp builds his account of the ontological *status* of values, and consequently, his foundation of the pre-givenness of the law in values, raises the issue of the significance of this need. This need is a tendency that is essential for the being of values and human persons: the satisfaction of such a need is a necessary condition for the meaningful existence of both values and persons. This need implies that without values, there is no personal existence worthy of being lived and no rational-mutual contract worthy to be concluded. As already noted, the concept of "existence" involved here by Schapp is always a qualitative one: it is the quality of existence of persons as well as the quality of the existence of mutual contract based on the quality of existence of values. Indeed, Schapp is not interested in the conditions of a merely physical, space-time individuated existence, be it that of human persons, values, or the rational-mutual contract. Schapp's phenomenology of law has therefore, the great merit of showing that the law is a human and "personal issue," not in the sense of a subjective and relativistic issue, but in the sense that its fundament is the qualitative and motivational, but constitutively pre-given, structure of the existence of persons.

It is because human persons tend essentially to savor values to the full in order to make their existence a meaningful one, that they tend to evaluate their world of values and the world of values of other persons, that they tend to take decisions on certain values to be exchanged with other persons, that they tend to declare such decisions to each other, and so tend to perform mutual contracts. None of these passages is necessary, but still, each of these passages is motivationally grounded in that essential tendency of human persons.

In other words, Schapp's idea of the existence of "pre-givennesses" of the law, that is, the idea of the existence of legal structures that preexist the positive law and are a priori with respect to the positive law, is a humanly and anthropologically deep-rooted idea: there are pre-givennesses of the law because the meaningful existence of both values and persons depends one upon the other, and the law, in particular the rational-mutual contract, regulates the process by which values can be savored to the full by persons, and persons can savor values to the full. Indeed, the need of human persons to savor values to the full leads them to exchange and share values, and, by doing so, human persons satisfy also the need of values to be savored to the full. This is the fundament on which the rational-mutual contract takes place, as a pre-givenness of the law that permits the regulation of those sharing and exchanging of values.

Schapp's phenomenology of law opens up a perspective on the *existential foundation* of the law, grounded on the essential tendency of human persons to savor values to the full, on the one hand, and on the *relation of motivation* between values and the rational-mutual contract, on the other, that represents the beginning of a completely new and compelling inquiry by social ontology into the *quality* of the existence of legal entities.

Notes

1 I coined and used for the first time the expression "qualitative social ontology" in De Vecchi (2016a), and then, I developed my account of a qualitative social

ontology phenomenologically embedded in De Vecchi (2017), (2020), 2022), (2024). I previously worked on Schapp's phenomenology of law, precisely on its a priori foundation of the law and its relation with Reinach's *A priori foundations of the civil law*, in De Vecchi (2016b), where I also pointed out Schapp's position in the phenomenological tradition. In this chapter, I take up again the work I have already done, and I develop it further by placing it in the frame of the qualitative social ontology.

2 This is a thesis shared by Husserl 1994: Third section, Stein 1922, Scheler 1954. I further developed this thesis as one of the main theses of the qualitative social ontology in De Vecchi 2022. It needs to be pointed out that Husserl's position about values is less clear-cut than that of Stein and Scheler. See, for instance Husserl's *Crisis of the European Sciences*, where he limits himself against the Galilean mathematization of the *plena*, to a rehabilitation of the solely sensory qualities and also not of value-qualities in his account of the lifeworld (Husserl 1976); see the distinction he continues to make between "real predicates" (*reale Prädikate*) that are sensory and natural qualities and "meaning predicates" (*Bedeutungsprädikate*) that are cultural qualities in *Nature and Geist* (Husserl 2002: 124–5), and see also how he continuously returns to and addresses the issue of the ontological status of value-qualities without reaching a definitive position, in his manuscripts on *Gefühl und Wert* (Husserl 2020).

3 On the personal or "personalistic attitude," see Husserl 1994: Third section on *The constitution of the spiritual world.*

4 Of course, the main reference here for the idea of different spheres of value is Scheler (1954).

5 I do not have time here to develop this point on the structure of the wholes as unitary foundation, see De Vecchi 2022, Ch. II.

6 The "personally living" has to be distinguished from the "naturalistic way of living": on the one hand, we live in the personal attitude that is our natural attitude toward the world, on the other hand, we can also assume a "naturalistic way of living" that extracts all the qualitative from things, as it is irreducible to the data of positive sciences (Husserl 1976, 1994).

7 This is also the title of the second chapter of the first part of Schapp's book: *Der Unterbau des gegenseitigen Vertrages. Die Welt der Werte.*

8 "Der vernünftige gegenseitige Vertrag besteht nun darin, daß aus der Wertwelt des andern etwas verpflanzt wird und umgekehrt" (Schapp 1930: 27).

9 In the philosophy of law, existential, and phenomenological approaches to the foundations of the law are, among others, those of Bobbio (1934), Weil (1949), Cossio (1983), Hersch (2008).

10 Very surprisingly, Schapp does not refer to Scheler at all and behaves as if Scheler's phenomenology of values (Scheler 1954) did not exist, see Schapp 1930: 184.

Schapp's neglect of Scheler's account constitutes a real theoretical *lacuna* in his theory. If he had considered Scheler's account, he would have avoided problems like the confusion, or the insufficiently clear distinction, between values and goods. Schapp's neglect of Scheler is truly puzzling because Schapp was aware of Scheler's account on values, see Schapp 1959.

11 Scheler's characterization of values implies a very strong distinction between values and goods, see Scheler 1954: First part, first section on "Materiale Wertethik und Guter-Respektive Zweckethik," §1 on "Guter und Werte."

12 See Schapp 1930: 7. It is necessary to remark that the early phenomenologists' works on values had already identified the act of grasping values as an affective act, the so-called "*Wertfühlen*," and spoke of a capability to grasp values which can be more or less developed, and in some cases not developed at all (as is the case of blindness to values). Concerning all these issues, see Scheler (1954), Hildebrand (1916 and 1922) and Reinach (2012).

13 "Wir erleiden z.B. einen Schmerz. Der Schmerz als Qualität hat dabei den Charakter des Unwertes" (Schapp 1930: 10).

14 Also concerning the issue of the double polarity of the world of values, positive values and negative disvalues, see Scheler (1954), Hildebrand (1916 and 1922) and Reinach (2012).

15 "Diese Welt der Werte und der Unwerte ist die eigentliche Welt in welcher wir leben. [. . . .] Ohne diese Werte wäre sozusagen die Welt nur noch ein Schema, etwas rein Mathematisches ohne jedes Interesse für uns" (Schapp 1930: 11).

16 "Der Gegenstand hat diesen Wert, auch wenn er zufällig nicht genossen wird, ebenso wie der Gegenstand existiert, d.h. nach unserer Meinung existiert, auch wenn er nicht wahrgenommen wird" (Schapp 1930: 12).

17 "Die Werte, welche nicht genossen werden, haben für den Menschen ihren Zweck verfehlt" (Schapp 1930: 11).

18 "Ebenso wie die Erkenntnis dem Gegenstande mehr oder weniger adäquat sein kann, kann auch das Genießen mehr oder weniger vollkommen sein" (Schapp 1930: 11).

19 "Diesen Begriff der Adäquatheit müssen wir festhalten. Er bedeutet ein Auskosten des Wertes bis zum Letzten. Erst im so verstandenen Genuß erreicht der Wert die vollste für ihn mögliche Lebendigkeit" (Schapp 1930: 12).

20 It is worth noting that Reinach makes a similar observation on the quality of existence of claim and obligation: the meaningful existence of claims and obligations is the one which is satisfied by the corresponding realizing action, by which they end their existence "in a natural way" and thus, are not compelled to last in senseless agony. This quality of the existence of claim and obligation is something inscribed in the ontological paradigm of these entities, see Reinach 2012: 32). On this passage by Reinach, see De Vecchi (2013), and on the issue of the "quality of

the existence" and of "degrees of existence" in Reinach (2012) and also in Stein (1925), see De Vecchi (2016a) and (2017). More in general, I developed the issue of "qualitative existence" in De Vecchi 2022: first chapter.

21 "von diesem Genießen strömt eine Kraft aus für das weitere Leben nach den verschiedensten Richtungen" (Schapp 1930: 12).

22 "Das Genießen scheint vielmehr daneben noch der eigentliche Lebensquell zu sein, welcher das Leben trägt, aus dem das Leben Kraft und Mut zum Weiterlebe schöpft" (Schapp 1930: 13).

23 See the similar concept of "*Lebenskraft*," presented by Stein (1922).

24 "Dasselbe Verhältnis findet aber nicht nur dem Einzelnen gegenüber statt, sondern der ganzen Umgebung gegenüber, die Kreise, in dem wir leben, der Stadt, in der wir leben, dem Lande in dem wir leben, der Zeit, in der wir leben" (Schapp 1930: 13). See similarly Husserl's idea of the constitution of the social and cultural world (Husserl 1994: §51).

25 "Wertbeziehungen, welche natürlich gegenseitig sind, sind in Wirklichkeit das soziale Leben. Ohne sie hätte es keinen Sinn, von sozialem Leben zu sprechen" (Schapp 1930: 13). See also Husserl's idea of social reality as grounded in mutual intersubjective and interpersonal relations, Husserl 1994: §51.

26 "Man braucht sich nur vorzustellen, was das Leben des Einzelnen verlieren würde, wenn es keine spielenden Kinder, keine Frauen, keine Männer von Bedeutung in seinem Leben mehr geben würde" (Schapp 1930: 13).

27 "Man könnte fragen, ob es überhaupt werte gibt, welche der einzelne für sich allein nicht genießen kann, welche nur die Gemeinschaft in der Gemeinschaft voll genießen kann. Zu solchen Werten scheint z.B. ein Dom oder ein Münster zu gehören" (Schapp 1930: 20).

28 "Für das Wesen des Staates scheint es uns nun eine Hauptfrage zu sein, ob irgend etwas zum Staate Gehörendes Eigenwert für den Menschen hat und in welcher Weise es diesen Eigenwert hat, ob etwa in der Weise, wie der Sonnenuntergang für viele seinen Eigenwert hat, so dass jeder Einzelne ihn genießen kann, oder eher in der Art des Münsters und Gottes, dass ein Zusammengehen von vielen, ein Zusammengehen der gläubigen Gemeinde dazu gehört, um die Werte auszuschöpfen" (Schapp 1930: 25).

29 "Ob dabei der Einzelne in der Gemeinschaft geniest oder ob es Sinn hat, zu sagen, dass die Gemeinschaft genießt, wagen wir nicht zu entscheiden" (Schapp 1930: 20). The problem of the identity of the subject of collective intentionality, whether a "collective subject," a "group mind," or rather only single individuals as the bearers of collective intentionality, is a crucial problem in studies of collective intentionality. To cite only a few of the main philosophers' positions on this issue, see Searle (1995) and (2010), Tuomela and Miller (1988), Gilbert (1989) and (2014). In the phenomenological domain, see the analysis of the "common person" (*Gemeingeist*)

by Husserl (1994, §51), of "collective person" (*Gesamtperson*) by Scheler (1954), of "Individual and Community" (*Individuum und Gemeinschaft*) by Stein (1922).

30 "Wir haben davon gesprochen, daß eine Wertwelt einer bestimmten Seele zugeordnet sei und daß diese Wertwelt von der größten Mannigfaltigkeit sei" (Schapp 1930: 21).

31 "Zu dieser mir zugeordneten Wertwelt gehört der Sonnenaufgang, den ich von Spitzengewebe der Wall-Allee dazu, welche in Winter auf dem lichten Hintergrund in immer neuen Münstern und Formen sich abhebt. [. . .] es gehören dazu die Menschen, denen ich gern begegne, kurz, es gehört eine Unendlichkeit dazu" (Schapp 1930: 21).

32 "Demgegenüber scheint die Möglichkeit, andern solche Werte zu verschaffen, auf andere Werte zu übertragen [. . . .]. Ich kann wohl anderen auf manche Art und Weise den Zugang zu Werten erleichtern. Ich kann sie auf Werte hinweisen, an welchen sie vorübergehen, ohne sie in ihre Wertwelt aufgenommen zu haben" (Schapp 1930: 21).

33 "Ein Wertkomplex, welcher einer Person zugeordnet ist, kann zugleich einer andern Person zugeordnet sein, ohne daß [. . .] der Wert dieses zugeordneten Komplexes für den einzelnen Beteiligten sich mindert, er kann sich sogar durch die Beteilung mehren. Geteilte Freude ist doppelte Freude" (Schapp 1930: 23).

34 "Die dem Mann und der Frau zugeordneten Wertwelten bilden in Wirklichkeit zum großen Teil eine einheitliche Wertwelt, welche zwei zugleich als Einheit genießen" (Schapp 1930: 23).

35 See Scheler (1954), Gilbert (2005), Durkheim (1912).

36 On this issue, see De Vecchi (2015), and Gilbert (2005) (in Gilbert 2014). Moreover, is the problem of what it means to share a value analogous to the problem of what it means to share a feeling? On the latter, see Schmid (2009): Chapter four, "Shared feelings."

37 "Der vernünftige gegenseitige Vertrag besteht nun darin, daß aus der Wertwelt des einen in die Wertwelt des andern etwas verpflanzt wird und umgekehrt. Ohne Beziehung auf einen Wertwelt gibt der gegenseitige Vertrag keinen Sinn" (Schapp 1930: 27).

38 "Wenn nun die Voraussetzungen für den Abschluss eines gegenseitigen Vertrages gegeben ist, d.h. wenn ein Stuck der Wertwelt des einen gegen einen Stuck der Wertwelt des andern irgendwie ausgetauscht werden soll, so *fragt es sich, in welcher Weise dieser Austausch zustande kommt.* Damit sind wir in dem eigentlichen Gebiet der Jurisprudenz angelangt" (Schapp 1930: 27, my italics).

39 "Wenn zwei Stücke aus zwei Wertwelten gegeneinander ausgetauscht werden sollen, *so fragt es sich, wie dies im einzelnen vor sich geht.* Für den Laien ist nichts einfacher als dies. *Der Jurist hat aus diesem Austausch eine Wissenschaft gemacht, welche in entwichelteren Gesetzen in Tausenden von Paragraphen behandelt wird.* Der Weg

des Austausches ist der gegenseitige Vertrag für den Juristen. Diesen betrachten wir nun genauer. Die Voraussetzung des *gegenseitigen Vertrages* ist das eigenartige Verhältnis von zwei Wertwelten, von welchen je ein Teil zum Austausch mit einem Teil der andern Wertwelt drängt. Diese Voraussetzung bezeichnen wir als *Unterbau* des gegenseitigen Vertrages, den Austausch selbst entsprechend als *Oberbau*" (Schapp 1930: 28, italics mine).

40 "Bei allen [Verträgen] besteht der Unterbau in der Abschätzung der umzusetzenden Werte und der Oberbau in Kundgebung, welche diese Umsetzung bewirken" (Schapp 1930: 34).

41 "Diese Willenserklärungen sind aber nicht beliebige Willenserklärungen, sondern *soziale Akte*" (Schapp 1930: 40).

42 Schapp assumes Reinach's idea of social acts and affirms that "the essence" of social acts "was established by Reinach, with rare clarity, according to the phenomenological method" Schapp (1930: 56). The fourth section of the first part of Schapp's work refers very explicitly to Reinach: this section is entitled *Studie über die Kundgebungen im Vertragsschluß. Die Akte*, and takes up Reinach's analysis of social acts, in particular, the "making known" (*Kundgeben*) of the social acts, pinpointed by Reinach as one of the essential moments of social acts, see Reinach (2012: §3). Moreover, Schapp illustrates two new paradigms of social acts: (1) Social acts whose *addressee is not a human being*, but either a non-human animal or God (concerning God, Reinach, too, had already pointed out the possibility of social acts addressed to God, such as praying; see Reinach (2012: §3); (2) Social acts that are *original* (*Originalakte*) and social acts that are *artificial* (*Kunstakte*): differently from original social acts, artificial social acts do not have a correspondence in the sphere of the pre-givenness of law (examples of original social acts are: promising [*versprechen*] and commanding [*bestellen*]; examples of artificial social acts are: admonishing [*anfechten*] and contesting [*mahnen*]). See Schapp (1930: 59) and following.

43 "Die Formeln, welche wir für den gegenseitigen Vertrag im Unterbau und Oberbau gefunden haben, stehen nicht zu irgendeinem positiven Recht in besonderer Beziehung, und doch sind sie in irgendeiner Weise die Grundlage jeden positiven Rechtes. Die Formeln sind auch nicht auf dem Wege der Verallgemeinerung aus den bekannten positiven Rechten gewonnen, sondern das positive Recht findet diese Formeln vor und wählt die aus, welche ihm zweckmäßig erscheinen und gibt ihnen eine erhöhte Bedeutung" (Schapp 1930: 35–6).

References

Aristotle. (2002), *Categories and De Interpretatione*, trans. J. L. Ackrill, Oxford: Oxford University Press.

Bobbio, N. (2019 [1934]), *L'indirizzo fenomenologico nella filosofia sociale e giuridica*, ed. P. Di Lucia, Torino: Giappichelli Editore.

Cossio, C. (1983), "La logica juridica y su denominacion," in *Estudio de filosofia del derecho y ciencia juridica*, Madrid: Faculdat de derecho de la universidad complutense – Centro de estudio constitucionales.

De Vecchi, F. (2013), "Ontological Dependence and Essential Laws of Social Reality," in M. Schmitz, B. Kobow, and H. B. Schmid (eds), *The Background of Social Reality. Selected Contributions from the Inaugural Meeting of ENSO*, 233–51, Heidelberg, Dordrecht, London: Springer-Verlag.

De Vecchi, F. (2015), "The Plural Subject Approach to Social Ontology and the Sharing Values Issue," *Phenomenology and Mind*, 9: 84–97.

De Vecchi, F. (2016a), "The Existential Quality Issue in Social Ontology: Eidetics and Modifications of Essential Connections," *Humana.mente. Journal of Philosophical Studies*, 31: 187–204.

De Vecchi, F. (2016b), "A Priori of the Law and Values in the Social Ontology of Wilhelm Schapp and Adolf Reinach," in H-B. Schmid and A. Salice (eds), *The Phenomenological Approach to Social Reality. History, Concepts, Problems*, 279–316, Heidelberg, Dordrecht, London: Springer-Verlag.

De Vecchi, F. (2017), "Eidetics of Law-making Acts: Parts, Wholes and Degrees of Existence," *Phenomenology and Mind*, 13: 86–95.

De Vecchi, F. (2020), "Common-surrounding World and Qualitative Social Ontology—Phenomenological Insights for the Environment and its Crisis," *Rivista di Estetica*, 3: 33–51.

De Vecchi, F. (2022), *La società in persona. Ontologia sociale qualitativa*, Bologna: Il Mulino.

De Vecchi, F. (2024), "A personally embedded qualitative social ontology—issues from Stein and Husserl," in M. Lebech and R. Hagengruber (eds), *Person and Intersubjectivity. Edith Stein's and Edmund Husserl's Phenomenology of the Social 1916-25 with Focus on Ideas II*, Dordrecht: Springer, (forthcoming).

Durkheim, E. (1912), *Les formes élémentaires de la vie religieuse*, Paris: Alcan.

Gilbert, M. (1989), *On Social Facts*, New York: Routledge.

Gilbert, M. (2005), "Shared Values, Social Unity and Liberty," in M. Gilbert (ed.), *Joint Commitment. How we Make the Social World*, 11–44, Oxford: Oxford University Press.

Gilbert, M. (2014), *Joint Commitment. How we Make the Social World*, Oxford: Oxford University Press.

Hersch, J. (2008), *L'exigence absolue de la liberté. Textes sur les droits humains (1973-1995)*, ed. F. De Vecchi, Genève: MetisPresses

Hildebrand von D. (1916), "Die Idee der sittlichen Handlung," *Jahrbuch für Philosophie und phänomenologische Forschung*,3: 126–251.

Hildebrand von D. (1922), "Sittlichkeit und ethische Werterkenntnis," *Jahrbuch für Philosophie und phänomenologische Forschung*, 5: 462–602.

Husserl, E. (1950), *Ideen zu einer reinen Phänomenologie und phänomenologischen Philosophie. Erstes Buch: Allgemeine Einführung in die reine Phänomenologie*, hrsg. von K. Schuhmann, Hua III/1, Martinus Nijhoff: Den Haag.

Husserl, E. (1973), *Zur Phänomenologie der Intersubjektivität. Texte aus dem Nachlaß. Erster Teil: 1905-1920*, hrsg. I. Kern, Husserliana XIII, Den Haag: Martinus Nijhoff.

Husserl, E. (1976), *Die Krisis der europäischen Wissenschaften und die transzendentale Phänomenologie. Eine Einleitung in die phänomenologische Philosophie*, ed. W. Biemel, Husserliana VI, Den Haag, Martinus Nijhoff.

Husserl, E. (1984), *Logische Untersuchungen*, hrsg. von U. Panzer, Hua XIX/1, XIX/2, Den Haag: Martinus Nijhoff.

Husserl, E. (1994), *Ideen zu einer reinen Phänomenologie und phänomenologischen Philosophie. Zweites Buch: Phänomenologische Untersuchungen zur Konstitution*, hrsg. von M. Biemel, Hua IV, Den Haag: Martinus Nijhoff.

Husserl, E. (2002), *Natur und Geist. Vorlesungen Sommersemester 1919*, hrsg. von M. Weiler, Hua Mat IV, Dordrecht: Kluwer.

Husserl, E. (2020), *Studien zur Struktur des Bewusstseins*, hrsg. von U. Melle e Th. Vongehr, Hua XLIII/2, Dordrecht: Springer.

Reinach, A. (2012), *The Apriori Foundation of the Civil Law*, trans. J. F. Crosby, Amsterdam: De Gruyter.

Schapp, W. (1930), *Die neue Wissenschaft vom Recht. Eine phänomenologische Untersuchung*, Berlin: Rothschild.

Scheler (1954), *Der Formalismus in der Ethik und die material Wertethik*, in *Gesammelte Werke*, vol. II, hrsg. von Maria Scheler, Bern-München: Francke.

Scheler, M. (1973), *Wesen und Formen der Sympathie*, in *Gesammelte Werke*, vol. VII, hrsg. von Maria Scheler, Bern-München: Francke.

Schmid, H. B. (2009), *Plural Action Essays in Philosophy and Social Science,* Dordrecht: Springer.

Searle, J. R. (1995), *The Construction of Social Reality*, New York: Routledge.

Searle, J. R. (2010), *Making the Social World. The Structure of Human Civilization*,Oxford: Oxford University Press.

Stein, E. (1922), "Beiträge zur philosophischen Begründung der Psychologie und der Geisteswissenschaften," *Jahrbuch für Philosophie und phänomenologische Forschung*, 5: 1–283

Stein, E. (1925), "Eine Untersuchung über den Staat," *Jahrbuch für Philosophie und phänomenologische Forschung*, 7: 1–123.

Stein, E. (2008), *Zum Problem der Einfühlung*, in *Edith Stein Gesamtausgabe*, Bd. 5, hrsg. von M. A. Sondermann, Freiburg-Basel-Wien: Herder.

Tuomela R. and Miller, K. (1988), "We-Intentions," *Philosophical Studies*, 53: 367–89.

Weil, S., (1949), *L'enracinement. Prélude à une déclaration des devoris envers l'être humain*, Paris: Gallimard.

Part III

The Hermeneutics of Stories

9

The Power of Storytelling

Being Entangled in Stories as a Core Feature of Human Identity

Susan Gottlöber

0. Introduction

We are of the opinion *that being human is exhausted in being entangled in stories* [my emphasis], that each human being is the one being entangled in stories.[1]

It is a widely recognised belief that the essence of human existence lies within the intricate web of narratives that envelop us. Each individual is undeniably enmeshed in stories that shape our identities, both on a personal and collective scale. Today, the significance of storytelling, not only for defining human identity but also for charting the course of personal and cultural development, stands as an established theory. This acknowledgment has been greatly reinforced by the insights of prominent thinkers such as Paul Ricœur, Roland Barthes, and Walter Benjamin, who have expanded our understanding of storytelling beyond the confines of pure philosophy (cf. Ricœur1984–90; Barthes 1975; Benjamin 2019). Yet, by and large it remained strongly connected to the concept of text or a textual schema that is important for most cultures to put an order to experience and knowledge (cf. Stierle 1984: 398).

Certainly, Wilhelm Schapp, *the* philosopher of stories, connects his own philosophy stories strongly with this claim: In both, the *Philosophie der Geschichten* (*Philosophy of Stories*) from 1959 and *In Geschichten verstrickt* (*Entangled in Stories*)[2] from 1953, the great stories of human culture and their writers (if known) feature prominently: from Homer and the *Iliad* and the *Odyssey* to Hesiod to the *Bible* and the *Bhagavad Gita*. Included in his reflections are not only the famous *Wozu-Dinge* (what-for-things) but also a number of concepts closely related to textual analysis: speaking, listening, understanding, and language; even silence and "quiet speaking."

Yet, the direction of his thinking, starting from phenomenology and then, later, as a pushback and moving away from Husserl's phenomenological standpoint goes beyond the hermeneutical: for Schapp, stories—in the shape of being entangled in stories—become the essential feature not only of being myself, of social, and individual identity, but of being human: *there is no being human* outside of being entangled in stories. Or, to phrase it somewhat differently: Schapp's answer to the questions "what is the human being?" and "what does it mean to be human?" is *being entangled in stories*—a strong anthropological claim that deserves attention and that quite uniquely brings the hermeneutical aspect of Schapp's concept into conversation with philosophical anthropology.

This quite bold anthropological assertion meant a further reconsideration of the direction of this paper: my original idea was to develop Schapp's concept of being entangled in stories mainly within the context of and in relation to hermeneutical theories. However, I quickly noticed two obstacles to this approach: first, that despite the similarities between the classical historical hermeneutics of concepts such as Dilthey's historical hermeneutics and its concerns, and Schapp's being entangled in stories their respective approaches should not be equated too easily, not least of all because for thinkers like Schleiermacher or Dilthey, the question was not so much an anthropological concern but rather almost exclusively that of human understanding. Secondly, the anthropological concern is much more central to Schapp's theory than I originally realized: Schapp's philosophical questioning does not just solely concern *understanding* but actually *being* human. Thus, while on the surface being more related to the hermeneutical approach, Schapp's theory belongs—at least in parts and if we take his claim serious which we intend to do—as much into the area of philosophical anthropology, where it has—with few exceptions—received little attention to date.[3] Methodologically, this becomes complicated even further by Schapp's relationship to (especially Husserl's) phenomenology, both as his philosophical "up-bringing" as well as his later pushing away from his phenomenological origins.

These preliminary considerations result in a clarification of our question which unfolds now on three levels: what being entangled in stories means for: (1) being human, and, by extension, Schapp's understanding of what it means to be human (which will be our main focus); and (2) our individual identity, the starting point of all philosophical investigations for Schapp. While we can discuss these questions separately, they are intrinsically related, or, as Schapp would phrase it: entangled. Answers to these questions are mainly found in *In Geschichten verstrickt*. Our goal for this paper will be to detangle these aspects and to conclude by investigating the potential of Schapp's theory for twenty-first-century debates.

1. From Understanding Human Activities to Being Human: Being Entangled in Stories as a Primordial Phenomenon?

As Karen Joisten points out in her introduction to *Philosophie der Geschichten*, that Schapp heard both Dilthey (on Husserl's *Logical Investigations*) and Simmel lecture is undoubtedly of importance for our understanding of Schapp's philosophical development (Joisten in Schapp 2015: 5; see also Lübbe 1972: 55f.). And indeed, at first glance, Schapp's philosophy of stories seems much more closely related to Dilthey's historical hermeneutics, but also, in some aspects, to Simmel's life philosophy, such as Simmel's concept of world and his particular take on the *Ur-phänomen* or primordial phenomenon (even though Schapp does not follow in the footsteps of life philosophy (cf. Simmel 2010, esp. the chapter "The Turn Towards Ideas")) rather than it is to the Husserlian phenomenology. A possible exception here is Husserl's concept of the lifeworld (*Lebenswelt*) as "backdrop" to human consciousness which, according to Husserl's description in the *crisis*-book, functions as the foundation of meaning, our conscious universal horizon that we all share, a fact that has been forgotten by the natural sciences (cf., for example, Husserl 1996: 52ff.), and a description reminiscent also of Schapp's understanding of the relationship of being entangled in stories with the natural sciences.

But while Schapp's own reference points clearly indicate phenomenology, especially Husserl, the key ideas of the philosophy of stories are, in many ways explicitly, a pushback movement from classical phenomenology (cf., for example, Gottlöber 2020: 48–64), taking inspiration, as Joisten points out, from the philosophical positions mentioned above without it being possible to be assigned to any particular one.[4] It might be due to its quite syncretic nature and its rather unconventional inter-philosophical approach that Schapp's theory could not be clearly identified as belonging to one tradition of thought or another. There are, therefore, good reasons to situate the philosophy of stories quasi "at the crossroads" of especially phenomenology and hermeneutics who, of course, themselves are quite intertwined both in their origins as well their philosophical concerns around existential situatedness in the world, human experience, and interpretation. It comes, therefore, as no surprise that the terminology Schapp uses—either directly or implicitly—reminds one often not only of similar concepts in phenomenology but also hermeneutics; well captured in Pohlmeyer's description of Schapp's philosophy of stories as "story-hermeneutics," developed "on the basis of a phenomenological style and philosophizing" (Pohlmeyer 2004: 5).

These similarities can be found on many levels: beyond the already mentioned lifeworld, frameworks such as the notion of background (*Hintergrund*) remind one of, for example, Gadamer's concepts of horizon and pre-judices (*Vor-Urteile*). Schapp himself refers to the concept of horizon repeatedly (e.g., Schapp 2012: 101). These notions have a common framework, namely, allude to the inevitable conditions inherent in any form of understanding. The same is true for Schapp's idea that we cannot identify a first pre-story (*Vorgeschichte*) but that certain parts of the story will be "lit up" looking back into history (Schapp 2012: 88ff.; see also Gadamer 1990: 275ff. or 31ff.). Equally important, if not more so, is the close correspondence between being entangled in stories and the idea of historicity, "that something past has remained effective despite its being the past" (Renthe-Fink, c. 404). Or, as Arnold Gehlen had put it in his article "Historicity," the "historical mode of being of the human spirit" (Gehlen quoted in Renthe-Fink 1974: c. 404). To express it in another way: Gadamer's notion of the historicity of understanding (Gadamer 1990, pp. 270ff.) transforms into the idea of being entangled in stories as a fundamental aspect of human understanding. These resemblances have not gone unnoticed, and scholars have repeatedly drawn our attention to the connection between the hermeneutical tradition and Schapp's use of stories (see, for example, Thiemer 2010), a relationship supported by substantial evidence: for example, Schapp consistently underscores the notion that our *sole* gateway to understanding the individual human being is through stories—a realization that, perhaps more than any other thinkers, Schapp would have because of his background as a practicing lawyer, an occupation from which he derives numerous examples (for example, Schapp 2015: 64ff).

Yet, the differences between Schapp and the classical hermeneutical tradition are equally important: the emphasis of thinkers like Dilthey but also Gadamer was not only on human understanding but also on the special place of the human sciences within the overall body of human knowledge, clearly demarcating them from the natural sciences. In this way, they do not only assert the autonomy of the humanities but also underscore their indispensability. A similar trend can be observed with philosophers like Paul Ricœur, a pivotal figure in contemporary hermeneutics and whose influence extended beyond the realm of philosophical hermeneutics as his concepts, such as the narrative, found their way into mainstream discussions, literary, and psychological discourses. To the best of my knowledge, Ricœur refers to Schapp only on two occasions, but does not provide a detailed exploration of Schapp's ideas. In *Time and Narrative*, vol. 1, Ricœur, referring to a case Schapp himself uses, highlighting the significance of the passive voice in *being* entangled in stories as something that happens *to* me (cf. Ricœur 1984: 74f).[5] Here, Ricœur draws our attention to the fact that for Schapp, the story happens before it is being told; entanglement then "seems more like the 'prehistory' of the told story, whose beginning has to be chosen by the narrator. This 'prehistory' of the story is what binds it to a larger whole and gives it a 'background'," with the narrating becoming a secondary process and telling stories, understanding them, etc. is simply a continuation of these untold stories, quasi making them visible (Ricœur 1984: 85).

The second instance where Schapp is mentioned by Ricœur occurs in *Onself as Another*. Here, Ricœur explores the intricate relationship between self and narrative, and he credits Schapp specifically with the crucial discovery of entanglement which highlights the difficulty to attribute a sequence of actions to a single agent as each of us is intertwined with the actions of others:

> We have insisted elsewhere, following W. Schapp, on the idea, proper to the narrative field, of being "entangled in stories" (ref. Schapp [*In Geschichten verstrickt*]); the action of each person (and of that person's history) is entangled not only with the physical course of things but with the social course of human activity. How, in particular, are we to distinguish in a group action what belongs to each of the social actors? (Ricœur 1992: 107)

While Ricœur in this passage, underscores the significance of the intersubjective element and emphasizes that the self cannot truly be disentangled from it, he does not quite recognize the inherent radicality within Schapp's thought here, particularly concerning anthropological consequences, even though he does acknowledge it in *Time and Narrative*, where he concedes that Schapp performs an "existential analysis" (Ricœur 1984: 75). As we have stated before, if we take Schapp by his word, then not only can no human knowledge be understood outside of the context of stories (including the natural sciences which is a topic we will not follow further here but which, as we have pointed out earlier, seems to be a reminder of the lifeworld of the later Husserl),[6] but being entangled in stories is an *essential anthropological criterium*. We can therefore, at this stage, draw the first following conclusion: while Schapp's alignment with the concept of an inescapable horizon of understanding (to borrow, once again, the concept from Gadamer) mirrors aspects found in Husserl and Gadamer, the transformation of this essential *hermeneutical* aspect into a fundamental *anthropological* characteristic appears genuinely innovative and merits further examination.[7]

Within the context and at the intersection of hermeneutics and phenomenology, a concept emerges that holds the potential to connect all the previously mentioned approaches, including Schapp's work, in a surprising manner and could help us in elucidating what being entangled in stories means for being human: the primordial phenomenon. Scholars have repeatedly commented on the fact that Schapp's idea of being entangled in stories is treated by Schapp as a primordial phenomenon or primordial factum (*Urfaktum*) (see, for example, Joisten in Schapp 2015: 7). Indeed, Schapp frequently emphasizes the notion of being entangled in stories as the quintessential and inescapable characteristic of being human. Yet to me, at least, the question if being entangled in stories can be treated as an *Urphänomen* is not as clear as it may first appear; at the same time, however, it is a promising avenue that I would like to explore further in the light of our anthropological question.

While Schapp does make reference to Husserl's use of the term *Urphänomen*, it is worth considering a return to the thinker who coined the term as a foundational point that both Husserl and Schapp, among others, draw upon Johann Wolfgang von Goethe. Schapp, an avid reader of Goethe like most intellectuals of his generation, would have been familiar with the term that seemed to have become, according to Heidegger, one of the predominant problems of contemporary philosophy (Heidegger 2007: paragraph 4). Goethe himself had described the primordial phenomenon "not [. . .] as a principle from which manifold consequences result, but as a basic phenomenon within which the manifold is to be seen" (Goethe in a letter to Christian D. von Buttel from May 3, 1827, in Goethe 1988: 231). He uses the example of beauty to illustrate: "Beauty is a primordial phenomenon that never appears itself, but whose reflection is visible in a thousand different expressions of the creative spirit" (Goethe in conversation with Eckermann April 18, 1827, in Eckermann 1948: 617). From this point onward, the concept began its triumphant march within German philosophy. Notably, figures like Schopenhauer, Nietzsche, Dilthey Husserl, Simmel, Scheler, and Gadamer all incorporated the concept to some extent into their work, albeit with distinct variations in its interpretation and application.

Crucial to our understanding is the fact that Schapp would have encountered the term not only through his study of Goethe but also during his lectures by

Dilthey and Simmel, and notably, through his engagement with Husserl himself. It seems already Husserl reinterpreted the term insofar as for him it was a way to describe the foundational experience of a phenomenon before it was categorized, especially with regard to the flow of temporality: "The 'primordial phenomenon' of flowing is the phenomenon of all phenomena. [. . .] everything is in the primordial-phenomenal flowing as that which is 'given' therein and [. . .] as the same enduring unity" (Hua Mat VIII: 1-2).

In *Auf dem Weg zur Philosophie der Geschichten* (*On the Way to a Philosophy of Stories*), Schapp shows that he is familiar with Husserl's use of the term: Schapp contends that while in Husserl's terminology the story might be considered the primordial phenomenon, it does not align with his own perspective as for him, such a characterization would contradict the fundamental notion of being entangled in stories. "We only know an ego or a person that executes intentional acts or is aimed in its intentional acts towards the world." A story cannot be reconstructed from those acts or with the help of those acts (Schapp 2017: 132).[8] Rather, Schapp argues that if one were to draw a connection between his own thought and Husserl's, it would be that the stories and being entangled in stories replace Husserl's notions of thing and perception and the extension of the thing in relation to the world and perception in relation to other acts. The story itself, Schapp continues, is its own phenomenon.

These remarks indicate that the question whether Schapp considers being entangled in stories as a primordial phenomenon, or not, cannot be so easily answered as it appears at first glance. Much hinges on how Schapp interprets the concept, a matter that remains somewhat ambiguous within his texts. However, a second avenue would be to approach this question by proceeding from the original idea itself as we find it presented in Goethe. For him, the core of this concept is the phenomenon not as a governing principle but as something that continually appears or manifests itself, which means we can only observe the primordial phenomenon in its "manifestations" but never the phenomenon in itself.[9] How would this look when applied to being entangled in stories?

In *In Geschichten verstrickt*, Schapp describes stories, first of all, as formations (*Gebilde*), not as objects (*Gegenstände*), precisely because of the fact that "something is only a story insofar as I am entangled in it."[10] This means in turn that being entangled in stories and the stories themselves cannot be separated; the same is true for knowing the story and being.[11] Finally, stories can only appear when they have happened to someone who thus necessarily belongs to it (cf. Schapp 2012: 86f). Hence, stories, the state of being entangled in them, and knowing them are inseparable and collectively describe the same phenomenon. All these remarks suggest very strong hermeneutical elements that only get emphasized further when he adds later that our last access to the human being is through stories (Schapp 2012: 103). This approach gets extended in other passages to the external world (mediated through the what-for-things), including animals, thus aligning with the concept of stories as hermeneutical framework.

However, Schapp does move in a next step from the hermeneutical perspective to much more substantial philosophical anthropological assertions: not only is that which is essential of the human being captured in their stories and the stories that surround them (Schapp 2012: 105), but "[t]he human being is not the human being of flesh and blood. In its place pushes their story as the actual."[12] These anthropological statements carry not only a phenomenological and hermeneutical dimension, but have also a distinctly existentialist flavor: what makes our essential being *is* both our story and the stories that surround us. The focus, therefore, changes from what stories *are* to *their relationship with our being human*: "The story stands for the man"[13]—and this is where the being entangled in stories becomes interesting from a philosophical anthropological perspective. If we were to assume here that Schapp is talking about the human individual in its entirety, then, of course, we can question the one-sidedness of this assumption, especially since Schapp continues later, "[t]he human being is the not the human being of flesh and blood."[14] However, I do not think that this is the case.

A valuable clarification on this matter is offered by a fellow contemporary phenomenologist, Max Scheler (1874–1928), who in his 1928 published work "Man's Place in the Cosmos" ("Die Stellung des Menschen im Kosmos"), investigates one of the urgent questions of his time (as evidenced by the number of the publications on the topic with the same name), namely, the place of the human being in nature and in the cosmos in the light of scientific advances, especially in biology, zoology, and evolutionary theory. Here Scheler makes the point that when we speak of "the human being," we actually refer to two very different, even antagonistic concepts: firstly, we refer to the notion of the human being as *homo naturalis*, who stands in a long line of mammals and was, is, and always will be, an animal.[15] Secondly, however, the term human being (*Mensch*) is used in strongest opposition to the animal and which concerns the nature (*Wesen*) of the human being (Scheler 1995: 11f.).

When Schapp speaks of the fact that the story stands for the human being I would suggest that he refers to this conceptual understanding—the *Wesen*—of what it means to be human. This does not mean, of course, that Schapp has the same focus on the distinction in the qualitative nature between human and other animals as Scheler and others would have. For example, *Geist* (spirit) which plays such pivotal role in a number of these debates and for thinkers like Scheler is, as far as I can see, not mentioned by Schapp at all—although one could argue that—at least from a Schelerian perspective (but also thinkers like Dilthey)—the phenomenon of stories in themselves is a manifestation of what Scheler calls the primordial phenomenon of *Geist*.

If I am right in this and Schapp actually talks about a *Wesen*-consideration, then the rather obvious biological but also phenomenological criticisms that Schapp does not pay enough attention to the human being as embodied would not hold, as the human being as *homo naturalis* was not what Schapp had in mind in the first case. This remains the case even when we take into account his reflections on embodiment as developed in *Philosophie der Geschichten* as Schapp emphasizes that also the *Leib* (body) only becomes comprehensible via stories (Schapp 2015: 115). It is worthwhile to mention in this context—without being able to develop it any further at this moment—that the what-for-things, which already play a crucial role in our engagement with the external world also are of pivotal importance here, for example, with regard to our limbs: "We do not say too much if we mean that these limbs appear or meet us in connection and reciprocity with the what-for-things."[16] The important point for our argument at this stage is that there is no going beyond being entangled in stories, the hand only materializes with or "on" a human individual, which is, of course, in itself, also a biological entity. At this juncture then, it is reasonable to assert that there is a valid argument in favor of stories being considered indeed a primordial phenomenon in Schapp's philosophy of stories. It is from these conceptual clarifications that we have now circled back to the starting point for all philosophical inquiries, including those related to stories, namely, our individual selves.

2. The Emergence of the Individual Self as Being Entangled in Stories and Its Relationship to the "We"

Schapp's idea that we begin with our own concrete entangled story is, of course, also a phenomenological and, indeed, an existential starting point: as soon as one discovers one's own entanglement in stories, one discovers that this entanglement has been at the core of one's identity all along, including the intersubjective element. It is worthwhile noticing, however, that Schapp seems to be here much closer to the first generation phenomenologists like Husserl or Scheler, who do not see the individual in opposition to the social aspect but rather the individual existence simultaneously intrinsically related with and emerging from the intersubjective. Likewise, we do not see in Schapp's thought the need to free ourselves from the harmful impact of society (*das Man* in Heidegger or the gaze of the other in Sartre) in order to be authentic; rather, who I am as an individual is inexorably tied to being entangled in stories; without this connection, I would cease to exist as the person that I am.[17] At the same time, without the I or person being entangled in stories, there would neither stories nor any entanglement—both (in themselves inseparable, according to Schapp) do not exist outside their "materializing" simultaneously on individual and social level.[18]

Schapp underscores how profoundly intertwined the (individual) self and stories are right from the outset in *In Geschichten verstrickt*: "To every story belongs someone who is entangled in it,"[19] whereby the distinction between the individual human being and the self is often not made clear and, potentially, deliberately left vague. Once more, Schapp initiates his investigation from a hermeneutical standpoint, asserting that access to the human being can only be attained through stories. (Schapp 2012: Vorwort, V; 103ff). The primary aim here is understanding—a goal that Schapp substantiates with numerous examples drawn from law, his own primary field of expertise. Only through stories, according to Schapp, are we able to "touch" the self.

At the same time, Schapp emphasizes that the individual story is intertwined from the very beginning in a "we": "it belongs to every story that there are fellow entangled persons."[20] And even stronger later in the same work: "already the smallest individual story entails the we."[21] Every encounter with ourselves already encompasses the encounter with others (cf. Schapp 2015: 145).

However, this fact extends beyond those individuals who are directly entangled with us such as family, the town, etc. A closer investigation reveals not only that stories have no absolute beginning but begin in other stories. If we follow this train of thought, we find ourselves through an entangled-with (*Mitverstrickung*) connected to an even bigger story that Schapp calls the all-story (*Allgeschichte*), a notion that we will return to in our conclusion.

Schapp's methodological approach is almost classic existentialist-phenomenological as it follows the path from the individual experience to the other and the "we" to the quasi-open horizon of the all-story—a process of discovery that reveals the fact that the story of the "we" that we eventually uncover has, in truth, been present from the outset, and we have been inherently embedded within it all along. While this so far does not capture much more than the intersubjective element that we see discussed repeatedly in phenomenology, Schapp, again, adds another perspective: "it is not only that I am entangled in stories together with others, but the same story may actually look different depending on the different perspectives of the people being entangled in it" (cf. Schapp 2015: 32). This is a quite unique way of bringing together the universality of being entangled in stories (ultimately in the all-story which replaces traditional concepts of the unity of humanity such as biological features, culture, etc. (cf. Schapp 2015: 198)) with the irreplaceable unique individual person who is entangled in the story.[22] It is thus that, as Joisten puts it, "the individual, unmistakable person, with his or her own unique stories, once again comes into the field of vision" (Joisten in Schapp 2015: 11).

This uniqueness of the individual self is an important feature in Schapp's considerations on the question of the human self. I would argue that this was Schapp's way of engaging with the challenge of considering the individual person as unique in the face of scientific abstraction and the species-thinking of evolutionary theory.[23] In this way, Schapp also found a way of addressing what many intellectuals of his time would have thought of as the problem of massification, especially in the face of the totalitarianisms of the early part of the twentieth century that had shown itself without any concern of the destruction of the individual.[24] A concern that we can see likewise in the Catholic personalism of the early twentieth century. However, while the concerns seem the same, down to structural similarities, it is essential to acknowledge that these conjectures must remain speculative in nature. As far as my knowledge extends, Schapp does not make reference to either the existentialists or the Catholic personalist movement.

What complicates this investigation into the relationship between self and stories even more, is the fact that Schapp normally talks about human being (*der Mensch*) and it is often up to the reader to decide if Schapp is talking about being human or an individual human person with their own self-identity. But again, I think Scheler's conceptual approach to the person could be helpful here. Schapp states himself regarding his methodology in *In Geschichten verstrickt* that he is *not* attempting an examination of the essence or nature of something (*Wesensuntersuchung*), as such an attempt would counter what he intends to do, namely, to investigate the living connection of stories with each other (Schapp 2012: 94f.). Yet, he is presenting us with a *Wesensuntersuchung* in kind; only it is not about *what stories are* but what does it mean *to be human*, namely, being entangled in stories. While this is the universal aspect of our humanity, so to speak, understanding the *specific and individual stories* and being entangled in them gives us an understanding of the individual self, akin to Scheler's individual *ordo amoris*.[25] If one were to compare the two approaches then one could say that—to some extent only—Schapp replaces Scheler's acts with stories. We can see then how thinkers like Ricœur, who are concerned with the self are much more "willing" to follow Schapp in his analysis of the self that is so entangled in stories that it cannot be distinguished from them—it *is* them. It is in this way, that García Serrano rightly speaks of the pragmatic narrative holism as the basis of Schapp's approach (cf. García Serrano 2020: here 194).

If we look back over our analysis, then we have discovered the following: starting with ourselves, we realize that who we are is being entangled in multiple stories that in some way precede us—no one becomes who they are out of a vacuum. Each of these entanglements—and therefore each of us—is unique this way, as no entanglement can be the same as another, even when it looks from the outside that more than oneself are entangled in the same story. Discovering the "we"-story in this way leads us then further to the all-story or stories that connect both the individual stories and the we-stories with each other; being entangled in these all-stories is what unites humanity. Finally, we discover that this being entangled in stories not only connects human beings with each other and throughout the ages but that we have arrived at an essential defining feature for being human: being entangled in stories, or to phrase it differently: that our humanity gets realized or individuated in a unique way anew in each individual self. The ramifications of fully embracing this concept, if we take it at face value, are profound—to an extend that, I believe, takes us beyond Schapp's own application.

3. Conclusions: The Untapped Potential of Schapp's Theory for Twenty-First-Century Debates

Schapp's theory is compelling in its simplicity and, at the same time, distinguished by its being "in-between" and flexibility, which, in my view, constitutes its greatest strengths. Its potential for contemporary debates remains still largely untapped.

In times when the search for universal features or structures of human existence becomes more and more challenging, Schapp's approach provides an interesting nuance in distinguishing the different human experiences both on individual and social level as well as finding access to it: the access (*Zugang*) is through the individual story or stories, encompassing not only the history of a culture, people, or group but also their interpretations and reinterpretations over time. The impact of being entangled in stories in this way on our human self-understanding should not be underestimated in its radicality, since it combines the extraordinary plasticity that we see in, for example, existentialist approaches with an intersubjective approach to self and society, that embeds the self in the social surroundings in such a way that it cannot be detached from them—the stories in which the individual self is entangled would disappear, and the self with it. The hermeneutical thereby, remains the starting point for philosophical investigation: through stories, we gain understanding and thus access to both ourselves and the other person, but stories are also who we are—and in directing our investigative philosophical "gaze" beyond our subjective starting point, it also gives us (phenomenologically speaking) what makes us human.

Concerning our individual and social self-identity, it could potentially open up new ways of dialogue in, for example, the debates surrounding identity politics. Being entangled in stories would then be seen not just be the story of a people or cultural, other, group, but that story *is* who one *is*—the person being entangled in the stories and the entanglement in the stories themselves then become indistinguishable and experiences etc., that were part of the story become part of the self.

As Ricœur points out, being entangled in stories is, first of all, passive; it is something that happens *to us*. These happenings are, as Ricœur reminds us, not ethically neutral, nor are we entangled in only one story at a time; rather, we are entangled "with the social course of human activity" (Ricœur 1992: 107, 140)—here, Ricœur emphasizes his interpretation of both his own narrative concept and Schapp's idea (which he acknowledges following in this context), highlighting their alignment along similar lines. At the same time, the story can and may be changed. While we do not choose the stories we are entangled in (they happen to us), we are not imprisoned by them either; in becoming part of them, we actively shape them but also challenge them by looking for parts that may have been left out. In this way, we can literally rewrite the stories of the past, including aspects left in the dark or stories previously untold.

On the one hand, this extraordinary malleability of the stories themselves contains both possibilities and dangers and shows the care with which they need to be treated. On the one side, they have a liberating power for both individuals and groups and societies, even cultures. Just because a story has been told and remembered in a certain way, does not mean it has to stay like that; on the other hand, stories are fragile structures: they can be retold to liberate as well as to oppress, to build or to destroy, to be inclusive or to discriminate. This extraordinary power of telling the story also raises the awareness that some stories may have been irretrievably forgotten or altered in such a way that they become unrecognizable from one of the lived experience of the person or group once entangled in it.

On the other hand, Schapp himself did not seem to always follow through with the radicality of his own thought. This becomes especially striking in his reflections on women where he connects the eternal way of the woman with the absolute (cf. Schapp 1965b: Vorwort, no page number). This establishing of eternal ways of being seems problematic within the context of a philosophy of stories, and appears to stem from arguments for the traditional family and from a biological essentialist viewpoint. Likewise, the metaphysical elevation of motherhood does not seem to fit within the being entangled in stories (see Schapp 1965b; Joisten 2010).[26] The interesting question is, how much Schapp himself was aware of the discrepancy of his writing in this regard. One may argue here—and rightly so—that identity, especially with regarding gender or sexuality, were not discussed in the same intense manner as they are discussed today. This, however, is not the case when it comes to the social roles of women, including motherhood. This example shows, in its own way, the great power (which Schapp implied rather than reflect on explicitly) of the stories we are entangled in. In this way, we are thinking with Schapp beyond and engaging with Schapp reminds us of the care we need to take with stories and of the potential impact we may have telling them in a particular manner.

In relation to the specific anthropological enquiry, I have argued that aspects of Schapp's theory of being entangled in stories present a not only phenomenological but also hermeneutical inspired response to the question: Who is the human being? We can thus say that he adds to the famous definitions of *homo sapiens*, *homo ludens*, *homo faber*, *homo religious*, *homo symbolicus*, etc. the definition of *homo implicatus in fabulis*, who encompasses all the previous definitions. If we were to use Cassirer's critique of Aristotle's definition of human being as the rational animal, arguing that the latter is only a moral imperative while we cannot "escape" being symbolic animals (Cassirer 1944: 43f.), we could make a similar argument here: humans may be thinking at times, playing, have the capacity for religion, etc., but they are always already entangled in stories. This being entangled in stories, which happens or appears together with the individual who, at the same time, cannot be who they are without already being entangled in stories, makes it a primordial phenomenon in the original sense.

As Schapp himself states, his theory is not at all to be considered a systematic account of the matter. And since he does not aim for it either to become a science or to deliver a philosophical foundation for the sciences (cf. Schapp 2012: 87), a number of questions remain unanswered.[27] Therefore, rather than building a complete anthropological theory on Schapp, one should consider his ideas adding an interesting additional feature to existing concepts. It would be an interesting next step to bring Schapp's philosophical anthropological considerations into conversation with other, (often more explicit) philosophical anthropologies to tease out in more detail, what Schapp's ideas can add in this regard while taken into account also its potential shortfalls (I would argue, for example, that Schapp, despite attempting to show otherwise, underestimated the importance of the biological (Scheler would say life-) element as determining factor on stories both for our being human and our self-identity).

In addition, for those coming from a personalist perspective of the early twentieth century, one cannot help recognizing a number of features of Schapp's idea of being entangled in stories both in its anthropological conclusions and consequences for our (singular and collective) self-understanding, as akin to personalism, varied as it was in itself. It is, thus, somewhat curious that personalist thinkers such as Max Scheler did not, as mentioned above, get a mention in Schapp's work—although one may argue that these thinkers and ideas may well have been part of the stories Schapp himself was entangled in.

We all start out at least by believing the stories we were told and the ones we tell ourselves. Schapp's powerful vision is a reminder that while we are born into a story and therefore are not clean slates, we are in our being not determined by them. In this way, Schapp's concept offers a compelling philosophical argument for valuing the continuous re-investigation of our stories, personal and cultural, with regard to identities and how we consider our own humanity. For Schapp, stories keep the horizon open. But in an interesting, and not at all relativist way, it means that even the individual stories can also always be a little different.

Notes

1 "Wir sind der Meinung, dass sich das Menschsein erschöpft im Verstricktsein der Geschichten, daß der Mensch der in Geschichten Verstrickte ist" (Schapp 2012: 123). Unless indicated otherwise, all translations are my own.

2 Both are parts of a trilogy of which the *Metaphysik der Naturwissenschaft* (*Metaphysics of the Natural Sciences*) from 1965 forms a third part (Schapp 1965b).

3 One of these exceptions is Nicole Thiemer's contribution, "Essentia oder existentia? Vom wesentlichen und geschichtlichen Verstricktsein des Menschen in Geschichten" in *Die Rezeption der Geschichtenphilosophie Wilhelm Schapps* (Thiemer 2020). Here, Thiemer investigates the question from the perspective of the classic *existentia-essentia*-distinction. While I am not sure that I fully agree with her conclusion that Schapp's philosophy of stories in general is bound back to an essentialist-philosophical approach (Thiemer 2020: 162), I will agree, as I will show

here later, that being entangled in stories can indeed be interpreted as a primordial factum of being human.

4 Joisten points to Rickert and Pfänder as additional sources with whom similarities can be shown (Joisten in Schapp 2015: 5). Hermann Lübbe, in his second preface to *In Geschichten verstrickt*, points out that while Schapp's analysis shows structural similarities to Heidegger's existential analysis (*Daseinsanalytik*), it has not been influenced by Heidegger. Cf. Lübbe in (Schapp 2012: IX).

5 Ricœur refers here to Schapp (2012): 86 (p. 85 of the edition he uses), where Schapp emphasizes that stories can only appear in their happening to someone. For a more detailed discussion on Schapp and Ricœur see, for example, Haas (2002).

6 With this, but that cannot be further discussed here, Schapp also provides a radical critique of one of the key principles of the classical phenomenology of Husserl and his followers: a science without prerequisites (*voraussetzungsfreie Wissenschaft*) is not possible—a critique that first generation phenomenologists like Scheler would share. For Schapp, see (Schapp 1965a).

7 Especially the relationship between "*Geschichten*" (stories) and "*Geschichte*" (history) could be of interest here. Without going into more detail at this point, it seems to me that history is part of the story we tell ourselves in a group context.

8 I thank Daniele Nuccilli for drawing my attention to these passages.

9 Scheler whom Schapp does not mention, describes it as follows: "as that given to perception, which can *never* be observed, but only *seen*" ("als das Anschauliche, das *nie* beobachtet, sondern nur noch *erschaut* werden kann" (Scheler 1976: 87).

10 "etwas Geschichte nur insoweit ist, als ich in die Geschichte verstrickt bin" (Schapp 2012: 85f.). Curiously, Schapp also refers to human beings as *Gebilde* (cf. Schapp 2015: 95).

11 Interestingly, this somewhat contradicts Ricœur's interpretation of Schapp from above.

12 "Der Mensch ist nicht der Mensch aus Fleisch und Blut. An seine Stelle drängt sich uns seine Geschichte auf als sein Eigentliches" (Schapp 2012: 105).

13 "Die Geschichte steht für den Mann" (Schapp 2012: 100).

14 "Der Mensch ist nicht der Mensch aus Fleisch und Blut" (Schapp 2012: 105).

15 "er war Tier, er ist Tier und wird ewig Tier bleiben" (Scheler 1972: 191).

16 "Wir sagen wohl nicht zuviel, wenn wir meinen, daß diese Gliedmaßen im Zusammenhang und Wechselseitigkeit mit den Wozudingen auftauchen oder uns begegnen" (Schapp 2015: 113). A detailed analysis would also need to take in to account Schapp's reflections on the face, however, we cannot develop these points in more detail at this moment.

17 For me, these ideas resemble very closely both Scheler's personalist philosophy as well as his theories of knowledge, especially the later Scheler. But seeing that Scheler is not mentioned by Schapp, although one may assume safely that he was at least familiar with the most famous aspects of Scheler's work, we will not follow this avenue any further here.

18 Again, this basic concept of how being entangled in stories appears (phenomenologically speaking) reminds one very much of Scheler's personalism as developed in his key work *Formalism and Non-Formal Value Ethics* (Scheler 1980).

19 "Zu jeder Geschichte gehört ein darin Verstrickter" (Schapp 2012: 1).

20 "so gehört es zu jeder Geschichte, dass es Mitverstrickte gibt" (Schapp 2015: 32).

21 "wobei aber die kleinste Einzelgeschichte schon das wir enthält" (Schapp 2015: 201).

22 If Schapp is right in this regard is a different question for a number of reasons: one could, for example, argue that we have evidence of peoples so isolated that they do not have a connection with our all-story at all.

23 Schapp engages with the idea of species and series both in *In Geschichten verstrickt* and in *Philosophie der Geschichten*, questioning the traditional approach to individual and species (*Gattung*) (cf. Schapp 2012: 56ff); in *Philosophie der Geschichten* where he distinguishes, using again the example of a lion, between the lion that is entangled in a "lion-story" and the "biological formation" lion. Schapp suggests that a series is the more useful approach (cf. Schapp 2015: 62ff.).

24 We can see this in a great number of philosophies developed especially after the Second World War—one may only think of the French existentialists or thinkers like Hannah Arendt, who argues passionately for the uniqueness of each human being: "men, not Man live on the earth and inhabit the [. . .] earth plurality is the condition of human action because we are all the same, that is, human, in such a way that nobody is ever the same as anyone else who ever lived, lives, or will live" (Arendt 1958: 8).

25 "*Who has the ordo amoris of the human being has the human being.*" ("*Wer den ordo amoris eines Menschen hat, hat den Menschen.* [italics in the original]") (Scheler 1986: 348). Note that also Scheler speaks here of *Mensch*, in this case, the moral subject who is the individual person.

26 Joisten treats Schapp's consideration, maybe more kindly than myself, as a "conversation starter."

27 For example, in my opinion it remains unclear if, for Schapp, the individual human being is completely explained by being entangled in stories, since he presents arguments which give rise to different interpretations. Schapp's theory, therefore, does not have the comprehensive strength with regard to answering philosophical anthropological questions as would, for example, Scheler or Plessner.

References

Arendt H. (1958), *The Human Condition*, Chicago: University of Chicago Press.

Barthes, R. (1975), "An Introduction to the Structural Analysis of Narrative," *New Literary History*, 6 (2), *On Narrative and Narratives*: 237–72.

Benjamin, W. (2019), *The Storyteller. Essays*, ed. Samuel Titan, New York: NYRB Classics.

Cassirer, E. (1944), *An Essay on Man. An Introduction to a Philosophy of Culture*, London: Yale University Press.

Eckermann, J. P. (1948), *Gespräche mit Goethe in den letzten Jahren seines Lebens. Gesamtausgabe, Vol. 24*, ed. Ernst Beutler, Lahr: Schauenburg.

Gadamer, H.-G. (1990), *Wahrheit und Methode. Grundzüge einer philosophischen Hermeneutik*, Gesammelte Werke 1, Tübingen: J.C.B. Mohr (Paul Siebeck).

García Serrano, M. (2020), "Die narrative Entstehung der personalen Identität", in Karen Joisten, Jan Schapp, and NicoleThiemer (ed.), *Die Rezeption der Geschichtenphilosophie Wilhelm Schapps*, 192–229, München: Alber Verlag.

Goethe, J. W. von (1988), *Goethes Briefe und Briefe an Goethe: Briefe der Jahre 1821–1832,* Hamburger Ausgabe, Vol. 4, ed. K. R. Mandelkow, München: C.H. Beck.

Gottlöber, S. (2020), "Phänomenologie," in K. Joisten, J. Schapp, N. Thiemer (eds.), *Die Rezeption der Geschichtenphilosophie Wilhelm Schapps. Kommentare und Fortsetzungen*, 48–64, München: Karl Alber

Haas, S. (2002), *Kein Selbst ohne Geschichten. Wilhelm Schapps Geschichtsphilosophie und Paul Ricœurs Überlegungen zur narrativen Identität*, mit einem Nachwort von Jean Greisch. Studien und Materialien zur Geschichte der Philosophie, Vol. 61, Zürich/New York: Georg Olms Verlag Hildesheim, Magisterarbeit.

Heidegger, M. (2007), *Die Phänomenologie der Anschauung und des Ausdrucks, Gesamtausgabe 59*, ed. Claudius Strube, Frankfurt am Main: Klostermann.

Husserl, E. (1996), *Die Krisis der europäischen Wissenschaften und die transzendentale Philosophie*, Hamburg: Felix Meiner.

Husserl, E. (2006), *Späte Texte über Zeitkonstitution (1929-1934): Die C-Manuskripte (Hua Mat VIII)*, ed. Dieter Lohmar, Dordrecht: Springer.

Joisten, K. (2010), "Wilhlem Schapps unzeitgemäße Betrachtung *Zur Metaphysik des Muttertums*. Grundzüge und Gesprächsanlässe", in K. Joisten (ed.), *Das Denken Wilhelm Schapps. Perspektiven für unsere Zeit*, 172–89, München: Alber.

Lübbe, H. (1972), *Bewußtsein in Geschichten. Studien zur Phänomeologie der Subjektivität. Mach—Husserl—Schapp—Wittgenstein*, Freiburg: Rombach.

Pohlmeyer, M. (2004), *Geschichten-Hermeneutik. Philosophische, literarische und theologische Provokationen im Denken von Wilhelm Schapp*, Münster: LIT Verlag.

Renthe-Fink, L. von (1974), "Geschichtlichkeit," in J. Ritter (ed.), *HwbPhil*, Vol. 3 (G-H), 404–8, Basel: Schwabe & Co.

Ricœur, P. (1984), *Time and Narrative, Vol. 1*, trans. K. Blamey and D. Pellauer, Chicago and London: University of Chicago Press.

Ricœur, P. (1988), *Time and Narrative, Vol. 2*, trans. K. Blamey and D. Pellauer, Chicago and London: University of Chicago Press.

Ricœur, P. (1990), *Time and Narrative, Vol. 3*, trans. K. Blamey and D. Pellauer, Chicago and London: University of Chicago Press.

Ricœur, P. (1992), *Onself as Another*, transl. Kathleen Blamey, Chicago and London: University of Chicago Press.

Schapp, W. (1965a), *Metaphysik der Naturwissenschaft*, Den Haag: Martinus Nijhoff.

Schapp, W. (1965b), *Zur Metaphysik des Muttertums*, Den Haag: Martinus Njhoff.

Schapp, W. (2012), *In Geschichten verstrickt. Zum Sein von Mensch und Ding*, Frankfurt a. Main: Klostermann.

Schapp, W. (2015), *Philosophie der Geschichten*, ed. K. Joisten and J. Schapp, Frankfurt a. Main: Klostermann.

Schapp, W. (2017), *Auf dem Weg einer Philosophie der Geschichten*, München: Alber.

Scheler, M. (1972), "Zur Idee des Menschen," in Maria Scheler (ed.), *Vom Umsturz der Werte. Abhandlungen und Aufsätze* (GW III), 171–95, Bern and München: Bouvier.

Scheler, M. (1976), "Manuskripte zur Erkenntnis- und Methodenlehre der Metaphysik als positive Erkenntnis (Auseinandersetzung mit Gegnern)," in M. S. Frings (ed.), *Schriften aus dem Nachlaß II: Erkenntnislehre und Metaphysik* (GW XI), 72–117, Bonn: Bouvier.

Scheler, M. (1980), *Der Formalismus in der Ethik und die materiale Wertethik. Neuer Versuch der Grundlegung eines ethischen Personalismus* (GW II), ed. Maria Scheler, Bern: Francke.

Scheler, M. (1986), "Ordo amoris," in Maria Scheler (ed.), *Schriften aus dem Nachlaß, vol. 1: Zur Ethik und Erkenntnislehre* (GW X), 345–76, Bonn: Bouvier.

Scheler, M. (1995), "Die Stellung des Menschen im Kosmos," in M. Frings (ed.), *Späte Schriften* (GW IX), 7–71, Bonn: Bouvier.

Simmel, G. (2010), *The View of Life. Four Metaphysical Essays with Journal Aphorisms*, Chicago: University of Chicago Press.

Stierle, K. (1984), "Narrativ, Narrativität", in J. Ritter and K. Gründer (eds), *HwbPhil*, Vol. 6 (Mo-O), 398–401, Basel: Schwabe & Co.

Thiemer, N. (2010), "Das 'stille Sprechen' in der Geschichtenphilosophie Wilhelm Schapps under Universalitätsanspruch der Hermeneutik im 20. Jahrhundert," in K. Joisten (ed.), *Das Denken Wilhelm Schapps. Perspektiven für unsere Zeit*, 142–58, München: Alber.

Thiemer, N. (2020), "Essentia oder existentia? Vom wesentlichen und geschichtlichen Verstricktsein des Menschen in Geschichten," in K. Joisten, J. Schapp, and N. Thiemer (eds), *Die Rezeption der Geschichtenphilosophie Wilhelm Schapps*, 149–63, München: Alber.

10

Philosophy of Histories I: *In Geschichten verstrickt*

Approaches and Reflections

Nicole Thiemer

0. Preliminary remarks

As humans, we are all entangled in stories, in histories. We are shaped by and through them; we are imprinted by our stories, living with them and through them, which comprises our entanglement in histories. This refers to the undeniable facts that both life philosophers and existential philosophers have repeatedly emphasized: thrownness, projection and possibility, bondage, being in relationship and in webs of references in a historical, social, cultural manner, along with further aspects.

Today it is more commonly held that narratives are relevant in understanding and communicating about human beings, as well as for questions of identity, and that mere factual, objective "explanations" cannot capture the significance of narratives, of stories, for humans and their horizons of understanding.

But when Wilhelm Schapp published his writings on his philosophy of histories, neither depth psychology, nor narrative ethics, nor cultural philosophy were in vogue. Their philosophical implications were not openly discussed, nor were they recognized as subjects of scientific inquiry. Shortly thereafter, however, thinkers such as Hans-Georg Gadamer, Jean-François Lyotard, Emmanuel Lévinas, and Alasdair MacIntyre, as well as Paul Ricœur and Jean Greisch, accepted the consideration of stories and histories as an inevitable challenge to philosophical thinking and placed them at the center of philosophical discourse.

The phenomenon Wilhelm Schapp seeks to bring to light—namely, histories and being entangled in histories (*Geschichten*)—cannot be reduced to an illustration like a digital blog post that merely conveys what has just happened.

It is not a news message or an item of information that one may or may not be affected by. This would be a misleading and inappropriate reduction. Moreover, though the phenomenon Wilhelm Schapp pursues can find its expression in novels or films, it cannot be reduced to them. The philosophical debates about, and the disclosure of, what the notion of *Geschichten* encompasses within the horizon of human beings and humanity, as well as across generations, form the impetus for Wilhelm Schapp's philosophy.

Schapp's philosophy is not abstract, and it does not develop a philosophical system. It focuses on concrete human beings, on the lived world, and on everything that is part of it. It describes the particular in order to give expression to a universal, structural understanding, yet without assuming that this could ever be achieved through "concepts." As humans entangled in histories, all we can offer are purely human approximations, as we "write" and "read" those histories or "are written" by them or through them.

In-Geschichten-Verstrickt-sein contains an unavoidable "web of references" inherent to human existence. Here I recall Hannah Arendt's words regarding this phenomenon, which, in my opinion, speak for themselves:

> The realm in which human affairs take place consists of a system of references that forms wherever humans live together. Since humans are not thrown into the world by chance but are born into an already existing human world, the web of human affairs precedes all individual action and speech, just as the new beginning that action sets in motion is like threads that are woven into an already pre-existing pattern, thereby changing the fabric as they in turn affect all the threads of life they come into contact with within the fabric. [. . .] The fact that the span of human life between birth and death ultimately takes the form of a narratable story with a beginning and an end is the [. . .] condition for there being something like history in the existence of humankind. (Arendt 1987: 174f.)

These insightful lines emphasize the interconnectedness of human existence within the web of human affairs. They highlight the role of storytelling, the role of a narrative horizon, in giving shape to our lives and creating a sense of history/histories/stories/narrative entanglement. The contents of being entangled can be changed by oneself or by external circumstances, and can continue to be changed. But here it is important to consider that humans are never solely authors of themselves; a co-authorship always exists as well (cf., among others, MacIntyre 1995). From a structural perspective, the "*Bezugsgewebe*" (or "reference-network") remains, with threads reaching backward and forward.

Schapp's philosophy of histories deals with entanglements that embrace all of us (*Ich-Verstrickung, Wir-Verstrickung, Fremd-Verstrickung, All-Geschichte*). In its own way, it gives voice to the freedom and possibility and the binding and thrownness that human existence always is.

In the following, I would like to account for the title of the chapter—"Approaches and Reflections"—by placing the idea of "approaches" in the forefront.[1]

1. On Wilhelm Schapp's Philosophical Perspective

The philosophy of histories is an original philosophical approach developed by Wilhelm Schapp throughout his entire life. Schapp published this approach in the 1950s and 1960s through three works: *In Geschichten verstrickt. Zum Sein von Mensch und Ding, Philosophie der Geschichten,* and *Metaphysik der Naturwissenschaft* (Schapp 2009, 2012, 2015).

The works address the fundamental themes and concerns of the philosophy of histories in many ways, and are often referred to as a "trilogy of histories" (cf. Joisten 2013). With these writings, the horizon of the philosophy of histories is opened, a horizon that—viewed from today's perspective—is ahead of its time (though Schapp does not use contemporary terminology) and places the fundamental perspective in an anthropo-ontological reflection concerning histories, narrations, and storytelling. Thus, it is a matter of "*Wirkungsgeschichtlichkeit*" (in the sense of Hans-Georg Gadamer), of social and cultural situatedness, of figurations and configurations of meaning, of authorship and co-authorship, of birth, of temporality, of death and life, of identity, of "being-in-relation-to," of the oblivion of histories, and so on (see Joisten 2010, 2013, 2015; J. Schapp 2004a, 2004b, 2007, 2020, 2022; Greisch 2010; Liebsch 2010; Joisten, J. Schapp, and Thiemer 2020).

Two points should be emphasized here. First, Schapp's representations of the contents of the philosophy of histories do not align with or merge into the published writings mentioned above. Second, Wilhelm Schapp did not begin his philosophical thoughts directly or immediately with a focus on a philosophy of histories (see for the following Joisten 2016; Schapp 1964, 1976, 2025).

At the beginning of his studies, Wilhelm Schapp became one of the philosophers in the early phenomenological circles. He studied law and philosophy at the University of Freiburg, beginning in the Winter Semester of

1902–3. He then moved to Berlin, where he described his experiences in his brief biography:

> I listened there to Simmel, Schmoller, Wagner, von Liszt, Kohler, Dernburg, all renowned teachers. Dilthey was no longer lecturing. However, in my 6th or early 7th semester, I was able to attend some seminar sessions that he held in his house. These lessons also included reading Husserl's *Logical Investigations*, which Dilthey highly esteemed. While I had to prepare for the first legal state examination, I continued to study philosophy diligently, especially the works of Kant. (Schapp 1964: 54)

And Schapp's philosophical studies did not end with the successful completion of his law studies. During his time as a trainee lawyer, he continued his studies in Göttingen, where he sought out Edmund Husserl. Just as Schapp had thoroughly studied the writings of Immanuel Kant in Freiburg, he now meticulously and energetically worked through Husserl's *Logical Investigations* with "enthusiasm increasing daily, reading day and night for several years" (Schapp 1976: 7, 2025: 228). In 1909, he obtained his doctorate under the supervision of Edmund Husserl with the dissertation *Beiträge zur Phänomenologie der Wahrnehmung*, which was published in Halle in 1910 (Schapp 2013).

It would not be inappropriate to point out that Wilhelm Schapp cannot be regarded as a faithful disciple of his doctoral advisor, Edmund Husserl. Two aspects stand out in Schapp's case. First, he had already embarked on the path of a lawyer and remained active as a jurist and notary throughout his life. Second, Schapp did not identify his philosophical approach as representative of what he called classical phenomenology. He perceived this movement as being unduly influenced by mathematics and logic. Schapp sought a different path, and in doing so, he encountered the phenomenon of histories.

In his first published book of the history trilogy, *In Geschichten verstrickt*, Schapp himself acknowledges a clear contrast to Husserl's position: "If we start from histories, our starting point is diametrically opposed to Husserl's. The difference is comparable to the difference between the Pythagorean theorem and the fairy tale of Little Red Riding Hood. It may not be surprising that the world presents itself differently depending on this starting point" (Schapp 2012: 172). Nevertheless, the philosophy of histories reveals a phenomenological orientation rooted in an approach to or an attitude toward philosophizing, as Schapp himself expresses in an early publication: "I only hope that I wrote nothing I did not myself see" (Schapp 2013: ix).

Wilhelm Schapp's extensive literary estate, which he did not publish during his lifetime and which comprises over 20,000 typewritten pages, illustrates his original approach even more clearly. Research has been conducted on this collection since 2006 at the *Wilhelm-Schapp-Forschungsstelle*, and since 2016, works from the *Nachlass* have been published. Regarding this aspect of Wilhelm Schapp's philosophy, I will paraphrase passages and thoughts recorded by the editors of Wilhelm Schapp's posthumous writings (Karen Joisten, Jan Schapp, and Nicole Thiemer), which can now be presented for the first time in English (Schapp 2016, 2017, 2018, 2019).

Parts of Wilhelm Schapp's literary estate are preserved in the archives of the Bavarian State Library, while others remain in private possession. Some of the manuscripts that illuminate the comprehensive horizon of the philosophy of histories are published in the series: "*Wilhelm Schapp. Philosophischer Nachlass*."

The documents encompass Wilhelm Schapp's philosophical discussions and reflections from 1920 to 1965, and the pages mainly contain written dictations, corrected preparatory work for manuscripts, and notes; the *Nachlass* also includes letters. In addition to the publications, these documents demonstrate Wilhelm Schapp's intense philosophical contemplation throughout his entire life, as well as his consistent and continuous pursuit of the development of his own approach. The *Nachlass* shows that, for example, Wilhelm Schapp had already written *Zur Metaphsysik des Muttertums* (Schapp 1965) in 1937, as part of his reflections on the problem of values, a problem that occupied him throughout his life. It also reveals that the phenomenological questions of his dissertation were further developed and transformed. Moreover, it provides insights into Wilhelm Schapp's readings, such as his intellectual engagement with the phenomenology of Edmund Husserl, the early phenomenological circles in Göttingen and Munich, Sigmund Freud's psychoanalysis, Ferdinand de Saussure's philosophy of language, and the re-reading of pre-Socratic thinkers. It also offers glimpses into biographical and contemporary history, including numerous published articles by Wilhelm Schapp on debtor protection, as well as correspondence with Rudolf Smend, Hermann Noack, Roman Ingarden, Friedrich Kambartel, Alexander Pfänder, and Herbert Spiegelberg.

Wilhelm Schapp documented his philosophical thoughts throughout his life by dictating in the mornings and afternoons. He then reviewed, corrected, and further developed these dictations. This independent approach corresponds to the linguistic style of Wilhelm Schapp's published writings. When reading them, one gets the impression of following a free lecture, sometimes referring back and sometimes ahead, rather than a strictly objective and rational discourse. This characterizes the unfolding of his philosophy of histories.

2. A close "Re-reading" as an Approach

The two central thoughts of *In Geschichten verstrickt* highlighted in the present chapter refer to the diverse themes and horizons of the philosophy of histories. All of the contents of the philosophy of histories are vividly interconnected. Trying to reduce them to a system (even in a mere representational retelling) is misguided. The notion of systematics, in the broadest sense of the term, readily suggests the idea of a closed system. However, the approach of the philosophy of histories is opposed to such a notion. The philosophy of histories does not establish a philosophical system, but pursues the web or network of relationships among histories in ever deeper and broader circles. In this web or network, the lifeworld is given to humans, humans are given to themselves and to others, and fellow humans are constantly interconnected through histories. The contents of the philosophy of histories can be understood, metaphorically speaking, as a vivid organism within which no part can be adequately comprehended without recognizing its place in the overall context.

To support this, I cite the following words of Wilhelm Schapp:

> We do not want to separate the individual history from the context in which it arises and then compare it as an independent entity with other histories, attempting to attain general statements about histories. Such a procedure would, in our view, distort the structure (*Gebilde*). If we see correctly, it is not that one history is connected to another, nor is each history merely a drop in a sea of histories; rather, each history is connected with other histories and perhaps with all histories within this vivid nexus. (Schapp 2012: 94)

Formulated from another perspective, Schapp emphasizes that histories themselves are "fundamental," since they provide access to the understanding of human beings and their world. Moreover, being human implies being entangled in histories, as the title *In Geschichten verstrickt. Zum Sein von Mensch und Ding* expresses. This is the central topic that emphasizes the significance of histories for the (anthropo-ontological) approach.

A. Wozudinge

Let's begin with the topic of "*Wozudinge*" (one of Wilhelm Schapp's most well-known neologisms), the topic to which the first section of *In Geschichten verstrickt* is dedicated. This approach can be regarded as the fundamental starting point of the philosophy of histories. The descriptions in *In Geschichten verstrickt* initially aim to characterize access to the external world through *Wozudinge*. In this context, Schapp examines the relationship between human beings and the (external) world, demonstrating that the philosophy of histories departs from a traditional epistemological approach such as Cartesianism. Such an approach to the philosophical challenges concerning the relations or the "web of references" of the human-world connection would be misguided. It posits a thinking subject that perceives the world and its objects merely as objects of knowledge, thereby highlighting the epistemological primacy of the subject and relegating the primacy of the prior human-world relationship to the background. The philosophy of histories is fundamentally opposed to and undermines such a subject-object dichotomy.

If we want to consider Schapp's approach from a different point of view, we find that focusing on the idea of "being in relation" easily evokes echoes of other expressions such as *Bewandtniszusammenhang* or *Zuhandenheit*. However, it is important to emphasize that the development of Wilhelm Schapp's thinking does not merge into a fundamental ontological endeavor, such as Martin Heidegger's *Sein und Zeit*, nor does it align with an analysis of the "world-with-others," as in the case, for example, of Karl Löwith.

What is important for Wilhelm Schapp to demonstrate? First and foremost, he is concerned with a modified phenomenological approach that addresses the relationships of "human being/thing/world" through the phenomenon of histories. In this regard, Schapp states: "The *Wozuding* we are dealing with in this section, and which serves as a connection between history and the external world, is the thing created by humans. It is the work of human hands. Such *Wozudinge* include cups, tables, chairs, houses, cathedrals, streets, and railways" (Schapp 2012: 11).

The *Wozuding* is something created. It is not merely an object for a subject, as would be claimed from an epistemological perspective. It is neither "world-poor" nor "worldless," nor is it simply "occurrent," as one might say in line with other philosophical currents of the twentieth century.

In *Metaphysik der Naturwissenschaft* (see Schapp 2009: 126f. and 109), Schapp describes his lack of understanding regarding the fact that the particularity of the "emergence of the world" (*Auftauchen von Welt*)—the how of its emergence—is rarely or not at all addressed in classical, scientifically influenced models of world-explanation. With the concept of *Wozuding*, Schapp distances himself from the successful possibility of any such conceptions (see J. Schapp 2004b).

Jan Schapp refers to the significance of characterizing the *Wozudinge* for Wilhelm Schapp's philosophy of histories in his article "Erinnerungen an Wilhelm Schapp":

> My father later told me more often about the moment when the significance of histories became clear to him. In a discussion group, they philosophized about the perception of a teacup on the table. This cup had a crack. It was this crack that made the importance of histories evident to him, histories in which things first emerge that he then referred to as "*Wozudinge*." In *In Geschichten verstrickt*, the discovery of the crack in the cup is mentioned, of course, without any indication of the significance of this moment for the philosophy of histories itself. (J. Schapp 2004a: 17)

Things are not just things; in the philosophy of histories, the focus lies in the fact that something emerges as something, here referred to with the term "*Wozuding*." Within this terminological innovation, the "*Wozu*" should not be understood solely in terms of function. Time, age, and location, as well as relation to and from human beings, are all taken into account. *Wozudinge* are not things in themselves. In their "condition," and in the way in which they are handled and encountered, they are not just something; instead, from a philosophical perspective, they serve as an access point, as a seam or interface—in Schapp's words, a "*Nahtstelle*." "We see this access point (*Nahtstelle*) between histories and the external world in the formations (*Gebilde*) we call *Wozudinge*" (Schapp 2012: 3).

Wozudinge reveal themselves in their "definiteness"—specifically, in their age, with a past: within them, temporality is given. With *Wozudinge*, then, a horizon emerges. The topic of the horizon has been particularly emphasized by Hans Rainer Sepp (see for the following Sepp 2010). With Sepp, it can be emphasized that in *In Geschichten verstrickt*, Wilhelm Schapp undertakes the task of analyzing the *Wozudinge*—as things of active engagement—in order to explore the connection between histories and the external world.

Wozudinge have a genesis that grants them a horizon in their present use, their manufacture, and their context of use. In the philosophy of histories, the concept of horizon can also be described, following Sepp, as a *Sinnzusammenhang* (meaning-context). The significance of a *Wozuding*, arising from its current use, its past real uses, its manufacture, and its potential functions, constitutes "meaning-determinations" that are inherent in this thing as a horizon. Although they are fundamentally related, they do not necessarily need to be explicitly addressed. Since each *Werk-Ding* has its own "history of meaning" (*Sinn-Geschichte*), it is connected to the meaning-histories of all other products in the active lives of people. The horizon acts as a link that establishes these interconnections.

Following Wilhelm Schapp, it can be emphasized:

> *Wozudinge* emerge in or with their determinations, with their characteristics. Closely related to this is that they do not appear in a punctual present or as only punctually present, but with a past, with a history, with an age. This past, this history is always present as well. Here we use the expression that the past appears within the horizon. This horizon can be more or less filled in its emergence. However, it is also more or less present without being filled. The cup from which I drink daily has a crack. Yesterday, this crack was not there. Now, within the horizon, the question arises about how this crack came to be. Thus within the horizon, which is always present [. . .], an island appears. In its way, the horizon of each *Wozuding* includes its production, as if it were the moment of its birth. With the act of production, a producer emerges within the horizon—a human being. In this way, through the *Wozuding*, we somehow encounter this being "human," to which all our efforts ultimately apply. (Schapp 2012: 17)

Within the horizon of the *Wozuding*, its production—for example, the moment of its emergence—is situated, as are the events that have happened to the *Wozuding* along with its connection to human beings. *Wozudinge* always appear with their respective specific horizons, within a specific meaning-context, which is demonstrated in terms of spatial location and temporal aspects (*räumliche und zeitliche Verortetheit*) in the philosophy of histories (see, for example, Schapp 2012: 56ff. and 72ff.).

To speak of *Wozudinge* as a phenomenon in the sense of the philosophy of histories means articulating the emergence of a meaning-context. The "determination" of something based on categories such as matter, substance, or form, is accordingly subverted within the philosophy of histories; indeed, it could perhaps even be called "objectless" or "non-representational."

From here, it can be clarified to what extent Wilhelm Schapp adopts the expression "*Auswas der Wozudinge*" to describe his approach:

> The material is a derivative, an offspring of the *Wozudinge*. The *Wozudinge* are not things among other things; they are not things at all. They cannot appear as

> purely material entities, but rather the material is always just the *Auswas* of the *Wozudinge*. If, now, seemingly alongside or among the *Wozudinge*, something appears that is merely material, it borrows its character and determinations from the dependent "*Auswas*" (from-what) of the *Wozudinge*, which is artificially made or becomes independent. (Schapp 2012: 31)

The contributions of Jan Schapp (Wilhelm Schapp's son), which contain an examination of his father's philosophy of histories (see J. Schapp 2022), emphasize the extent to which the philosophy of histories also includes an implicit examination of the early work *Beiträge zur Phänomenologie der Wahrnehmung*, which specifically focuses on the phenomenon of object-perception as a point of reference. The philosophy of histories introduces new approaches. This is demonstrated in the portrayal of the phenomenon of *Wozudinge*, where the topic of perception is not treated from an epistemological perspective. Rather, the *Auswas* of the *Wozuding* only comes to the foreground through "working with the things." Access to the *Wozuding* is achieved through actions such as "sawing, drilling, hammering, filing," and other forms of activity, along with their multiple variations, always within the framework of stories in which human beings are entangled (see, among others, Schapp 2012: 20). Access always takes place in a "history-like manner" (*geschichtenhaft*).

In an analogy, *Wozudinge* could be conceived in terms of *Werke* (works), in which, human beings are always entangled insofar as such works emerge. The *Wozudinge* are also part of the world of histories, the circle of histories, as Wilhelm Schapp expresses it in his philosophical approach. The oblivion of histories, which is a central theme of the *Philosophie der Geschichten*, is particularly evident in the fact that this was undermined in the course of the *Sonderwelt des Abendlandes* (special world of the Occident) (cf. J. Schapp 2004b). From the perspective of that time, this is the subject of the investigations taken up in *Metaphysik der Naturwissenschaft*.

The apprehension of thing, world, and human as a "state of affairs" (*Sachverhalt*), as it can also be called, is a notion that is subject to critique in the philosophy of histories, taking into account different philosophical lines of traditions. This becomes evident in *In Geschichten verstrickt*, though it is more extensively explored as a separate topic in *Philosophie der Geschichten*. These explorations lead Wilhelm Schapp to his original philosophy of histories. A state of affairs thinking "skips over" being entangled in histories, thus bypassing the anthropo-ontological situatedness of philosophical reflection. In other words, blind spots or omitted aspects become conspicuous by their absence in state of affairs thinking, which the elaboration of the philosophy of histories responds to and makes its subject-matter. To conclude this part, I quote Wilhelm Schapp's own words:

> Phenomenology, for example, would say that even the fairy tale of Little Red Riding Hood consists of sentences that have their clear meaning, just like the sentences of the Pythagorean theorem, with the difference that in one case, they are individual sentences, and in the other case, they are general sentences, which may also be founded again in individual sentences, similar to the way the general sentences of natural science are founded in individual sentences as they are formed, for example, in the description of an experiment. [. . .] We have repeatedly attempted to grasp the structure (*Gebilde*) of history using these constructions or the means that [such an approach] [. . .] provides us. We have tried to grasp the structure, on the one hand, as a combination of sentences consisting of concepts, and on the other hand, as a state of affairs corresponding to these sentences. All our efforts to grasp the structure of history (*Gebilde Geschichte*) in its peculiarity with this have failed. (Schapp 2012: 172f.)

History, in the sense of the philosophy of histories, is not simply composed of sentences, and does not dissolve into a representation of states of affairs coinciding with a (re)objectifying process. Today, one might also speak of breaking away from the lifeworld situation by assuming the possibility of a "worldless" or "third" observer, which is, indeed, possible in the act of thinking—but what is thereby encountered is not at all what is pursued in the philosophy of histories.

B. "*In-Geschichten-Verstricktsein*"

At the beginning of this section, I would like to refer to lines written by Karen Joisten, Jan Schapp, and the author of the present contribution as editors of Wilhelm Schapp's posthumous writings in the preface to Volume 4: *Geschichte und Geschichten* (see Schapp 2019: 7). Here they quote the—presumably—most frequently cited sentence from *In Geschichten verstrickt*: "The history stands for the man" (Schapp 2012: 103), that is, the heading given by Wilhelm Schapp to Chapter 2 of the second section of *In Geschichten verstrickt*. In the posthumous writings, there is a further, and perhaps more appropriate, paraphrase of the thought, as stated in a manuscript from May 27, 1959: "If we previously said that history stands for man, now I want to propose the statement: history stands for a people, or even for a world and a time" (Schapp 2019: 32).

Wilhelm Schapp begins *In Geschichten verstrickt* with the meaningful lines: "We humans are always entangled in histories. To every history belongs someone entangled in it. History and being entangled in histories are so closely connected that one perhaps cannot even separate them in thought" (Schapp 2012: 1).

Being human means being entangled in histories (*In-Geschichten-verstrickt-sein*) (see, among others already cited, Haas 2002; Pohlmeyer 2004; Lübbe 1972). Being entangled in histories means both "*Eigenverstrickung*" (self-entanglement) and "*Fremdverstrickung*" (other-entanglement), but also the "*Wirgeschichte*" (we-history) (see Schapp 2012: 121ff., 148ff.) as an ineluctable *Geschichtengewebe* (fabric of histories), even if we are not always aware of it.

This thought, this approach, this perspective serves as the foundation of the philosophy of histories, expressing that the human being is intertwined in a multitude of histories, from birth to death, as well as from a standpoint, in the sense of Gadamer's "effective history" (*Wirkungsgeschichte*). Humans are authors, but they are always also co-authors. At the same time, this signifies that access to understanding humans happens through histories and can only happen in the sense of the philosophical approach of histories. In this context, Schapp emphasizes that "encountering histories (*Begegnen mit Geschichten*) is equivalent to being human" (Schapp 2019: 76). And it is here that the anthropo-ontological perspective of the philosophy of histories is located.

In *In Geschichten verstrickt*, Schapp vividly describes the approach of the philosophy of histories with the following words:

> If one surveys one's acquaintances, one will see that one actually knows them all only through histories, and that perhaps many small histories may come together to form a picture of life. The essential thing we know about human beings seems to be their histories and the histories surrounding them. Through the history [of a man], we come into contact with a self. A Man is not the man of flesh and blood. Instead, his history imposes itself on us as his true essence. (Schapp 2012: 105)

It is important to remember that the notion of being "entangled" (*Verstricktsein*) in the philosophy of histories does not have a negative connotation, but refers to the fact that histories comprise a network or web of relationships and references in which the human being, as a human being in the lifeworld, is always already located. Human beings can move from one history to another in the sense that the content of histories may differ, but they are never without histories, both from a structural and an anthropo-ontological perspective. A complete detachment from being entangled in histories is existentially and essentially impossible. An idea like that is only possible through an intellectual act of abstraction, which, if used as a point of reference for philosophical reflection, inevitably surpasses its foundation.

To illustrate the idea of being entangled in histories, I cite the well-known example given in Chapter 6 of the second section of *In Geschichten verstrickt* (see Schapp 2012: 103–6). The impressive opening lines of the chapter are as follows: "The history stands for the man. By this we mean that we have ultimate access to the human being through histories about him. We seek to illustrate this with a few examples" (Schapp 2012: 103).

This example vividly illustrates the dynamic network or web of references, which, from the perspective of the philosophy of history, characterizes the concept of being entangled in histories in relation to human beings. Here Wilhelm Schapp appeals to webs of references in practical life, always keeping in mind a "depth semantics" perspective in order to let the philosophical significance of being entangled in histories emerge.

As previously mentioned, Wilhelm Schapp was active not only as a philosopher but also as a lawyer. In this regard, I recall the following statement by Jan Schapp:

> That Wilhelm Schapp was not only a philosopher but also a lawyer was certainly of an importance for the development of his philosophy of histories that should not be underestimated. Perhaps one could even argue that his long-term experience as a lawyer and notary was as crucial to the emergence of this philosophy as his origins in Edmund Husserl's phenomenology. (J. Schapp 2010: 65)

The example we are concerned with, which deals with a case and with the perspective of a judge toward a defendant, provides a fundamental insight into the concern of Schapp's philosophical approach. It begins with a "report against a respected man [. . .] with many delicate details" (Schapp 2012: 103), or in other words, the content of the case file. According to Schapp, "Our question now is: How does the structure of history (*Gebilde Geschichte*), which has appeared in front of the judge on the basis of the case file, relate to the man himself who now confronts him (the judge), next to whom he is perhaps sitting, with whom he enters into a conversation?" (Schapp 2012: 103).

Through the case file, the judge becomes acquainted with "a history" that reflects the person of the accused. This history continues within the judge's thoughts, initiating a kind of "co-entanglement (in histories)," as it can be called, using the terminology of the philosophy of histories. Based on the case history, the individual human being in question appears in the world for the judge. At the same time, the encounter with the defendant may also bring other histories of the judge himself to the surface. This is reflected in the following lines:

> We assume that the judge is convinced of the accuracy of the report. His conversation with the man will be very chilly. However, considering the [courtroom situation], he cannot avoid observing the proprieties in the conversation. In this example, it is evident that the judge believes that he knows the man from the case file, from this history recorded in the files, in a completely different and better way than from the encounter with him in society. We can also modify the scenario slightly, where the judge finds the report's accuracy to be highly doubtful, and has reasons to assume unfair motives behind it. Then he might compare the entity (*Gebilde*) "man" that emerges from the report itself with the man he gets to know. (Schapp 2012: 103)

Only histories provide approach, access—and not just one mode of access but rather a multitude.[2]

Schapp seeks to demonstrate with this example that the histories (in the case file) and the vivid experience do not necessarily lead to the same impression about the person. However (and this is the deeper meaning), what Schapp pursues through his description is that access to this person is always (only) given and (only) possible through and via a multitude of histories in which the person is entangled. Thus, in the above example, the judge is entangled through the file histories as well as through the encounter. Concerning this topic, Jan Schapp writes:

> What we refer to as a "case" here are actually histories. They may be histories with a legal focus. But there is hardly a case that does not also reveal human qualities and provide insights into the human soul. We would like to emphasize that the cases represent the individual humans, and that the lawyer reaches the individuals through the cases. (Schapp 2012: 104)

3. Reflections

Looking ahead, I would like to remain close to Schapp's philosophy of histories while offering a suggestion regarding the importance of revisiting and reflecting on the philosophy of histories in our present times. The currently accelerated—actually, over-accelerated—process of digitization and the technological transformation of our lifeworld goes hand in hand with a mathematized conception of human beings and the world, which overlooks our "being-entangled-in-histories" (see Thiemer 2023). Here one can recall Husserl's reflections concerning the lifeworld (see Husserl 2012) and the overlooking of embodiment. Also, overlooked is an "appropriate" measure of the possibility of "authentic" human existence and being. Digitalization shapes a new *Sonderwelt* (special world) whose boundaries and localizations can be critically addressed through the philosophy of histories.

In Wilhelm Schapp's philosophy, histories and being entangled in histories are relational meaning-contexts that point forward and backward, never seamless, never indifferent. They contain differences and distinctions, and they are always relational, including the notion of being bound on one hand and free on the other—the very tension that characterizes human beings, whether considered concretely, philosophically, or ethically.

And here I would like to raise once again the idea of the horizon. In the philosophy of histories, it is written: "History is constantly ahead of itself, and it is constantly attached to the past. It imperceptibly transitions into pre-history and post-history. In it, there is no resting point in the sense of the present, but only in terms of the deconstruction and construction of future horizons" (Schapp 2012: 161).

At the same time, the "entanglement in histories" discussed in the philosophy of histories does not imply that a person, as an entangled being in stories, is once and for all essentially determined by a single story or history. Rather, the concept of being entangled in histories allows us to reflect upon the interplay of relational conditionality, relational freedoms, and relational possibilities.

To illustrate this connectedness, we can turn to a passage where Schapp speaks of the "arcs" of histories, of being entangled in histories. Regarding natality (as Hannah Arendt has termed it), thrownness (as Martin Heidegger has termed it), and our temporal finitude and spatial situatedness (as emphasized in various life-philosophical, cultural, or social-philosophical approaches), humans are relationally bound, yet always also retain a possibility, a "design" or "projection" that can be "mastered": "From the beginning, an arc stretches out, already having a direction toward an end. However, this arc does not fully unfold. The direction it points to is abandoned, dismantled, and new arcs emerge" (Schapp 2012: 91).

The phenomenon of histories, as presented in the philosophy of histories, does not merely look into the thought of narrative texts, of narratives. Schapp succinctly formulates the dimension of the philosophy of histories: "For us, histories are primordial phenomena (*Urphänomene*), primordial structures (*Urgebilde*), more primal than the formations (*Gebilde*) of science" (Schapp 2015: 26). And here I would like to cite these additional lines:

> Thus the question repeatedly arises for us whether we have done justice to what the phenomenologist understands as the ultimate sphere of objects and verifications, or whether there exists, beyond and alongside or behind the histories, some kind of world of objects. In our perspective, histories as primordial phenomena consume the entire world of objects, or perhaps we could also say that the world emerges only from the histories. (Schapp 2016: 71)

Finally, I would like to propose for reflection the following lines by Maurice Merleau-Ponty, which, in my opinion, aptly describe the profound significance of Schapp's philosophical approach: "Philosophy, in truth, means learning anew to see the world, and in this respect, a simple narrative—a story that is told—can mean the world just as 'deeply' as a philosophical treatise" (Merleau-Ponty 1966: 18).

Notes

1 The thoughts expressed here refer to contents addressed (albeit with varying degrees of emphasis) in Thiemer (2020a, 2020b, 2022), and other unpublished lectures concerning the philosophy of Wilhelm Schapp.

2 Here the topic of narrative identity could also be linked with the threefold theory of mimesis, as Paul Ricœur especially emphasized during his middle phase.

References

Arendt, H. (1987), *Vita Activa oder Vom tätigen Leben*, 5th edn, München/Zürich: R. Piper.

Greisch, J. (2010), "Phänomenologie als Philosophie der Geschichten: eine vierte, stille Revolution der philosophischen Denkungsart?" in K. Joisten (ed.), *Das Denken Wilhelm Schapps. Perspektiven für unsere Zeit*, 190–214, Freiburg/München: Alber.

Haas, S. (2002), *Kein Selbst ohne Geschichten. Wilhelm Schapps Geschichtenphilosophie und Paul Ricœurs Überlegungen zur narrativen Identität*, Hildesheim/Zürich/New York: Olms.

Husserl, E. (2012), *Die Krisis der europäischen Wissenschaften und die transzendentale Phänomenologie. Eine Einleitung in die phänomenologische Philosophie*, ed. E. Ströker, Hamburg: Meiner.

Joisten, K. (2010), "Von dem 'Verstricktsein,' der (Gerichts)Akte und dem Erzählen und Hören. Zur Geschichtenphilosophie Wilhelm Schapps," in P. Gödicke, H. Hammen,

W. Schur, and W.-D. Walker (eds), *Festschrift für Jan Schapp zum siebzigsten Geburtstag*, 283–97, Tübingen: Mohr Siebeck.

Joisten, K. (2013), "Wilhelm Schapp," in T. Bedorf, A. Gelhard (eds), *German Philosophy in the 20th Century. Ein Autorenhandbuch*, 246–8, Darmstadt: WBG.

Joisten, K. (2015), "Wilhelm Schapps Philosophie der Geschichten. Ein Zugang," in W. Schapp (2015), *Philosophie der Geschichten*, ed. K. Joisten, J. Schapp, 3rd ed., Frankfurt am Main: Vittorio Klostermann: 5–11.

Joisten, K. (2016), "Wilhelm Schapp. Eine biographische Skizze," in W. Schapp (2016), *Auf dem Weg einer Philosophie der Geschichten. Teilband I*, ed. K. Joisten, J. Schapp, N. Thiemer, 360–72, Freiburg/München: Alber.

Joisten, K., Schapp, J., and Thiemer, N., eds. (2020), *Die Rezeption der Geschichtenphilosophie Wilhelm Schapps. Kommentare und Fortsetzungen*, Freiburg/München: Alber.

Liebsch, B. (2010), "Die Idee der Phänomenologie im Lichte ihrer narrativistischen Verabschiedung im Werk Wilhelm Schapps," in K. Joisten (ed.), *Das Denken Wilhelm Schapps. Perspektiven für unsere Zeit*, 22–48, Freiburg/München: Alber.

Lübbe, H. (1972), *Bewußtsein in Geschichten. Studien zur Phänomenologie der Subjektivität: Mach, Husserl, Schapp, Wittgenstein*, Freiburg: Rombach.

MacIntyre, A. (1995), *Der Verlust der Tugend. Zur moralischen Krise der Gegenwart*, 6th edn, Frankfurt am Main: Suhrkamp.

Merleau-Ponty, M. (1966), *Phänomenologie der Wahrnehmung*, trans. R. Boehm, 6th edn, Berlin: De Gruyter.

Pohlmeyer, M. (2004), *Geschichten-Hermeneutik. Philosophische, literarische und theologische Provokationen im Denken von Wilhelm Schapp*, Münster: LIT.

Schapp, J. (2004a), "Erinnerungen an Wilhelm Schapp," in K.-H. Lembeck (ed.), *Geschichte und Geschichten. Studien zur Geschichtenphänomenologie Wilhelm Schapps*, 13–24, Würzburg: Königshausen & Neumann.

Schapp, J. (2004b), "Positive Welten und Sonderwelt des Abendlandes in der Geschichtenphilosophie Wilhelm Schapps," *Phänomenologische Forschungen*: 133–149.

Schapp, J. (2007), "Verstrickung und Erzählung," *Phänomenologische Forschungen*: 125–144.

Schapp, J. (2010), "Geschichtenphilosophie und Recht," in K. Joisten (ed.), *Das Denken Wilhelm Schapps. Perspektiven für unsere Zeit*, 65–85, Freiburg/München: Alber.

Schapp, J. (2020), "Eine Einführung. Wilhelm Schapps Geschichtenphilosophie," in K. Joisten, J. Schapp, N. and Thiemer (eds), *Die Rezeption der Geschichtenphilosophie Wilhelm Schapps. Kommentare und Fortsetzungen*, 15–38, Freiburg/München: Alber.

Schapp, J. (2022), *Zugänge zu Geschichtenwelten*, Freiburg/München: Alber.

Schapp, W. (1964), "Kleine Autobiographie des Verfassers, " *Eckart-Jahrbuch 1964/65*: 54–6.

Schapp, W. (1965), *Zur Metaphysik des Muttertums*, Den Haag: Martinus Nijhoff.

Schapp, W. (1976), *Erinnerungen an Edmund Husserl. Ein Beitrag zur Geschichte der Phänomenologie*, Wiesbaden: Heymann.

Schapp, W. (2009 [1965]), *Metaphysik der Naturwissenschaft*, 3rd edn, Frankfurt am Main: Vittorio Klostermann.

Schapp, W. (2012 [1953]), *In Geschichten verstrickt. Zum Sein von Mensch und Ding*, 5th edn, Frankfurt am Main: Vittorio Klostermann.

Schapp, W. (2013 [1910]), *Beiträge zur Phänomenologie der Wahrnehmung*, 5th edn, Frankfurt am Main: Vittorio Klostermann.

Schapp, W. (2015), *Philosophie der Geschichten*, ed. K. Joisten and J. Schapp, 3rd edn, Frankfurt am Main: Vittorio Klostermann.

Schapp, W. (2016), *Philosophischer Nachlass. Teilband I: Auf dem Weg einer Philosophie der Geschichten*, ed. K. Joisten, J. Schapp, and N. Thiemer, Freiburg/München: Alber.

Schapp, W. (2017), *Philosophischer Nachlass. Teilband II: Auf dem Weg einer Philosophie der Geschichten*, ed. K. Joisten, J. Schapp, and N. Thiemer, Freiburg/München: Alber.

Schapp, W. (2018), *Philosophischer Nachlass. Teilband III: Auf dem Weg einer Philosophie der Geschichten*, ed. K. Joisten, J. Schapp, N. and Thiemer, Freiburg/München: Alber.

Schapp, W. (2019), *Philosophischer Nachlass. Teilband IV: Geschichten und Geschichte*, ed. K. Joisten, J. Schapp, and N. Thiemer, Freiburg/München: Alber.

Schapp, W. (2025), "Recollections of Husserl," trans. E. A. Behnke, in D. De Santis and D. Nuccilli (eds), *The Philosophy of Wilhelm Schapp: From Phenomenology to Jurisprudence and the Hermeneutics of Stories*, 227–238, London: Bloomsbury.

Sepp, H. R. (2010), "Welt und Grenze. Wilhelm Schapps Philosophie der Geschichten," in K. Joisten (ed.), *Das Denken Wilhelm Schapps. Perspektiven für unsere Zeit*, 283–97, Freiburg/München: Alber.

Thiemer, N. (2020a), "Essentia oder existentia—vom wesentlichen und geschichtlichen Verstricktsein des Menschen in Geschichten," in K. Joisten, J. Schapp, and N. Thiemer (eds), *Die Rezeption der Geschichtenphilosophie Wilhelm Schapps. Kommentare und Fortsetzungen*, 149–63, Freiburg/München: Alber.

Thiemer, N. (2020b), "Welt ohne Kosmos!? Ein Beitrag zu Wilhelm Schapps Geschichtenphilosophie," in H. R. Sepp (ed.), *Natur und Kosmos. Entwürfe der frühen Phänomenologie*, 116–32, Nordhausen: Bautz.

Thiemer, N. (2022), "Wilhelm Schapp," in *Enzyklopädie Recht und Literatur*. https://doi.org/10.17879/71089503293; URL:https://lawandliterature.eu/index.php/de/inhalt?view=article&id=24&catid=11.

Thiemer, N. (2023), "Zur Bedeutung der Erzählung im Zuge der Digitalisierung. Eine technikethische Reflexion des Grenzverlustes der Information," in E. Barbagallo, I. W. Gerhartz, and N. Thiemer (eds), *Erzählhorizonte. Inter- und transdisziplinäre Herausforderungen einer narrativen Ethik*, 69–83, Wiesbaden: Springer Nature.

11

Philosophy of Histories II: *Philosophie der Geschichten*

Approaches and Reflections

Karen Joisten

0. Preliminary remarks

Wilhelm Schapp can be called the father of the "philosophy of histories" (*Philosophie der Geschichten*). It is important to note that his *Philosophie der Geschichten* should not be understood in the sense of a traditional *Philosophie der Geschichte* (philosophy of history). A traditional philosophy of history can be understood—with the help of the French Enlightenment philosopher Voltaire—as a *philosophie de l'histoire* that has the intention of providing a comprehensive, overall philosophical interpretation of the course of world history. Probably the best-known representatives of such a traditional philosophy of history in the eighteenth and nineteenth centuries are Georg Wilhelm Friedrich Hegel and Karl Marx, with whom the overall philosophical interpretations of a philosophy of history, in a narrower sense, also came to an end.

Wilhelm Schapp's philosophy of histories is termed a "trilogy of histories" (see Joisten 2013: 246–48) because it comprises the three books that Schapp published during his lifetime, each book representing a different approach to his philosophy of histories. This trilogy includes, first, his 1953 work *In Geschichten verstrickt. Zum Sein von Mensch und Ding*; second, the extensive book *Philosophie der Geschichten* that followed in 1959; and finally, *Zur Metaphysik der Naturwissenschaft*, which was published in 1965.

Without the public being aware of it, however, Schapp continued to develop and differentiate the basic idea of the primacy of histories throughout his life. Most of his legacy, which covers the period from 1920 to 1965, is housed in the archives of the Bavarian State Library, where it is kept in twenty-seven different boxes. It contains typewritten documents, manuscripts, handwritten notes, published and unpublished articles, and letters. If one concentrates on the manuscripts from the 1950s that were put together by Wilhelm Schapp himself, possible further perspectives, transitions, and developments of the philosophy of histories become apparent (see Schapp 2016, 2017, 2018, 2019).

For our task of presenting the central ideas of Schapp's comprehensive book, *Philosophie der Geschichten*, and making those ideas accessible to an international audience in a critical-constructive way, the reference to his material legacy is indispensable. This legacy includes a lengthy manuscript to which Schapp gave the title *In Geschichten verstrickt. Fortsetzung.*[1] This manuscript is, as it were, the seam between *In Geschichten verstrickt* (1953) and *Philosophie der Geschichten* (1959). In this manuscript, Schapp offers an interpretation of human beings as always woven into a vivid historical nexus, bodily disclosing their "world" with so-called "things-for" (*Wozudingen*), gradually opening up access to it. And in the course of these reflections, there emerge new perspectives, aspects, and facets of his philosophy of histories that are not included in the books already published.

However, it should not be overlooked that a great deal of material from the manuscript was indeed able to find its way into *Philosophie der Geschichten*. Thus, the three volumes of his legacy *In Geschichten verstrickt. Fortsetzung* can more precisely trace (and make comprehensible) the path that Schapp took between *In Geschichten verstrickt* and his final version of *Philosophie der Geschichten*. If one allows oneself to become involved in the conceptual correspondences, deviations, and differences between this manuscript and the final version of *Philosophie der Geschichten* authorized by Schapp for publication, one finds expressions of annoyance, questions, and provisional positions that invite one to take a constructive stance toward Schapp's work, giving it new impulses and perhaps even opening up new fields of research beyond the already established contexts.

In these preliminary remarks, another reference may be relevant with regard to Schapp's *Philosophie der Geschichten*. As mentioned, Schapp published the book in 1959. He was able to check this first edition. In 1981, the book was published in a second edition, but minor changes were made. Since Jan Schapp and I wanted to provide access to this book in the form authorized by Wilhelm Schapp, we published a third, revised edition in 2015, which represents a return to the first edition. With this in mind, it is advisable to use the first or third edition as the basis for citation.

1. The Claim: Three Revolutions and the Fourth One

The second volume of the trilogy of histories, *Philosophie der Geschichten*, takes a historical perspective on the position and rank of a philosophy of histories. While Edmund Husserl presents an "oblivion of the lifeworld" (*Lebensweltvergessenheit*) in the course of the crisis of the European sciences, Martin Heidegger exposes an "oblivion of being" (*Seinsvergessenheit*) in the Western history of metaphysics.[2] And carrying out its "destruction" requires us to take a "step back" before the beginning of this development so that overcoming it becomes possible. Similarly, in the context of thinking about histories, Schapp too recognizes the necessity of overcoming the oblivion of histories (*Geschichtenvergessenheit*). Whether this overcoming will succeed, Schapp is not able to answer. But he does concisely highlight the positions of Thales of Miletus, Francis Bacon, and Immanuel Kant, each of which caused a specific revolution (to be understood literally), which—taken together—function as distinctive stages leading to the supremacy of science and the displacement of histories. In the context of Schapp's conception, the crucial question now becomes "whether the next revolution must lead to man's self and thus to his histories" (Schapp 2015: 26).

Let's be more specific. In his preface to the *Philosophie der Geschichten*, Schapp refers to Immanuel Kant and his remarks in the foreword to *The Critique of Pure Reason* of 1787, in which he distinguishes three internally "interrelated revolutions in the way of thinking." According to Kant, each revolution leads to the foundation of a new science: while in the first revolution, mathematics is founded as a science by the Greeks through Thales of Miletus, Francis Bacon undertakes the foundation of natural science, and Kant sees his own achievement in the foundation of metaphysics as a science. These three revolutions and the resulting sciences demonstrate the supremacy of science as a discipline in which factual thinking prevails, proceeding objectively and methodically to achieve statements that are as universally valid as possible. Science is thereby valued more highly than, for example, philosophy, unless the latter intends to become a science itself, to fulfill the claim of science.

But Schapp sees a blind spot in this reading: namely, Kant does not ask "the question about the meaning of these revolutions." This could be pursued if one pays attention to the word "revolution" and realizes the connection it has to the political realm—for example, the storming of the Bastille in 1789. Schapp is convinced that Kant certainly "felt" this connection, but did not take it up and think it through. Thus, he overlooks the "relations between science and its founders and the revolutions in technology and politics" (Schapp 2015: 24).

For Schapp, a "fourth revolution" is therefore necessary, one in which a radical reconsideration and a reversal take place in order to return to humans themselves and their histories:

> If we want to approach ourselves, we cannot do it through the sciences, not through facts, but only through histories. We ourselves are not bloodless ghostly points of relationship that intend facts; but [we are] heroes, kings, knights, priests, seers, saints, prophets, poets, or someone from the people, all with their special histories, entangled in histories. Yet these histories are all connected from the beginning of time until today, forming a unity in which the most miserable has a place as well as (and here one sees clearly how the circles close) the prophet and the founder of religion. (Schapp 2015: 25)

If the next revolution toward the philosophy of histories is to succeed, then one will have to understand the task of philosophy as teaching us wisdom, allowing the previously sharp division between knowledge and belief to be revealed as subordinate. The phenomenon of the histories in which we are entangled then becomes the "certain phenomenon," serving as a point of departure. And from here, one can allocate the appropriate place to the other areas such as the strict sciences—but also the sayings of the "Seven Sages" and their successors (see Schapp 2015: 27).

2. Modes of Interpretation and In-Depth Reading

If one takes the entanglement of humans in histories seriously as a certain phenomenon, it is necessary to adopt a hermeneutic-phenomenological attitude of deepening interpretation, daring to jump into the vivid nexus of histories and becoming aware of their inseparable interweaving (see Joisten 2010: 283–97). If histories are *Urgebilde* and *Urphänomene* before, above, beside, and behind which one cannot penetrate, one has to move within their fabric, immersing oneself in them ever more deeply. In this way, they can be illuminated and penetrated from the inside and conceived more and more clearly in their progression. An absolute separation that assumes the perspective of an outsider and makes history comprehensible as an object is therefore not possible in the strict sense. Absolute separation would be a pure abstraction and construction that makes history into an object of research, thereby obstructing access to it.

Against this background, Hans Rainer Sepp presents an apt characterization of Schapp's philosophy:

> Schapp's philosophy of histories is smooth-edged; here everything is circular. Like the daily cycle, histories emerge from their horizons, manifest themselves, remain in the foreground for a while, and then recede once again into the darkness of their horizons; things emerge, tell their history, and thereby refer to the chain of histories on which they are based, which in turn lead to the individual thing. The world becomes a stage, but a stage without an audience, for [as Schapp writes], "one falsifies the picture if one looks at it through the eyes of an audience member or an outsider." (Sepp 2010: 52)

Another aspect is also important in this context. If one turns to seemingly the same history, this is a fallacy. In the strict sense, a single "finished" and fixed history doesn't exist, but rather a variety of readings, versions, or interpretations. Thus, it changes its mode of givenness according to the approach one chooses, just as it always appears in a different light in the specific experience of a person who is entangled in history and immerses herself/himself in it, so that it changes again and again, especially when we look back at it.

Every history—be it the individual history in which one human being is entangled or the "universal history" that has "the greatest breadth" in the "we-entanglement" (*Wir-Verstrickung*)—accordingly always carries an ambiguity with it, an ambiguity that one can and must approach interpretively, yet without ever being able to "exploit" it fully (Schapp 2015: 201). Thus, Schapp explicitly writes:

> The same history, seen from the viewpoint of the different people entangled, necessarily looks different; even a love story like "The Sorrows of Young Werther" is even more a universal history. With this, we touch on a question that will constantly come up again. What does the *same* history in which Werther and Lotte are entangled mean here? Should it be that no history is unique? That each is *ambiguous* from the beginning? (Schapp 2015: 32)[3]

Against this background, a philosophy of histories has the task of identifying different modes of interpretation through which one can approach the ambiguity of histories and try to conceive them as well as possible. The word "approach" and the comparative "as well as possible" refer to the fact that a complete interpretation—one through which "knowledge" merges into exact knowledge—is not possible. However, ways of interpreting can intersect with each other; they can partially merge or overlap, and then move away from each other again. And they can be repeatedly supplemented by new ways, whereby the network of approaches becomes more and more differentiated and far-reaching, deepening the interpretation. In this sense, Schapp's explanations in *Philosophie der Geschichten* can be read as ways of interpreting a philosophy of histories, which effectively invites readers to engage in a deeper reading, evolving their own interpretation in conversation with the text.

3. Histories and World

Schapp titles the first part of *Philosophie der Geschichten* "Histories and World" (*Geschichten und Welt*). The words "histories" and "world" refer to the horizons that each of these words opens. He turns first to histories, which he illuminates with the help of various approaches, and subsequently to the world, to which access is possible only in histories. Formally speaking, the world can therefore be interpreted as a secondary phenomenon that can only emerge via histories. Moreover, in a passage from April 22, 1955, Schapp notes: "More underpinning must be given to my teaching that beyond histories is nothingness, that one cannot speak of a world beyond histories. This is certainly the least understood" (Schapp 2017: 139).

Since we have mentioned the fact that Schapp begins his philosophy of histories with the help of various approaches, let us consider one of these approaches, which he terms "areas of histories" (*Gebiete der Geschichten*). If one wants to address the areas, the hermeneutic difficulty lies in the fact that the process cannot be carried out directly; Schapp does indeed cite, circumscribe, explain, and illuminate the areas, but always in a way that eludes a "final" determination. This methodical approach goes hand in hand with the fundamental conviction that wisdom cannot be fixed, but must be experienced step by step from different directions and perspectives. Only then is it possible for it to open and for its strength to emerge. Schapp, therefore, takes his readers spiritually by the hand so that together we can "go from one area into the other" (Schapp 2015: 35).[4]

Within the vivid nexus of the areas, Schapp specifically directs our attention to so-called "waking history" (*Wachgeschichte*). According to Schapp, the path then leads from there "to 'dream histories' (*Traumgeschichten*), 'histories in hypnosis' (*Geschichten in der Hypnose*), 'intoxication histories' (*Rauschgeschichten*), 'madness histories' (*Wahnsinnsgeschichten*), and whatever else there may be" (Schapp 2015: 34). If one looks at the headings of the areas, they stand for certain states in which a person may find herself/himself—wakefulness, dreaming, hypnosis, intoxication, and madness. If one also considers the deliberations in *In*

Geschichten verstrickt, "magic histories" (*Zaubergeschichten*) could also be cited as an additional area (see Schapp 2012: 146 ss.). However, one already notices that it is rather inappropriate—at least for today's listeners—to speak of being in a state of magic. Since human beings can indeed perform magic, just as they can perform other actions, performing magic does not itself seem to be a prevailing mood in which one finds oneself.[5]

If one wants to approach the areas of histories against this background, these areas stand for the basic possibilities for humans to disclose the meaning-contexts of histories in a special way, each in its own right. This disclosure does not happen in a purely rational way, but in fundamental states that display certain colorings. In wakefulness, for instance, we are entangled in histories differently than in the state of intoxication. And it must not be overlooked that the coloring of histories changes according to the human state. If the human being is inescapably entangled in histories, then the human being and the history are inseparably mediated and connected in a relationship of inner resonance and alternately permeated by specific—and corresponding—colorings.

The differentiation of the areas of the histories from each other does not, however, stand for a sharp separation between them, which would ignore their mutual "penetration" (see Schapp 2015: 231). As Schapp points out, he is "far from" wanting or even being able to make a conceptual division of the area of histories into different areas. In a history and between different histories, there are "transitions, occlusions, interlockings, and superimposition of layers" everywhere (Schapp 2015: 229).[6] Thus, it is impossible to draw clear delimitations between the areas. If one begins with the *Wachgeschichte*, Schapp tells us that it is distinguished by the fact that it is naturally given to every human being. It represents, so to speak, all that a human is, with all one's capacities, character traits, relationships, emotions, actions, etc.: "Whoever wants to understand us must have such a history ready, a history about love, life, honor, possessions, fame, hatred, revenge, preferably a private history of his own, with which he goes to bed at night and wakes up in the morning, from the time he reads these lines" (Schapp 2015: 31).

Moreover, one's own private *Wachgeschichte* is not simply present from time to time; instead, one is permanently occupied with it: it is "*constantly* present as a *whole* in its course" (Schapp 2015: 31). This being present means the presence of history as a representation of a vivid historical context in the extension between the past and the future, whereby it becomes problematic to speak of a "here and now," or even of a "point in time": "It makes no sense to indicate a point in time in relation to history, for instance how its being was on December

11, 1956, at 10 AM, because past and future always belong to history as to a whole." Thus, "one and the same history can [last] for months or years in old freshness," and sometimes "it stands still, then again achieves very fast progress" (Schapp 2015: 31).

If one takes what has been said seriously and tries to understand oneself in these terms, then the traditional request "Know thyself!" is transformed into the request to strive for a more in-depth understanding of one's own life based on the fabric of history into which one is woven. Especially within their *Wachgeschichte*, human beings are able to illuminate their lives and to reinterpret this reflexive self-knowledge to the effect that it represents an interpretation of one's own life in the context of history. However, in doing so, it is indispensable to comprehend oneself in one's finiteness as well, since life can only be led in a good way if something is at stake: one's own life in the unfolding of its possibilities considering—and despite—the conditionalities it has. Life and death, earth and underworld, the "realm of the dead and of life," therefore, cannot be separated. Both "sides" have their place in histories, whereby, as Schapp can clarify with recourse to Homer, "the spatial and internal separation of the realm of the dead and of life [is] abolished and both are united in one history" (Schapp 2015: 224).

If one thinks back to the beginning of the present section and recalls the heading *Geschichten und Welt* that Schapp gave to the first part, the order of the two words is important. If one wants to gain an understanding of the inner coherence of histories and world, "access [to the world] is only possible in histories."[7] However, this sentence is imprecisely formulated. Schapp is not content with the expression "world," but speaks instead of "*positive world* in reference to the expression *positive religion*" (Schapp 2015: 41; see Schapp, J. 2004). The relationship between histories and positive worlds is thus to be interpreted neither as a juxtaposition nor as a hierarchical relationship of superiority or subordination. Such an interpretation would erroneously introduce a separation between both supposed "sides"—here histories, there positive worlds. According to Schapp, "the reader must realize from the bottom up that an 'approach' to these worlds, a 'coming into' these worlds, a '*Heimischwerden*' in these worlds—all wrong, because we are constantly in them—is only possible through histories, and probably only through such entities as death, with its idiosyncratic central position in the histories" (Schapp 2015: 41).

If Schapp speaks of positive worlds, these represent religions, which appear in each case within a "universal history." The universal history has the widest horizon, within which innumerable other horizons can appear in turn. For example, besides the universal history of Homer and Hesiod, he refers to the monotheistic religions of Judaism, Christianity, and Islam. This is clearly expressed in the following:

> To be human means to be entangled in histories, but it also means to be or to live in a positive world at a positive time. To live in a positive world means again to live in a world in whose horizon other positive worlds emerge without end. Every human being is in such a positive single world and thus has the other positive worlds in the horizon. (Schapp 2015: 44)

From this perspective, individuals do not find themselves in a neutral space; instead, they are born into a web of sense whose preliminary lines have already been drawn. One belongs to a context in which interpretations, moral values, and the endowment of life with meaning exist and are passed on through histories.

If this dimension of the positive world is displaced—as happened, according to Schapp, by the so-called "special world of the Occident" (*Sonderwelt des Abendlandes*), which can also be paraphrased with the help of Schapp as "the physical world, the world of atoms"—then the "opposition to the positive worlds from Homer to Dante" arises in the occidental tradition. More precisely, what emerges is a contrast between an interpretation of the human being within a vivid nexus of histories in which wisdom has primacy, on the one hand, and, on the other hand, an interpretation of a mathematized world dominated by scientific knowledge.

4. Oblivion of Histories

If one looks with Schapp at the process that has led to the dominance of the "special world of the Occident"—which can also be called the "world of states of affairs" (*Sachverhaltswelt*)—this process can readily be characterized in terms of the oblivion of histories. Science, and the accompanying scientific knowledge, has step by step taken over the reins in the occidental tradition and triumphed over histories. In this way an understanding of histories was suppressed, an excellent example of which can be found in Homer and Hesiod, who "wrote poetry before the appearance of a science and before the emergence of an academic philosophy" (Schapp 2015: 213). In both poets, Schapp sees proximity to his own philosophy of histories: "By history, however, we will probably understand the same thing as these because the cosmos begins with histories and continues in histories, and without the histories one could not speak of the cosmos, nor without those entangled in histories" (Schapp 2015: 193).

The world unfolds out of and with the histories, and would no longer exist if the histories were deleted. As Schapp points out, chaos would then reign in Greek thought and speech. The opposition of chaos and cosmos (as the epitome of the ordered world) appears in the work of Schapp as the opposition of chaos and history, whereby he problematizes whether one could even assume an equivalent meaning in the word "chaos" (cf. Schapp 2015: 193).

The loss of "being at home" (*heimisch sein*) in histories in the occidental tradition, which allows the process of the oblivion of histories to appear, had already begun with the first Ionians: "With Thales, with Anaximander and Anaximenes the histories have no place, and the people entangled in history have no place as well. From these three philosophers, a philosophical direction goes straight to Democritus and his atomic theory. In this atomic world, a fortiori, histories have no place" (Schapp 2015: 234). This skein of the oblivion of histories becomes more and more dominant over the course of the occidental tradition. As part of this, wisdom, with its categories of meaning, understanding, and interpretation, is steadily displaced by scientific-technical progress. Wisdom is thereby replaced by the categories of virtualities, information, and facts—in short, by scientific knowledge and the dominion of a pure world of facts.

If humans are henceforth kept in check by the world of facts, "the facts, the object, the thing takes the place of histories [. . .]; cognition, the perception, thinking, imagining of facts take the place of being entangled in histories; the cognizant takes the place of the one entangled in histories" (Schapp 2015: 241). In this process of the oblivion of histories, it is "almost as if some force catapults the human being out of history into a sphere of facts" (Schapp 2015: 204). To take up a concise phrase used by Schapp, facts then "emerge as dictators of the universe," chasing histories "into the farthest corner, or better, out of the world" (Schapp 2015: 234).

It is not possible within the scope of these remarks to make further differentiations and consider other aspects. However, three more core ideas that are of central relevance can be highlighted in condensed form:

1) The beginning of our occidental tradition can be connected to the famous inscription "Know thyself!" (*gnothi seauton*). It was written above the oracle of Delphi at the temple of Apollo and was probably made by one of the Seven Sages, namely, Chilon of Sparta. It can be interpreted as an invitation to reflect on oneself and to perceive oneself in one's mortality in order to be able to live a responsible life in self-care and care for others. In our context, it can be transformed into the invitation, "Recognize yourself

in your entanglement in history!" It thus represents the admonition to be aware of being woven into the universal history of our religion and our histories, as transmitted by Homer and Hesiod. If the histories and our being entangled in them are forgotten, we also forget the starry sky above us and the death before and after us. Gods and the dead (which always belong to a universal history) then tell us nothing more, and we run the risk of losing anything to hold onto, becoming arrogant and exaggerated, and emptily spinning our wheels inside.

2) As Schapp emphasizes, humans are "lifted up" (*aufgehoben*) in a universal history (Schapp 2015: 244). Its wisdom and truth permeate us, just as it permeates all the other co-entangled persons (*Mitverstrickten*) that are woven into it. If we forget universal history, we also delete the broadest horizon within which we live together, horizons where "each one has his place across his history" (Schapp 2015: 208). We then attempt to build up a world from below, but we do not see that we are always already entangled in a universal history that leaves no one out, and without this, the individual then "has no proper name, but is ranked in the system only as a human being" (Schapp 2015: 208). The oblivion of histories thus leads to a loss of individuality. The proper name that represents a heading for the history of a distinctive human being disappears, making the individual interchangeable, merely appearing as one arbitrary human being among others.
3) If the oblivion of histories escalates, we tend to locate ourselves in a mathematical-scientific world of data, numbers, information, and facts. As a result, we lose our concrete connections, and we become restless wanderers or people who trap themselves. It then becomes apparent "that we have lost '*Haus und Hof und Heimat*' (house and farm and homeland), and restlessly move like pilgrims through the world" (Schapp 2015: 46).

At this point, we can briefly indicate the topicality of Schapp's core ideas for our time of digital transformation. The human being who has been woven into a virtualized context ever since birth is exposed to the danger of becoming either—in my terminology—a "mass autistic person" or a "mass vagabond" (Joisten 2015). Mass autistic persons are

> primarily related to themselves in an extremely imagined form, since we imagine them thrust out of the concrete fabric of reference, sitting alone in front of their screen and moving exclusively mentally in virtual worlds. The bodily present fellow human being, that irritating unknown, the unwieldy new, is not

> encountered by them concretely, but as a quantity of data that provides them with information. (Joisten 2015: 64)

Mass vagabonds, on the other hand, are distinguished by the fact that they

> align themselves with everything and anything, except themselves [. . .]. Restless and wandering, without duration, permanently on the way in a foreign land, they do not succeed in being at least gradually "*heimisch*" in themselves. They are literally always one step ahead of themselves, since they cannot integrate what they are experiencing into their bodilihood. Thus they do not "stand behind" themselves, and volatilize and scatter themselves into a multiplicity of moments. (Joisten 2015: 67)

If one understands the digitalized world as a radicalized form of the special world of the Occident—a world in which human beings exist far away from universal history—the possible consequences of the oblivion of histories highlighted in the three core ideas come true: (a) Humans no longer hear and pay attention to the admonition: recognize yourself in your entanglement in history! (b) One loses one's proper name and individuality, becoming a mere item in as a standardized data set. (c) We encapsulate ourselves in ourselves and wander "*heimatlos*."

What has been said can be summarized in the following quotation:

> If the universal history is lost, everything comes adrift. The outermost opposites are, for example, that man knows himself to be saved in a *Heilsgeschichte* (history of salvation), or on the other hand, that he feels like a patch of mold on some arbitrary star. This outermost contrast is expressed in another way in the contrast between history and facts. It is almost as if some force catapults man out of history into a sphere of facts. The universal history somehow has a different quality than the individual history. This is connected with the fact that the individual history rests in the universal history and that the universal history encompasses all individual histories, thus also already bringing the individual histories into a connection among themselves through their belonging to the universal history. (Schapp 2015: 204)

If one were to take a stance against the oblivion of histories, it would be necessary to take a courageous leap into a conception of histories. One would first have to comprehend the necessity of interpreting the histories that one experiences and that one can witness. Then, there is the admonition and request to penetrate one's own vivid historical nexuses more deeply in order to be able to understand them more and more adequately. To counteract the oblivion of histories would also mean facing the challenge of always having to make new interpretations and not being allowed to remain satisfied with any of them. The task of the philosopher would then be to ask new questions constantly in their historical context, to want to go increasingly into depth, and to comprehend the interconnections.

5. The Word and History

Another significant theme in Schapp's *Philosophie der Geschichten* is—as the fourth part of the book is titled—*Das Wort und die Geschichte* (The word and history). With regard to this topic (which is more precisely a thematic field), Schapp is particularly concerned with understanding the word, grammar, and speech within a philosophy of histories, which he illuminates from a variety of perspectives.

Turning first to the understanding of the word in a philosophy of histories, it should be emphatically noted that Schapp rejects a formulation of a question in which the word is approached through the function of the word (or even that of the sentence). If one adopts such an attitude, one picks out the word, literally clings to it, and considers it purely in terms of its functionality. The question of what the word itself is and whether it is then fades out (cf. Schapp 2015: 287). After all, the word could be understood differently in each sentence within a history, and, therefore, its meaning varies in each vivid historical nexus. Focusing on its function would be tantamount to removing it from this context, falsely thinking that one could "apprehend" it in this way.

We get an understanding of the word in the context of a philosophy of histories when we compare the "existence of words in books with their existence in heads."

> In the heads, words exist for fractions of seconds and then seem to disappear again. Where they come from, where they disappear to, we do not know. We cannot ask these questions in this way either. We would like to say for now that just like the histories, the words disappear without disappearing completely. With the histories, they also reappear. (Schapp 2015: 289)

If we consider this comparison between the "existence of the words in the books with their existence in the heads," we can continue what has just been said. Words do not exist purely in themselves, since they exist only "for fractions of seconds" in heads. Accordingly, they must become existent in a person in the context of histories, and they have to appear with a history and then disappear again. Schapp also refers to this process of the emergence of a word and its coming to exist in a person as "buzzing in the heads" (Schapp 2015: 289). With this phrase, which sounds strange at first glance, Schapp refers to the always latent presence of words, sentences, and language in the human being. Following this, he refers to the fact that the "buzzing" and "bubbling" of words and sentences (and the histories associated with them) are the primary phenomena in our heads. Thus, it is important that, for example, books or even dead languages find "connection to the buzzing"—otherwise, the existence of the words is lost. The "bubbling and buzzing in our heads" can therefore even be paraphrased by Schapp "as the shadow of being entangled in histories" (Schapp 2015: 291) by which the living presence of the words, sentences, and language(s) in the context of a history is indicated.

For example, if we read a book in our native language, we not only speak the words we are looking at, "but it bubbles and buzzes within the framework of the history we are reading, once far back, once far ahead with questions and answers, such as: Who was this person, after all? Or: Where does this chapter connect?" (Schapp 2015: 291). From here, if we once again follow Schapp's inquiry into what the word itself is and whether it is, it is only a word if it has found a foothold in histories from which it unfolds its meaning in buzzing and bubbling. Therefore, the word is externally "nothing in itself," and the same is true for the sentence.[3] Both only become something "in the context of the history and in view of those entangled in histories" (Schapp 2015: 232), insofar as words and sentences are connected with a speaker who lets them come to exist by buzzing and bubbling within a context.

However, there is another way that leads to the word with Schapp, for the word can also be interpreted as a "heading" for a history (approximately corresponding to what one can understand under "title, topic, keyword"). If one takes this path, one can encounter the word as a heading in different areas—for example, in naming, which can be grasped as a "title for a history," namely, for the life story of a newborn. Other areas in which the word is the epitome of a heading would be that of "things-for" (*Wozudinge*), that of the "from-what of things" (*Auswas der Wozudinge*), or also—following common categorizations in linguistics—that of noun, adjective, and verb. According to Schapp, for example, a "number of nouns, such as justice, love, goodness, pride, humility, can be taken as headings without further difficulty, and so can verbs, such as to fight and to quarrel" (Schapp 2015: 300). Each of these expressions, regardless of the field to which it belongs, can only truly be approached by engaging with its history and, therefore, understanding it as a gate opening the way to a history.

If this happens and one goes with a heading into a history, one finds, however, no words and sentences in this, but rather

> something similar like headings, I would like to say subheadings, which can often be arranged in stages. With these subheadings, histories are "targeted"differently than with the main heading. And yet it is part of the understanding of the history, of a history, that the subheadings come to life, or as we can now also say, to every history there belong sub-histories in obvious connections and in many degrees and stages. (Schapp 2015: 312)

To illustrate this, one can consider this fragment of conversation: *my aunt, the show jumper Elfi, drove with her horse to a tournament in France with a car and a horse trailer.* As in every history, this one has a person at its center—in this example, Aunt Elfi, to whom the history of the car, the history of France, and the history of horses and the tournament belong. If one wanted to follow all these subheadings as well as the heading for the ongoing history of Aunt Elfi, one would face an unsolvable task. With Schapp, one would be "lost. But one who does not have it somehow present is deaf and blind" (Schapp 2015: 312).[9] Thus, it should be a matter of deepening the understanding of a history, formulating it from another perspective, increasing its vividness by exploring its immanent degrees and stages in constantly new steps and completions of understanding, thereby gaining a complexity that is constantly differentiating further.

At this point, one can also turn (at least briefly) to grammar in a philosophical consideration of histories. For Schapp, the difficulty of such a consideration consists mainly in the fact "that grammar and linguistics do not know histories in our sense at all, while sentence and word have never become a problem to them as they are to us" (Schapp 2015: 315). According to Schapp, the blind spot in grammar is that it does not reflect upon its established categories. One deals naively with familiar divisions, such as those of word classes, without questioning and problematizing them. In the course of this, words are assigned to and subordinated to the respective word classes, they are pigeonholed, and they are manipulated. What remains is a rigid grid of categories that do not allow us to press forward to the ultimate units in a philosophy of histories, such as the "unity of the person." One then "stares" at the outside—at the unity of the person, for instance, at the body—without apprehending that these "only become what they are in this context [of histories] and in *their* history" (Schapp 2015: 316).

Furthermore, if one looks at "silent" speaking and speaking "aloud," one comes across a field of problems that deals with thinking and speaking. Connecting lines can be drawn to questions in the philosophical tradition concerning the claim of the universality of understanding (of hermeneutics) and the tradition of logos, which begins with Heraclitus. It should be noted that the topic of the connection between speech and thought is one of the central topics in the philosophy of histories, and it can be comprehended in the philosophy of histories in an original and transformed way. If in the tradition one defines the human being as an *animal rationale*, thinking receives a privileged position. Speaking then serves as a means and instrument to express thoughts—something that can never succeed completely, since speaking always fails to catch up with the truth that the thinking tries to comprehend.

If "being entangled in histories" is the primary phenomenon, "being occupied with histories" now takes the place traditionally reserved for thinking. But not only that:

> If thinking now loses its old place, speaking must also change its place. Speaking must then be brought into relation to histories, and the original form of speaking will probably have to be sought in the silent speaking by which every history is accompanied in its course. Maybe one must not even say *accompanied*, but perhaps the connection is a much more intimate one, and the speaking is as eternal as being entangled in histories. (Schapp 2015: 33)

If one pays attention to thinking and speaking in their inner relation to histories, thinking expresses the renewed movement back and forth between history and histories: "*Geschichte(n)*." It can therefore be conceived, as Schapp says, as a "silent" speaking familiar to anyone "caught up in histories"; one has only to visualize "thinking back and forth, taking a step forward, taking a step back, sinking into grief and despondency, taking heart again, reversing, going forward, fighting back" (Schapp 2015: 285). In this way, every human being's entanglement in histories becomes comprehensible through the "how" of being entangled, which takes place in immersion in silent speech. If this performance of silent speaking were missing, the anthropo-ontological interpretation of human beings as entangled in histories would be an abstraction that could not be comprehended in-depth by the individual.

6. In a Boat

The earth has shrunk. There is a worldwide interconnectedness between all of its areas, which is vividly expressed by the phrase World Wide Web. The World Wide Web enables the rapid exchange of data and information, accessible to all and free of charge, and connects even the farthest corner with world events. This worldwide process of digitalization presents enormous challenges in the twenty-first century because despite all the opportunities it provides, it also carries the risk of alienating people in subtle ways. In the course of the technologization of humans, one can be digitally suppressed since one has to subjugate oneself to the dictates of the measurement units that can turn one into a digitally measured quantity in the first place.

However, it is not only the global process of digitalization that involves enormous challenges in our time. Global climate change also challenges all people worldwide. Driven by the ruthless greed for profit within highly developed industrialized countries and companies, fertile areas have been and are being turned into wastelands in order to cultivate whatever increases wealth for the few and causes many to starve. The dominance of these economic processes can be selectively disrupted, but globally, it continues to operate indefinitely. Thus, even the best opportunities for a good life for as many people as possible come to nothing in order not to hinder the interests of a few.

The thinking of Wilhelm Schapp is very topical concerning these tendencies. It helps to direct our view toward the individual, and at the same time, it lets all humans appear. Conversely, in the view of all people in the "*All der Allgeschichten*," each individual is present at the same time. This belonging together of all people is vividly revealed in the fabric of the inner history within universal history:

> If one asks us what we aim at with our deliberations or whether we aim at anything at all, one may take what we present as the outline of a universal history in which all people and cultures have a place. It would be sufficient for us if we would all feel that we are sailing in one boat, slightly more than castaways in the nothingness, and as such we must stick together. (Schapp 2015: 346)

The basic insight that "Every human being is connected with fellow human beings in a universe of histories" can be interpreted as expressing Schapp's most deeply held convictions. It is a basic anthropological insight that always carries an ethical stance. More precisely, it is an ethical attitude that gives expression to profound wisdom and is to be situated *prior to* any specific ethics. In this attitude, the other person does not first appear as a stranger, adversary, enemy, or opponent, but as a fellow human being. Each is a "You" (or "Thou") close to me and can be addressed, according to Schapp, with "You are a unique person in your histories!" In such an attitude, the interpersonal differences that always arise are secondary, since what is first and foremost is the respect for and the affectionate orientation toward the other, who belongs to the "*All der Allgeschichten*."

We hear Schapp's ethical and anthropological conviction in the following words: "We are convinced that our considerations can be extended to all histories and universal histories on earth, and we even assume that there are not only parallels between universal histories and individual histories, but also inner and innermost connections, as they are expressed, for example, in the Indian word 'That is You'" (Schapp 2015: 210). A philosophy of histories can be understood from here as an invitation that belongs constitutively to the human being and to all human beings, despite all our differences—an invitation always to respect the unifying and connecting: we are all in the same boat!

Notes

1 The editors (Karen Joisten, Jan Schapp, and Nicole Thiemer) titled the three volumes: "Auf dem Weg einer Philosophie der Geschichten." The primary aim of the title was to avoid confusion, since if the three volumes had been titled "In Geschichten verstrickt. Fortsetzung," there would be two works with an almost identical title ("In Geschichten verstrickt").

2 In his eminent work *Die Krisis der europäischen Wissenschaften und die transzendentale Phänomenologie. Eine Einleitung in die phänomenologische Philosophie*, Husserl programmatically states: "The sense of being of the given lifeworld is a *subjective* construction; it is the achievement of experiencing, of prescientific life" (Husserl 1982: 75). In the oblivion of the lifeworld, which has taken place primarily through the mathematization of nature, the lifeworld is forgotten as the "foundation of sense."

3 See Rolf (2007).

4 Instead of "areas," Schapp also speaks of "regions" and "realms" (Schapp 2015: 35), but this happens only occasionally, which is why these expressions are of secondary importance.

5 Perhaps Schapp sensed this, and therefore did not include *Zaubergeschichte* as a history area in *Philosophie der Geschichten*.

6 In full, it says: "From the outset, we must not equate history with a scientifically established history, but we must willingly let ourselves be led by history itself. Besides the histories, which are, so to speak, transparent, there are the enigmatic histories, there are sagas, fairy tales, fables, myths, there are '*Traumgeschichten*,' there are '*Rauschgeschichten*.' All these expressions are only themes within a main theme. Everywhere there are transitions, occlusions, interlockings, superimposition of layers" (Schapp 2015: 229).

7 See the eponymous heading in Schapp (2015: 41).

8 In the context of histories, one encounters neither isolated sentences nor facts, but again and again, further histories. Schapp, therefore, writes that the sentence would be "nothing in itself," which means that its meaning remains nebulous when taken out of context. He tries to illustrate this with the frequently cited sample sentence "The queen is sick," which only becomes understandable in the context of a history. For example, he can point out that this illness is almost a stroke of luck since the queen does not have to perform an unloved task. Or, he can express that the illness is fatal, since an important agreement cannot be concluded (see Schapp 2012: 194).

9 From here, it can be pointed out that, according to Schapp, a distinction must be made between "headings for completed histories" and "headings for ongoing histories" that are constantly changing and whose "end is not yet in sight" (Schapp 2015: 308).

References

Husserl, E. (1982), *Die Krisis der europäischen Wissenschaften und die transzendentale Phänomenologie. Eine Einleitung in die phänomenologische Philosophie*, Hamburg: Meiner.

Joisten, K. (2010), "Von dem 'Verstricktsein', der (Gerichts)Akte und dem Erzählen und Hören. Zur Geschichtenphilosophie Wilhelm Schapps", in P. Gödicke (ed.), *Festschrift für Jan Schapp zum siebzigsten Geburtstag*, 283–97, Tübingen: Mohr.

Joisten, K. (2013), "Wilhelm Schapp", in Th. Bedorf and A. Gelhard (eds), *Die deutsche Philosophie im 20. Jahrhundert: Ein Autorenhandbuch*, 246–48, Darmstadt: WBG.

Joisten, K. (2015), "Der Massenautist und der Massenvagabund. Formen der Ent-Leiblichung im 21. Jahrhundert," in B. Beckmann-Zöller and R. Kaufmann (eds), *Heimat und Fremde. Präsenz im Entzug*, 61–9, Dresden: Text & Dialog.

Rolf, T. (2007), "'Die Geschichte steht für den Mann'. Ethische Aspekte der narrativen Repräsentation," in K. Joisten (ed.), *Narrative Ethik*, 151–67, Berlin: Akademie.

Schapp, J. (2004), "Positive Welten und Sonderwelt des Abendlandes in der Geschichtenphilosophie Wilhelm Schapps," *Phänomenologische Forschungen*: 133–49.

Schapp, W. (2009[1965], *Zur Metaphysik der Naturwissenschaft*, Frankfurt a. M.: Vittorio Klostermann.

Schapp, W. (2012[1953]), *In Geschichten verstrickt*, Frankfurt a. M.: Vittorio Klostermann.

Schapp, W. (2015[1959], *Philosophie der Geschichten*, Frankfurt a. M.: Vittorio Klostermann.

Schapp, W. (2016), *Philosophischer Nachlass. Teilband I: Auf dem Weg einer Philosophie der Geschichten*, hrsg. von K. Joisten, J. Schapp, and N. Thiemer, Freiburg, München: Karl Alber Verlag.

Schapp, W. (2017), *Philosophischer Nachlass. Teilband II: Auf dem Weg einer Philosophie der Geschichten*, hrsg. von K. Joisten, J. Schapp, and N. Thiemer, Freiburg, München: Karl Alber Verlag.

Schapp, W. (2018), *Philosophischer Nachlass. Teilband III: Auf dem Weg einer Philosophie der Geschichten*, hrsg. von K. Joisten, J. Schapp, and N. Thiemer, Freiburg, München: Karl Alber Verlag.

Schapp, W. (2019), *Philosophischer Nachlass. Teilband IV: Geschichten und Geschichte*, hrsg. von K. Joisten, J. Schapp, and N. Thiemer, Freiburg, München: Karl Alber Verlag.

Sepp, H. R. (2010), "Welt und Grenze. Wilhelm Schapps Philosophie der Geschichten," in Joisten K. (ed.), *Das Denken Wilhelm Schapps. Perspektiven für unsere Zeit*, 49–64, Freiburg: Karl Alber.

Appendix

12

Recollections of Husserl[1]

Wilhelm Schapp

[12] We are standing on Kant's shoulders and don't even reach the crown of his head—it is with this remark (whose author I don't know) that Rickert described the current situation of philosophy to us, his young students, around 1902.

I read the three critiques every day for two or three years; by reading them so often, I knew pages and pages of them by heart. The more I studied Kant, the more the citadel seemed solid and unassailable to me, as if its mighty building blocks fit seamlessly together. I don't need to go into the parts of this citadel and the connections between them—every philosopher is familiar with them: sensibility, understanding, pure reason, practical reason, forms of intuition, space and time, the thing in itself, appearance, synthetic a priori propositions, categories, the relationship between transcendental and transcendent. And on the other hand, God, freedom, immortality, and as a bridge into this unchartable terrain, the categorical imperative, which at the time may have had the same significance for one half of the old and new world as the Church had for the other half.

More generally, even if the categorical imperative gave us some support even in the infinite world, we were not so comfortable with Kant's doctrine. Instead, we felt overpowered, and saw no possibility of fruitfully philosophizing within the framework of the system. In contrast to Kant's doctrine, positivism or empiricism, along with everything else in this direction, played no great role for us—it seemed philosophically uninteresting to us, even if we were also concerned with refuting it.

[13] It was in this philosophical situation that I encountered Husserl. I was studying philosophy and jurisprudence, first in Freiburg, then in Berlin. After the first law examination, I began my graduate professional training, first near Göttingen, then in Göttingen itself, from the end of 1905 to 1909.

I had hardly heard Husserl's name in Freiburg and Berlin. I had merely attended a seminar with Dilthey, although not enthusiastically, shortly before my examination in Berlin. Other than this, Dilthey was no longer lecturing. In this seminar (in which Groethuysen also participated as Dilthey's assistant), some of the classes were devoted to the *Logical Investigations*, which had appeared in 1900 and 1901. Dilthey spoke of Husserl with the greatest respect. When one of the seminar members referred to the *Logical Investigations* as a "pamphlet," Dilthey, who was otherwise mild-mannered, was rather irritated and corrected him, saying, "That is not a pamphlet, it's a book." Since Dilthey had great influence in Berlin, this familiarity was certainly of some significance for Husserl. After the remaining examination, I went to Husserl in order to consider pursuing my further philosophical studies with him. (Due to the open-mindedness of my superiors, my graduate professional law training allowed me almost complete freedom for philosophical studies.)

I met a medium-sized, reserved, quiet, thoughtful, almost modest-looking, kind gentleman with a full beard, middle-aged, down to earth, almost ascetic, detached from the world.

I now attended his lectures and participated in all of the exercises, at the same time studying the *Logical Investigations* with my enthusiasm increasing daily, reading day and night for several years in what anyone but an insider would probably think was the driest book in the world. What was the value and attraction of this work? The phenomenological method.

Here I will not offer any presentation of this method, but only sketch the effect of this method on me and on my philosophical comrades, and in particular, the philosophical upheaval it brought about in us. It would be contrary to the spirit of the method if one were to present it as a system, although the temptation to do so is great (and one may constantly succumb to this temptation [14] to a greater or lesser extent). One could, for example, distinguish the following strata:

1. The objective, the objects, the matters (*Sachen*), or the world of objects and their relation to each other;
2. the states of affairs and
3. the propositions corresponding to the states of affairs, and
4. the judgments and acts of judging once again corresponding to the propositions, and then further in general
5. the sphere of cognitive acts in which a world is presented: representing, perceiving, intuiting, empty representation, questioning, doubting.

For phenomenologists, it is not only what is primarily objective that can become an object, but also the entire web or nexus in which the objective becomes an object—thus not only the bookcase and the room, but the states of affairs related to them, in their own right as states of affairs—and not only these state of affairs, but also the propositions related to them, along with the judgments and the acts in which the propositions become living propositions, as well as the perception of the bookcase on the other hand. The phenomenologist proceeds from the assumption that it is somehow possible to go back from the regard directed toward the object to the regarding, and—which is significantly more important—to everything else that comes to light in this regarding, in thinking -about, in being-occupied-with.

Were one to begin the presentation of the phenomenological method in this way, the listener would quickly come to an initial understanding, yet—at least in my view—this would still miss the phenomenological method completely. The first requirement for the phenomenologist is to avoid lapsing into rigidity or (which is not so far from this) into construction. To say "this is constructed" is the worst reproach that can be leveled against a phenomenologist. We should not be too hasty to circumscribe or to classify what emerges in the horizon of a thought. In the beginning of phenomenology, the individual investigation is everything, the system is nothing: the individual investigation is guided by striving for knowledge, for truth, for clarity and distinctness, for evidence. At first, this may merely be an ideal. In the course of the investigation, [15] it must be continually strengthened and brought to a conclusion. From this point of view it is understandable that mathematical investigations (and similarly, logic as well) attracted the greatest attention from Greek philosophy through Descartes, Leibniz, and Kant to Husserl, who himself came from mathematics. Phenomenology may now have developed in such a way that the phenomenologist—and first and foremost, Husserl—has come up with discoveries (or rediscoveries) that corresponded to those of, say, Archimedes or to other great discoveries. I don't need to go into detail about how Kant ingeniously accommodated number in his system, but still without ultimate clarity—namely, with regard to time and numbers—or how psychologism or empiricism, for which the world is divided into an inner and an outer world, tried to come to terms with number. Husserl was far from being satisfied with this attempt. He discovered number anew as an object—as a timeless object about which there were once again propositions, as an object that became (or could become) "visible" for humans, on the basis of acts of perception, in a new act founded in the perceptual act. So many propositions, so much at stake, which could nevertheless be immediately brought to light as grounded on the foundation of the proposition or the knowledge that the number becomes objective when one manipulates it or operates with it. With this there is, to begin with, a breakdown of the previously definitive division of the world into objects of the external world and objects of the inner world. This affected both the basic structure of empiricism and Kant, namely, by canceling the connection that had been constructed between time, counting, and number, thus putting in question the parallel connection between space and geometry. With this the entire system could become shaky.

Husserl now extended the assault. From the ideal object "number" (and further, "set") he came to the universal object, which he brought, by way of ideality, into ingenious connection with number, even going so far as to extend this to objects of sensuous experience. The universal object "lion" or "bookcase" was as timeless and ideal as number was. From the universal object he then came to the concept and [16] essence of the universal object, as well as to the proposition and its relation to the concept, to the universal object, and to any object whatever—to the proposition with its identical sense, i.e., to the proposition that in turn also displayed the closest kinship with the ideal objects. From the proposition he then came once again to the judgment in which the sense of the proposition became alive, which, however, was not essential to the proposition in itself

After the conclusion of the *Logical Investigations*, Husserl made new discoveries (though they were already prepared by the latter work) in the realm of the sphere of objects—new discoveries in the area of values and oughts. Values became a type of founded objectivities somehow adhering to bearers of value, but possibly, and probably, consolidated, in fine fixed orders, into a world of values and oughts, something then carried out by Beck and later by Scheler in particular, along with Reinach in the area of jurisprudence. The following series is instructive: the categorical imperative—Husserl's theory of value—Scheler's material ethics of value.

However, the most important epistemological discovery was the one revealing and securing synthetic a priori propositions, which was again closely associated with the other discoveries. The theory of synthetic a priori propositions proceeds from, or is connected with, the Kantian theory, but goes far beyond it in scope, grounding, and significance within the context of the investigation as a whole.

I had almost forgotten one highly significant point: itself-presentation, itself-givenness, and closely linked with it, the relationship of empty meaning-intending and fulfillment. In each case the investigation must be pursued up to the point at which what is being investigated is displayed in itself-givenness. This holds for every object of investigation, whether it is an object of the senses (in an older way of putting it), a state of affairs, a concept, a number, an act, or whatever else it may be. I could subsequently think of nothing more interesting than a critical investigation of this conception of itself-givenness (and of what it presupposes).

Can everything that is given be brought to itself-givenness, or is there also something that is surrounded as if by a quagmire, so that perhaps one can arrive in its vicinity, up to the [17] borders of the bog, but not reach it itself? Instead of the image of a quagmire or a bog, one can also think of a ditch or a wall in order to exclude the further connotations of a swampy marsh into which one might sink. Perhaps one can also speak of a hazy fog or a cloud. Yet one could still always say that one has to try to get as close to the object as its nature, its essence, and the circumstances permit, or one could also say that if one cannot bring the object itself to itself-givenness, one must at least lay bare the obstacles that still separate us from the object and bring these obstacles to itself-givenness.

I'm not going to say that this idea didn't also emerge in our circle early on. But it was probably not treated with the importance it deserves.

Another issue linked with itself-givenness is the question concerning the legitimacy of the separation of the objects, of the givens. There may be objects whose essence allows them to be grasped in their own right, completely without regard for a neighboring whole in space and time and without regard for anything coming before or after them. But as a rule, itself-givenness first leads only to a profile, to a givenness with a horizon (or with many horizons). Thus when we encounter Mr. Müller or the steamship "Bremen," they are always given within horizons. To be sure, in the case of the horizon, one can also speak of the itself-givenness of the horizon, but here the matter already gets complicated. Is, say, everything itself-given only within the horizon "world"—and what does "world" mean?

Now I had still almost forgotten the most important point of all, the phenomenological reduction. But I have never completely understood it, and so I must content myself with mentioning it. Husserl himself was only beginning to work out the phenomenological reduction in connection with his teachings during my stay in Göttingen, and mainly worked it out in the time following this. It had to do with the connection between being and being-thus, essence, and became linked in the must multifarious ways with his previous teachings.

When I return to the point of departure for my considerations—to Kant on the one hand and to empiricism on the other—[18] it is comprehensible how for us young phenomenologists, Husserl's teachings signified a breach of Kant's system, a system he was dismantling piece by piece, even if he could also take over important components (such as synthetic a priori propositions, and in the realm of the theory of value, the categorical imperative), albeit in a new version that was only identical to the original with regard to an innermost core.

With empiricism (or more precisely, psychologism), a certain connection would still be upheld with regard to the theory of acts, the most important points of which Husserl had taken over from Brentano, presenting them in partial agreement with Lipps. This was the most difficult part of Husserl's phenomenology.

Let me offer an overview of how through Husserl, we became free from Kant on the one hand and from empiricism on the other up to 1910 (or up to the First World War). On the positive side, what this meant was the opening up of an immense field of work within the framework of phenomenology, with countless individual investigations and with possibilities of investigating prior philosophies with regard to their phenomenological content and freeing them from constructions.

To be sure, we did wonder whether phenomenology and philosophy were one or whether phenomenology was merely a propaedeutic for philosophy. However, like Plato and his students, we had time; the decision did not need to be hasty. Every day we recognized the close connection between phenomenology and philosophy: many of the philosophers' grand constructions didn't hold up upon examination using phenomenological methods, yet on the other hand, important components of ancient philosophy were in agreement with the phenomenological findings.

To a large part of the scholarly world, Husserl's theory of ideal objects and universal objects seemed at first to be nothing but nonsense. People (and even the philosophically educated) were ruled by empiricism, along with the theory of evolution, to a greater extent than one would want to admit. As Husserl's theory of ideal objects became known, his colleagues—even specialists in the classics, who from their knowledge of Plato [19] really should have taken a broader view—labeled his theory a deplorable error. For them, Husserl was Don Quixote battling windmills he thought were giants. As Husserl himself told us, someone had even said: "Husserl's position is a long-winded way of having one foot in Platonism and the other in empiricism."

To stay with the image of a knight, to us Husserl seemed instead more like Dürer's knight riding forward with no thought of death and the devil, looking neither to the right nor the left. It was in this manner that Husserl was taking up the struggle with the most powerful scientific directions in the world, Kantian philosophy and empiricism.

Many students followed in the master's footsteps. Those allied with Husserl at that time had primarily pursued their philosophical studies in the school of Kant. With all the might of their young years, they threw themselves, as I did, into studying the *Logical Investigations*, and then tried to carry out independent investigations on the basis of this new standpoint. Philosophical-historical investigations were seldom practiced; each student attempted to cultivate a field (even if only a small one) with phenomenological methods. It was on this basis that there emerged the works of Reinach, Conrad, Hering, and those that succeeded them: Conrad-Martius, Ingarden, Spiegelberg, Stein, and Stavenhagen.

When I arrived at Göttingen in 1905, Husserl did not yet really have a circle of students. His oldest student was probably Neuhaus, who was somewhat older than I was, and after Husserl became a full professor, Neuhaus became his first doctoral student (shortly before I did), graduating with a dissertation on Hume.

And this was no accident. At the time, Husserl was very much occupied with Hume, both with regard to his theory and with him as a person. He recognized the strength of Hume's philosophical talent. But in his own way, Husserl reproached Hume for the fact that since his philosophical studies had no effect on English readers, he devoted himself to historical investigations, which then made him very well known, even though he did subsequently achieve a worldwide reputation on the basis of his philosophy. One had the impression that Husserl was criticizing Hume as if the latter were still alive. A certain bitterness emerged in these remarks from a man who was not quite fifty at the time [20], who first began his publishing career with his *Logical Investigations* when he was forty-two, having lived the life of a more or less unknown scholar until then. At the same time, however, there also emerged a satisfaction that he had unswervingly kept his goal of being a philosopher in mind, although even now, when he was beginning to be recognized, he was not quite ready to believe that he had brought about a turning point in philosophy.

The other students were von Sybel, Rosenbaum, Mahnke, Hoffmann, and Katz. Katz was a student of Georg Elias Müller, but he never succeeded in bringing Husserl into contact with Müller (or he hardly tried to). Hoffmann was first of all a positivist or psychologist, and at every class meeting he once again returned, with incredible tenacity, to the objections of the psychologists against Husserl's teachings. When the other students became impatient with these objections, which they thought had been refuted *ad nauseam*, Husserl waved them off—he obviously took pleasure in discussing such matters with psychologists, or defenders of psychologism, time and time again.

Husserl occasionally mentioned his followers in Munich to us, though he did so with reserve. He could take pride in his great successes there as such, but he didn't let himself pay much attention to them. Perhaps this corresponds to one of his basic feelings—his annoyance with small failures was stronger than his pleasure in great successes. Perhaps this is even necessary if one is to reach great goals.

One day (it had to have been in 1907), those from Munich were there—the invasion from Munich (I think it was in the summer semester). This included Reinach, Conrad, and the young Hildebrand; Geiger occasionally showed up. We took every opportunity to pursue philosophical discussions day and night with them, thinking that they were far ahead of us in every respect. They didn't have the unquestioning faith we did. Reinach reproached Husserl for turning toward the Marburg school, which was already attracting some attention in Munich at that time; he didn't think it was correct for Husserl to try to find support in the Marburg school for his metaphysical efforts. At that time we had founded a phenomenological society in Göttingen that met almost every week, [21] and for a time, Conrad led the discussions. I recall that—probably in connection with investigations in Munich—he attempted to bring the "signification" of a word to greater clarity. We were always examining new syntactic structures like "red wine," "wine that is red," "the wine is red," searching for the connection between word and signification, concept, and object. Occasionally a remark was made about the Munich approach and how they focused on the Platonic theory of *methekein* (the theory of participation in concepts), and moreover—joining Husserl and carrying his work further—they boldly proposed the theory that there is not only the ideal object, "two" (which Husserl did hold at the time), but also there must be many, infinitely many "two's."

The Munich group no longer believed in sensation as a constituent of perception, and explained any statements claiming this as construction; however, they still believed in acts and in psychology (the latter had not yet been placed in doubt).

In that era, we could discuss all these questions day and night. There was probably no place in Europe—and even in the world—that went back to Plato and his predecessors so resolutely and enthusiastically, taking up the work that Plato had left unfinished, if we may put it that way. Husserl occasionally listened or even lectured. At that time, Husserl indicated to me that he was playing with the idea of encouraging me to visit Brentano. I should go to see Brentano—Husserl's old teacher, who was about seventy years old and lived in Florence—for a fairly long time and give him a survey of the present state of phenomenology.

Unfortunately, nothing came of this plan, chiefly because it would take too much time away from my education as a law student. Instead, I decided that for the next semester, I would spend time in Munich in order to get to know Pfänder and Daubert and their circle of students. The law administration made it possible for me to continue my education in Munich. I let Pfänder and Daubert know that I had arrived. Daubert lived in a suburb (it must have been Schwabing), a long way up in the open air in an apartment with Biedermeier furniture. I told him about Göttingen and about Conrad's efforts concerning [22] signification. He immediately became absorbed in the conversation and spoke of living signification.

Regular weekly gatherings led by Pfänder took place in his apartment. Sometimes Daubert gave us fine cigars and served Italian wine. Once a week we all—including Pfänder and Daubert—met in the Italian restaurant. Up to that point, Lipps had taken up the philosophical space in Munich and had been teaching a significant number of intelligent and brilliant students. After the appearance of the *Logical Investigations*, they had split into followers of Husserl and followers of Lipps, striving in long discussions to conquer one another. One time Pfänder—who along with Daubert followed Husserl—told me that he had already come to results similar to Husserl's prior to the publication of the *Logical Investigations*. Be that as it may, he had immediately taken up Husserl's trains of thought. In a relatively short time, Lipps lost almost all his students to Pfänder—or better, to Husserl. Siding with Pfänder at the time were Geiger, Conrad, Reinach, Hildebrand, Löwenstein, von Gebsattel, the Voigtländer sisters, Fischer, Hirsch, and Welker. Lipps could not make any concessions anywhere, but continued to teach in the old style. However, younger students still took his lecture courses and seminars. Through Pfänder and Daubert, Husserl's phenomenology had triumphed in Munich. Scheler (for whom the young Hildebrand, with his good relationships, was a strong support) stood somewhat apart. I still remember a discussion in which "out of a clear blue sky," Scheler demonstrated how one has to broaden the sphere of the objective far beyond its customary extent. At the time, things were not going well for Scheler in the private sphere, but that didn't worry him. He would probably have liked to be more closely associated with Pfänder and his circle, but Pfänder held back—their two natures were probably much too different. Daubert played a major role in the spread of phenomenology in Munich; it would be worthwhile to study Daubert, who had never taken a final examination, but was well to do, living on private means. When he volunteered in 1914 (he was more than thirty years old) to join the army, he named the University in Munich—in fact, the philosophy department—[23] the heirs to his considerable fortune. This would probably have provided generous support for ten philosophy students for ages. Unfortunately, he lost most of his money after the war. With what remained, he became a farmer. Pfänder and Daubert remained close friends until Daubert's death, and today [i.e., when Schapp was composing his recollections], Daubert's widow is still living on the property. She also has Daubert's stenographic notes in her care; perhaps these will be handed over to the University of Munich for safekeeping.[2]

In Munich I was also searching for a theme for my doctoral dissertation, which I wanted to do with Husserl. I wanted to take perception and illusion as my starting point. I returned to Göttingen from Munich. Husserl approved of the theme, and I moved from Göttingen further into the countryside in order to have peace and quiet to finish the work. This lasted for about six months. Then I took the finished work to Husserl, who was quite taken aback when he saw it. He said, "This looks like a poem," alluding to my many paragraphs—in order to highlight the immense significance that each thought had for me, I had begun a new paragraph after almost every sentence, so that the reader could gather new energy for the following paragraph. We quickly agreed that there had to be fewer paragraphs. Then Husserl was tolerably satisfied with the work, correcting it in only two or three places.

The oral examination soon followed. National economics and psychology were my secondary subjects. During the examination, while everything went off smoothly with Husserl, I came off much worse with psychology. I had attended some of the psychologist's lectures with the best of intentions to make the examination less difficult for me. We began to speak of Ellen Key. I went a little too far and posed questions of my own, raising questions on a phenomenological basis. This didn't sit well with the examiner, who said, "Am I examining you, or are you examining me?" So this part ended on a sour note; it was similar in the part about economics.

At this point, Husserl had a hard time obtaining a fairly satisfactory grade for me. He came up with a compromise according to which the total result of the [24] examination was "good," but the work itself was judged "very good." Husserl was disappointed, but his wife was glad that I had so nonchalantly crossed swords with the psychophysicist, whom she didn't like.

Let me end my observations with a little more that is entirely about Husserl as a person. What strikes me in this regard is how little insight we all really had into his soul. He could reveal something about himself when he was speaking of truth and of service to truth—to the truth that is the same for all humankind.

Once in a while he referred to the racial problem, emphasizing the priority of the question of truth (in those days, truth itself was not in question for him).

He was remote from the things of the world, and perhaps a bit awkward with them. There were parliamentary elections while I was in Göttingen. The professors were liberal. Their champions were the historians, their opponents were the Guelphs.[3] The professors went door to door to campaign for their party. Husserl reported this to us at one meeting and said that he had never thought that one could do something like that, though he seemed to have gone along with it. The *Logical Investigations* had shielded him from the everyday world like a wall.

We students frequently talked about Husserl's personality. One—I think it was Reinach—brought up his erect posture, which one might interpret as unphilosophical. It turned out that Husserl had been a soldier, and retained his military posture for the rest of his life—perhaps he was not all that distant from the asceticism proper to a soldier. I can imagine that he wasn't a bad soldier.

Husserl could take a joke; he was pleased by the energy with which I tackled everything. And once, despite my youth, I even let myself get personal with him. From time to time Husserl intimated that he had no congenial students in Göttingen (naturally, he put it somewhat differently). I displayed interest, and invited him to say more about this complaint by recounting the following legend to him:

"Once upon a time," I began, "an Indian maiden gained such favor with Manitou[4] that he wanted to give her a gift. Manitou led her to the edge of a [25] huge field of corn and said to her: if you walk through this field and pluck the three most beautiful ears of corn, they will turn to gold in your hands. The maiden set off, reaching now for one ear and now for another, but always let her hand drop again, for she saw still more beautiful ears a little way ahead. She went on and on in this way until she was almost at the other edge of the field, where the ears of corn were smaller and scantier; now she really couldn't decide to pluck them. All of a sudden she was at the end of the field without having plucked any ears at all."

Naturally, as far as the small university in Göttingen was concerned, Husserl's view was basically correct. But at that moment, he didn't realize that the most beautiful golden ears were already ripening for him in Munich—Pfänder, Daubert, Scheler, Reinach, and Hildebrand, from my generation alone, to say nothing of Heidegger and Sartre.

According to Lübbe's bibliography, the secondary literature on Heidegger is approaching almost a thousand entries.[5] If someone wanted to produce a similar work on Husserl, there would surely be many thousands of names. When I think of the ordinary man in the lecture hall and at his desk, all that indicates much of this magical effect is the appearance of a truly great judge of character.

One time Pfänder said that there are giants, dwarfs, and humans. I might continue by saying that there are between ten and twenty philosophical giants. If someone asked me whether Husserl belonged among the giants, I might answer as follows.

From Thales to Kant, the emergence of philosophy recalls the battle of the Titans who assaulted—or defended—the heavens. One can take this image literally or less literally. The battle temporarily came to a halt with Kant in the eighteenth century, with his position on God, freedom, and immortality. What can phenomenology say about this? This depends on whether one may still count its founder among the giants, or whether the time of giants is over and darkness is setting in. This tallies with the fact that since Husserl or after Husserl, death has taken the place of God, freedom, and immortality.

Aurich, Ostfriesland

English translation by Elizabeth A. Behnke

Notes

1 Wilhelm Schapp, "Erinnerungen an Husserl," in *Edmund Husserl 1859–1959. Recueil commémoratif publié à l'occasion du centenaire de la naissance du philosophe*, ed. Herman Leo Van Breda and Jacques Taminiaux, La Haye: M. Nijhoff, 1959, 12–25.

2 [Since 1967, Daubert's manuscripts have been held at the Bavarian State Library in Munich; they have been accessible to scholars ever since Karl Schuhmann managed to decipher Daubert's unusual shorthand in 1976—*Trans.*]

3 [Schapp's actual word is "Welfen," the original German term for the Guelphs (who followed the Pope) in contrast to the Ghibbelines (who supported the Holy Roman Emperor) in medieval Italian politics—*Trans.*]

4 [In the Indigenous Algonquin tradition, Manitou is an impersonal, primal energy pervading and sustaining everything, although it is sometimes personified, as in the tale Schapp is telling—*Trans.*]

5 [See Hermann Lübbe, "Bibliographie der Heidegger-Literatur 1917–1955," *Zeitschrift für philosophische Forschung* 11 (1957): 401–52—*Trans.*]

Index

www.ingramcontent.com/pod-product-compliance
Ingram Content Group UK Ltd.
Pitfield, Milton Keynes, MK11 3LW, UK
UKHW020805290926
15470UKWH00003B/960

9 781350 3678